LULLABY FOR
MORONS

LULLABY FOR

MORONS

*Based on the True
Story of America's First
School Teacher Murder*

A NOVEL BY
Ronald Keith Siegel

NORTH COUNTRY BOOKS, INC.
UTICA, NEW YORK

LULLABY FOR MORONS

ISBN 1-59531-011-8

Library of Congress Cataloging-in-Publication Data

Siegel, Ronald K.
  Lullaby for morons : based on the true story of America's first school
teacher murder / by Ronald Keith Siegel.
     p. cm.
  ISBN 1-59531-011-8 (alk. paper)
  1. Teachers--Crimes against--Fiction. 2. Beecher, Lida--Fiction. 3.
Gianini, Jean--Fiction. 4. Trials (Murder)--Fiction. 5. Forensic psychi-
atry--Fiction. 6. People with mental disabilities--Fiction. 7.
Prejudices--Fiction. 8. Suicide victims--Fiction. 9. Psychological fiction. I. Title.
PS3619.I383L85 2006
813'.6--dc22

                                                                    2006030094

Front Cover: Jean Martinette Gianini
Back Cover: Herkimer County Courthouse

North Country Books, Inc.
311 Turner Street
Utica, New York 13501
www.northcountrybooks.com

For Frieda
For Jane
For Everything

Poland, New York, 1890

Author's Note

In 1914, many people in America were being wrongly diagnosed as "morons." Most were committed to asylums. Some committed suicide. Two were childhood friends who became involved in the tragedy of America's first school teacher murder.

The following is based on a true story but a few names and identifying or circumstantial details have been changed. The narrator's character has been reconstructed from historical archives including journals, letters, newspaper articles, trial transcripts, school and medical records, and interviews with surviving witnesses. Some aspects of his life have been created in order to fill gaps in the historical record.

moron. (From the Greek *moros*, meaning stupid or foolish)

> 1. The highest class of feebleminded or imbecile; a person having a mental age of between eight and twelve; as in "all morons are potential criminals" —Dr. Henry Herbert Goddard, 1914.

> 2. A sexual pervert.

> 3. A variety of venomous salamander.

> 4. The me you never want to be.

> *From the Journal of Noble Zoken*
> *Herkimer, New York*
> *December 1914*

1

Mama was my first teacher. She died when I was fourteen, and Father sent me to the Poland School near our farm in upstate New York. Since I was small for my age and had no formal education, the principal put me in Miss Lida Beecher's sixth grade class. Miss Beecher was only twenty and this was her first teaching position. I was nervous about being in a classroom for the first time and I could tell that she was too. It didn't make it any easier for her when the boys kept staring because she was so beautiful. All of us wanted to marry her when we grew up. No one looked forward to leaving her classroom at the end of the year. In a sense, I never did.

Two years later, at dusk on Friday, March 27, 1914, someone killed Miss Beecher as she was walking up Buck Hill Road leading from her house to mine. About half a mile out of town the killer struck her from behind on the head with a heavy metal wrench. He hit her twice more, knocking her to the ground, then stabbed at her with a sharp knife. Her hands were cut as she tried to ward off the attack. She was stabbed two dozen times. Several wounds punctured her neck, one cut into the spinal cord, and another cut the carotid artery. The killer dragged her body into a clump of willows, tearing off a piece of his coat on a barbed wire fence.

The following day my classmate Jean Martinette Gianini was

arrested for the crime and taken to the same cell in the Herkimer County Jail where Chester Gillette had been kept after he drowned his pregnant girl friend. Novelist Theodore Dreiser had referred to the Gillette murder trial as *An American Tragedy*. From the beginning the Gianini murder trial promised to be a far greater disaster. Jean Gianini didn't seem to care; he said he was happy Miss Beecher was dead. The village could not understand why any pupil would kill a teacher, especially one of such kindness, stunning beauty, and angelic voice. It was an unheard-of crime.

An alienist—one of those medical experts who study the mind—examined Jean Gianini and offered an equally unheard-of medical theory. He invented a new word and called my friend a "moron." At the trial he introduced a psychological test into an American courtroom for the first time. The test proved beyond the shadow of a doubt that Jean Gianini was a perfect moron, although one the public was least likely to recognize. The most famous alienists from across the nation came to testify. They said morons are a special type of imbecile and every one is a potential criminal. Morons are born that way and can't help themselves.

The jury acquitted Jean Gianini by reason of criminal imbecility, the first verdict of its kind in America. Then the same judge who had sent Chester Gillette to the electric chair for a far less vicious murder sentenced Jean Gianini to the Matteawan State Hospital. The newspapers referred to it by its former name—the Matteawan Asylum for the Criminally Insane—and reported that the asylum was simply a kennel housing vicious animals, but I know that the conditions were not fit for a dog. Despite the whitewashed cells and attendants in white coats, Matteawan was a dark hopeless prison for the mind as well as the body. Jean Gianini must have sensed it, too. It was reported in the papers that as the iron doors of his new home opened with a clang that shook the air, he trembled and sobbed convulsively. "I'll never go out of here alive," he cried. I'm sure he realized that an indefinite sentence in a madhouse was going to be worse than a few minutes in the electric chair.

After the trial I was beside myself with fright. It made me

aware of my own criminal potential. I am a grown man now yet I am still frightened. I have lived my entire life in the shadow of Jean Gianini, waiting for a similar fate. It is inevitable. I am a moron and nothing but a moron. That is what the doctors said to me, first calling me feebleminded, later using that other word. It sounded like they were cursing me and in my heart I refused to believe them. After a while, as others kept saying the same thing, that part of my heart which refused to believe broke and died. Then I realized that the underlying truth no longer mattered, the possibility of a wrong diagnosis no longer mattered, for I, like Jean Gianini, was truly cursed.

I do not look in the mirror, but I know I do not look like a criminal imbecile of the moron type. Most imbeciles are huge and ugly. I stand the same fifty-six inches high I did when Mama died. She said I inherited her thick chestnut hair and handsome looks, although I did not keep her beautiful smile. Most criminal imbeciles like Jean Gianini smile inappropriately. I never smile. And most imbeciles do not live long. I am now fifty-one years old, my body is strong, and my hair is still a soft reddish-brown like a young chestnut.

Imbeciles are of three basic types. Most are slow and stupid, and are of low-grade intelligence. They are called idiots and have a mental age of no more than two years. Those who have a mental age of three to seven years are known simply as imbeciles, but they are just as slow and stupid as idiots. Most can't even read. Morons have a much higher grade intelligence. They are the smartest of all.

My mind is quick and I have an excellent memory. Mama taught me Russian, Yiddish, and English at home; Father taught me Hebrew, and I learned to read other languages on my own over the years. Although we lived on a farm in the town of Russia, New York, only a few miles from the Poland School, we had our own copy of the 1903 edition of the *Encyclopedia Britannica* with all thirty-six volumes arranged in a wooden case. I began reading them when I was six and after finishing a volume I would return it to the case with the spine turned around. By the time I entered Miss Beecher's sixth grade class, all the volumes were turned around as were most of the other books in our house.

When I first met Jean Gianini I could tell he was well read. We talked about Julius Caesar and the Gettysburg Address, and he even quoted a few lines from *Hiawatha*. I was impressed, although I had never heard of the poem by Henry Wadsworth Longfellow. Afterwards, I borrowed a copy and memorized it. I can still recite every line and do so often when I am bored. The alienist who tested Jean Gianini for the trial found he had the mental age of ten years. I have never been tested but if it is true I am a moron I am certain that I have the mental age of twelve, which is the highest a moron can achieve.

Most people can not tell the difference between the types of imbeciles. They treat all of us as buffoons. They stare, play tricks, tell jokes, and laugh. Most people are cruel and heartless, and they act like idiots. Naturally I learned to stay away from most people, although I do not hate or mistrust my fellow man. I am not a misanthrope. I am a moron and it is I whom most people hate and mistrust.

I have mentioned that I am handsome. That is not exactly accurate. My face is slightly asymmetrical in that the shape of my eyes and the corners of my mouth do not tally. This is because my left eye is deformed and appears to be lower than the right one. When I was younger the eye could have passed for a normal one at a distance. Only if you were close would you see that it was surrounded by folds of pigmented skin that kept growing. Now there is so much extra skin that when I read I must hold the skin up by cupping my hand around it. Cupping my eye in this manner gives the appearance of a left-handed salute, which I enjoy doing because it is a way to honor the books I am reading. The longer the book, the longer I must hold the salute position. I do not look upon this as a problem, but when I remove my hand, the skin falls and I can no longer see clearly, since vision in my other eye has never been good for reading although it is excellent for distance. When I venture out of my room on some errand, I keep the left eye covered with a cloth patch. From time to time people have noticed a moisture coming from behind my patch, but I am not crying. The patch pushes the skin against the eye, which becomes irritated and tears. This necessitates constant washing of the patch, which I do every night. I let it dry on the sink in my room. I am embarrassed by the tears and prefer to go outside only at night when I do not wear the patch. I feel free in the dark.

There is a connection between my eye and the fact that I am labeled a moron. When the doctor saw it he knew instantly, from a single glance, that I was a moron. I was born that way just as Jean Gianini was born with a slight indentation on his head and protruding ears, although I am the type of moron more likely to be recognized. These are the stigmata of our affliction, the eyes and ears of our imbecility. We are helpless to change these things just as we are helpless to remove the label given to us.

I have worn my label so long that it has grown on me. My eye may scare people but I am not blind. I can still see. So they call me moron and treat me as one, yet I am not stupid. I can still think for myself. I know what is happening although I can no more remove the label that presses on my mind than the mass that enfolds my eye. Over the years the pressure from both has changed me. Things have happened to my brain. I have become increasingly sensitive to the light and now have frequent headaches and seizures. I have strange feelings and urges. Sometimes I go outside at night and gaze at the stars for hours. I have a terrible need to understand my place in the grand scheme of things before I do something...really terrible. I am afraid most of the time, although I hide it from people by hiding myself.

So I spend most of my time in a dark corner of the local public library. I read all the newspaper and magazine stories about the trial, and I study Jean Gianini's life as well as the lives of everyone else who was involved with the case. I follow the lives of the alienists and doctors who testified, and I read all their books and papers. I read every word ever printed about morons. I go back and read the trial transcripts again and again. I must have read them a hundred times. I read other books as well, including poetry, technical treatises, the great works of literature. I love to read. I read incessantly while constantly asking myself why I do it. I think it is because I am trying to find myself in the black ink on the pages, trying to see who I really am. I want to understand why you find me different, why you will never let me marry your daughter. I want to know why I have been forsaken.

I am not a fool. I am well aware that my very appearance confirms your darkest fears. You have allowed yourself to be influenced by shameless forces set in motion by the trial of Jean Gianini, instigated by the same individuals made famous at his expense and at the expense of all mental defectives. I have stood by and let them exert their eugenic influence in the so-called "progressive" America of the 1910s, in Leninist Russia in the 1920s, and, God forgive me, in Nazi Germany in the 1930s.

The conspiracy against Jean Gianini was hatched by the very forces sworn to protect and defend him: his father, his lawyers, and his doctors. They made it sound so simple at the trial: Jean Gianini committed a senseless murder because he was a moron. The real story is not so simple. I will offer new evidence that was either suppressed or ignored, that shows the murder did not occur for the reason stated and that an accomplice—perhaps the real killer—who might have changed the outcome of the trial was never found. It has taken me a lifetime to find him. I never believed that Jean Gianini would have acted alone and now I can prove it. And I will also prove that the alienists who testified based their opinions on a misunderstanding of their own findings. They were the real idiots. Their misconceptions changed the world—my world, the world of morons—and it was something neither your world nor mine deserved. Not all so-called morons are simpleminded folks. I, for one, am capable of complex feelings and thoughts, even moments of brilliant insight. I suspect others, including Jean Gianini, have similar capacities. I may wear a patch but it is the alienists who wear the blinders.

This grand illusion came about all because my beloved

teacher was murdered by a pupil, something that had never happened before in America. I have been a ghost trapped in that classroom all my life, cursed to haunt the past without any chance for a future. What promised to be a life of discovery and achievement turned out to be a wretched existence. When the trial of Jean Gianini ended I began a hunt for the accomplice who might free both Jean and me from the hell of our punishment.

My life may seem like fiction—it does to me at times—but if you could look me in the eye you would know it is true. I do not lie. I also do not sleep well. Read my story. Sing me a lullaby.

2

Sarah Cecelia McVey Gianini was twenty-seven years old when she gave birth to Jean Martinette Gianini on December 5, 1897, in New York City. Mama was also twenty-seven when she gave birth to me on Christmas, only twenty days later. I think there is a hidden meaning to these numbers and to the fact that Mama's name was also Sarah. It shows that Jean Gianini and I are truly connected although we were born miles apart. I have tried to trace our respective family roots to see if there was a connection between our parents that might have shaped our shared destiny.

Most people think Jean Gianini was Italian because of his name but his father's family was originally from the south slope of the Alps in Switzerland and his mother's family was from Ireland. His parents had both been born in New York City, where they met and married when his mother was twenty. Sarah Gianini, who was called Sally, was described as stylish, vivacious, a very bright woman who was accomplished in music. Her husband was known in the newspapers as Charles A. Gianini of New York and wore expensive suits and a tall black derby. He was privileged and educated, and served in the Seventh Regiment of the New York State Militia. After an honorable discharge, he went on to make a considerable fortune in the furniture business.

Mama was also twenty when she married my father back in

Russia, where she was a school teacher and he was a master woodworker. In 1896, they immigrated to America with only two suitcases: one full of clothes and another full of books, a few tools, and a silver wine cup that had been in the family since the time of the early Czars. My parents were poor compared to the Gianinis, and they were forced to share an apartment with another Russian family on Hester Street in the Lower East Side of New York. Father shaved his earlocks and beard and tried to fit in as much as possible but Mama couldn't adjust. Father said she was a greenhorn although he agreed with her that New York was crowded and dirty. The other family in the apartment threw the garbage out the windows into the street. There was already enough danger in the streets from crime, horses and carts, and aggressive street-vendors, so one certainly didn't need to duck flying garbage as well. It was no place to raise a family. After less than a year, Mama had enough and wanted to move.

She considered different sections of New York City including the Bronx, which was too expensive, and other areas where Jews were not particularly welcome. I don't know if she ever found her way to West 116th Street where the Gianinis were living at the time but I often wonder if they met. Perhaps they simply walked past each other on opposite sides of the street without saying a word. That would have been typical of Jews and Gentiles but eerie nonetheless. However, Mama did have an all too real encounter with a thug who threatened her with a gun and stole her purse. She told my father they had to move immediately.

Some Jewish families had already moved to the Mohawk Valley in upstate New York where there was a *shtetl*, or small community, in Utica that boasted a *shul* (synagogue) and a kosher meat market. My parents heard about the town of Russia only a few miles from Utica and assumed it would be more like their home country yet full of America's promise. Trains ran between Utica and villages near the town of Russia so they would not be totally isolated, but they heard that parts might not be safe for Jews. Some years earlier a Jewish salesman had been murdered in the area but the jury refused to convict the man for killing a mere "Jew peddler." The courtroom had cheered the verdict as did the village. "It would be best," Father told Mama, "to make our home our *shul* and keep our religion our own business." So they traveled north by train through Poughkeepsie and Albany, then west to Little Falls and Herkimer, then north to the village of Poland.

When they exited the train station at Poland they were appalled, as the air was filled with haze and the smell of charred wood. A recent fire had reduced several buildings in the center of town to ashes. Poland had been a growing community with businesses and stores, even some manufacturing plants, but sections of it now resembled a war zone. A stage coach took them through the scorched ruins to northern Herkimer County and the town of Russia, a tiny place consisting mostly of empty roads connecting dairy farms. There were cows everywhere but very few people and only one store. Father said it was primitive compared to New York City. He lamented the fact that there were no other Jews, which meant no Yiddish language newspaper, and that he would have to butcher his own kosher meat.

But Mama fell in love with the silence of the rural land compared to the noise of Hester Street. When they arrived, the open fields were covered with a blanket of fresh snow and she saw it as a place where life could be pure and good. She persuaded Father to buy a small farm with a barn and a large apple orchard, although he complained that he knew nothing about farming. "How hard can it be to farm apples?" Mama asked. "Nature does everything for us and we'll sell the fruit." And so they became apple farmers and Father also did carpentry jobs for neighbors. Mama hoped to get a teaching job at the school in nearby Poland, but she got pregnant instead and I became her one and only student. I shudder to think that the teacher killed by Jean Gianini might have been my mother.

My research failed to uncover a link in our backgrounds other than the fact that both our families had lived in New York City for a time. While there are more imbeciles in New York than elsewhere in the United States—and someone once joked you would have to be an idiot to live in such a crowded and noisy place—I don't think this fact has anything to do with crowds or noise. Otherwise anyone who worked in a factory would become an imbecile. I think it is more likely that the doctors at the Gianini trial were correct: our early development was either incomplete or abnormal. Both Jean and I are the product of difficult pregnancies and therein may lie the true cause of our affliction.

Sarah Gianini never had an easy pregnancy, I read in the newspaper accounts, which may be why she was always suffering from melancholia. Her first child, little Charlie, never learned to speak but merely made guttural sounds. He could not walk without tottering, so he moved about by sitting on the floor and pushing himself around. Little Charlie ate gluttonously and eventually choked to death on a piece of food when he was seven.

Five months after little Charlie was born, Sarah Gianini began drinking. At first, she drank a little brandy, later imbibing beer and whiskey as well. According to trial testimony, she appeared drunk throughout much of her pregnancy with her second child, Catherine. Catherine was normal except for the funny sailor hat and idiotic expression she wore at Jean Gianini's trial. When Sarah Gianini was carrying Jean she continued to drink and spent much time in a stupor. On one occasion she threw her husband's books out of the window in the middle of a rainstorm. Whenever I think about the horror of this senseless act I still get angry and have to beat my chest and recite prayers until the anger goes away. It helps if I remind myself that Sarah Gianini died from alcohol only six months after Jean Gianini was born. There can be justice for people who destroy books but there is never any justice for morons. Most of us are taken away from our mothers in one way or another. However, Jean Gianini can find some solace in the fact that his mother never learned the truth about him. She was so inebriated that she may have failed to notice he was puny at birth, weighing only five pounds. For weeks he hovered between life and death. His father, Mr. Charles A. Gianini of New York, stood vigil over him because his mother was probably too drunk. Jean Gianini's development was slow after that and he didn't speak until he was six years old. His first word was "Ma" but by then his Ma was rotting in the grave. It was too late for her to help him.

My Mama never touched alcohol except for holiday blessings and she was always there to help me. I mentioned that she had a difficult pregnancy with me. She was in constant pain. Years later, when she told me the story, there was a part deep inside me that seemed to stir with memories of those events. I know it is not possible for the brain to remember such things but I think my body remembers. Even now, if I close my eyes and try hard to think of the time before my birth, I can almost feel Mama's pain. I believe it is the weight of such memories that has kept my body from growing. I have consulted old almanacs and newspapers to confirm Mama's story and fill in the details. There was a series of celestial events that were as much signs of my condition as any marks on my body. It seems that God may recognize when morons are about to arrive on earth but He is as helpless as the rest of us to change matters.

In the spring of my conception in 1897, there had been relentless rains and floods. In the summer came lightning and shattering thunderstorms. These events apparently caused me to stir violently in Mama's belly, creating great pain for her. In the fall, terrifying winds lashed our apple trees. One roaring gust tore the roof off the barn which my father had just painted a deep crimson. He watched the roof twist and convulse as Mama's body did the same while blood the color of the barn trickled down her legs. Father ran to get the midwife, Zia Nardone, who lived on the adjacent farm. She told him it was nothing to worry about and refused to come over to check. Then two days before Christmas the worst ice storm in memory blew against the house so hard it cracked the glass in Mama's bedroom window. Suddenly, just at sunset, Mama saw a meteor of rare daylight visibility streak across the sky and detonate on the horizon over Lasher Creek in nearby Montgomery County. I often wondered if she was delirious with the pain of her labor or really saw such a wondrous thing, but in 1948, a meteorite weighing over one pound was finally found exactly where Mama said it fell. The fury of the storm and the fireworks in the sky told Mama the end was near. She reached for the nostrum bottle on the night table, then dabbed the thick licorice syrup on her lips.

"Aron!" Mama screamed to my father. "I'm dying."

Father left the house in a panic to find Zia Nardone. Mama's screams followed him until they were smothered by the howling wind. He didn't have time to put on his Sears rubber leg boots and was still wearing leather shoes, which caused him to slip and fall on his way down the icy hill to the midwife's house. Zia was home but she refused to go out in the storm. My father said he would stand on the porch and wait until she agreed, even if hell froze over. She finally said yes when she saw him crying but I know this was an illusion because Father never cried. It must have been the sleet stinging his cheeks and whipping into his eyes as he stood in the open that created the deception. He waited while Zia put on her boots and wrapped her neck with a frayed red muffler before following him back into the storm.

They passed the frozen pond at the edge of Zia's property. The wind was blowing the snow from the ice, piling it into pillowy drifts along the banks. When the children from the surrounding farms discovered it in the morning, they were certain to flock to the pond with their skates. Although Zia had delivered most of them into the world, she never approved of them playing and hollering and otherwise disturbing her peace. She was always swearing at them in Italian while carefully remaining outside the range of the snowballs they threw at "Z the Witch." Father said he was shocked to see Zia stop at the pond and break up the ice with her boot. He yelled for her to come quickly, but she didn't join him until water was gurgling through several breaks in the ice.

When the pair finally reached our house, they could hear Mama's screams punctuated by the crunch of their steps on the ice-encrusted porch. The wind took the door and held it open as Zia barged in with enough commotion to put out our Sabbath candles on the table in the front hall. She stripped off her muffler and coat, then scrunched her nose against her fist. I know she

14

was reacting to the smell in the house, an odor that stuck to the walls and furniture and filled the air with a barely perceptible mist. It was a mixture of cooking fat, onions, and boiled meat. To me it was the welcome smell of Mama's cooking. Zia later told people that it was the stench of a Jew house.

As Father rushed to relight the Sabbath candles, Zia ran into the bedroom where Mama lay in agonizing labor. Thirty more hours passed as the storm raged outside. Mama screamed until her voice was hoarse and all that remained was the sound of air rushing in and out of her throat like a frozen wind. She suffered strange contractions as if she wanted to hold me back. Mercifully, she lost consciousness and Zia seized the opportunity to pull me out with a tearing force. The umbilical cord was wrapped around my neck and I was not moving. Zia cut the cord, held my heels, and slapped me, but I still did not move. She slapped again, hard enough to cause spittle to fly from my mouth and spray Father with tiny droplets. Suddenly, I twisted my body around and partially opened my left eye.

Zia later said that the eye was grotesque and uglier than a toad's, and that the pupil dilated and looked in her direction. She wrinkled her nose and began to tremble so violently that she dropped me. For a moment Father thought that my head might have hit the floor but he dismissed the idea when I didn't cry. He quickly picked me up and placed me on the bed next to Mama while Zia grabbed her coat and rushed out the door. Father caught up with her at the bottom of the porch steps and handed her several bills. She seized the money, then spat at the house three times. Reflexively, the thumb of her right hand curled between the first and second fingers as her other fingers stretched out straight. Father said that the arrangement resembled a pair of horns.

"*Mal occhio,*" she yelled, then disappeared down the hill. The words hung in the air as clouds of frozen breath. *Mal occhio.* The evil eye.

Zia Nardone came from a small village in southern Italy where they believed that a person with an evil eye could kill you, or worse, capture your soul with a single glance. The evil eye aroused a raw primitive fear that crept along the spine and gripped one so tightly that it was impossible to move. It was the same paralyzing fear that people feel when fixated by a snake about to strike. I have tried to experience this myself by purposely facing a garter snake and staring at it but the snake turned away and slithered back into the grass. In Zia's village there was a legend that some people inherited the evil eye through a mistake in evolution. They were as feared as the serpents from whom they were supposedly descended. One didn't question such beliefs. It was enough to escape with your life. So Zia ran away from our house that day and never came back.

On the eighth day after my birth, a rabbi from Utica arrived on horseback to perform my circumcision. Mama told me he was dressed all in black with a long black coat and matching beard. When he removed his coat, he had on a white shirt that was so stained it, too, appeared almost black in several places. Mama watched as he took the knife from its case, then opened a leather-bound prayer book and asked for my name. Mama was going to name me after her uncle Nathan, a brave soldier who died fighting one of the savage mobs that attacked Russian Jews, but she paused for a moment to dab a drop of the licorice nostrum on my lips. As she capped the bottle, her gaze was transfixed by the label: "MOTHER NOBLE'S HEALING SYRUP." From a distance she heard herself speak a single word: "Noble."

The rabbi immediately repeated my new name, then added a blessing, giving my parents no time to make a correction. He placed me naked on a wooden board, binding my hands and feet with strips of cloth. As he began cutting, he paused because I was not crying. This was unheard of because resistance of any kind to circumcision, while futile, was always vigorous. Every baby cried and trembled under the rabbi's knife. I was different: Mama said I didn't even squirm. I had my eyes closed and appeared totally resigned and relaxed. My lack of reaction surprised everyone but Father. He knew I was a Zoken—that was his last name, and mine—and Zokens never cry. Most Zokens lived to fulfill the destiny of their surname, which meant old, old man. Old men have no tears left. I was born both Noble and old.

After wiping the beads of sweat from his brow, the rabbi resumed his work. Father said it was a slow, cruel final cut but true to my new name I didn't make a sound. The rabbi concluded the ritual by performing the *metitzah*, taking my newly-circumcised bleeding penis into his mouth and sucking the blood. At this point I apparently opened my eyes and watched.

When the rabbi finished swallowing, he looked up and saw my eye staring at him. His right fingers formed that odd horn-like sign as he mumbled another prayer. After I was released from the board and handed back to Mama, the rabbi accepted a large loaf of her delicious black bread for his services but he refused to share the traditional glass of schnapps. Father watched as he hurried out the door and rode away at a pace that was far too brisk for the steep hill. The horse slipped on the icy road, throwing the rabbi into a snow drift. As he struggled to his feet and brushed the snow from his coat, he glanced back at Father.

"*Ayin ra'ah*," the rabbi yelled. Father understood the Hebrew. The evil eye. Then the rabbi vomited. Tiny flecks of bright red blood sprayed against the white snow.

Mama laughed when she told me the story about the rabbi falling off his horse. I was old enough then to know the meaning of the Hebrew. Zia had said the same thing about my eye but she was an ignorant and superstitious old woman. Why would a learned man say such a thing if it wasn't true?

"He was angry at falling," Mama explained, "and didn't mean it. Proverbs says 'Eat not the bread of him that has an evil eye,' but the rabbi took our bread so he obviously didn't believe it," she smiled. "You're a good boy, Noble. My *ziskeit*, my sweet thing."

Mama patted my head, kissed my forehead, then sang a lullaby that always made everything better. There were no words to the lullaby; it was simply a soothing melody of caressing notes that wrapped me in a soft cocoon. I wish I could remember the tune but all I recall is that it made me feel like I was the center of the universe and the universe loved me.

Mama's cocoon nurtured and protected me through my early years. It hid my eye from everyone, even from me. There were no mirrors in our house for me to look at, and although I could see my reflection in a pond or a window at night it was never very clear or detailed. It was also never very bright, and this is how I came to believe there was something inherently dark about my appearance. Mama always made me wear my patch when I went outside because sunlight caused my eye to tear more. Only a few people other than my parents or the doctors saw my eye and nothing good ever came of this. Jean Gianini saw it and look what happened to him. And I saw my eye once. It happened on the day after the consumption took Mama.

In the middle of the night Father burst into my bedroom. In one hand he held a kerosene lamp so high the orange glow seemed to pour over his huge silhouette like liquid fire. In the other hand he held the knife we used for butchering chickens. Orange fire flickered and danced along the steel blade which was waving back and forth like a metronome keeping time with my racing heart.

"*Kriah*," Father announced as he entered my room.

I bolted from the bed and stood at attention, knowing full well what was going to happen. "No Father, no," I pleaded, praying it was a bad dream.

I stood as still as my trembling body would allow while the tip of the knife poked through the pocket on my flannel night shirt and tore it off. It was as if a tear, or *kriah*, had been made in my heart. Mama was dead.

Father and I carried Mama's body to the barn where he washed it with fancy Castile soap. Then he wrapped her in a white linen curtain from the living room and I stood vigil as he constructed a simple pine coffin. Under other circumstances I enjoyed watching Father work. He was very strong and had a man's hands, large and rough and covered with calluses. One finger was missing a nail and the nails of the others always seemed to have tiny blood blisters. As I watched him, a bead of sweat fell from his forehead onto the coffin, darkening the wood like a blister. That would be the closest thing to tears that he would shed. I heard the reason a thousand times: A man had to be strong like his hands. "Strong enough to shake a president's hand," Father would say. He liked to boast about once shaking President Teddy Roosevelt's hand outside the Hotel Carlton in Poland, New York. My hands were small, my fingers thin and delicate like Mama's. I knew I would never be as big as Father but I was determined to be as strong. As I helped hammer the nails into the coffin, I deliberately hit my middle finger, then watched proudly as the blood pooled into a purple circle under the nail. It hurt but I didn't cry.

Later that day at the cemetery I stood at the very edge of the open grave with Father and recited the burial kaddish. I was rocking back and forth and pounding my chest as hard as I could, trying on each forward swing of my body to peek down at the coffin. Suddenly I lost my balance and fell into the shallow grave, landing spread-eagled on top of the coffin, lips pressed against the wood. Just as quickly I felt Father's hand grip the collar of my jacket and yank me back to the graveside. As we resumed the kaddish, I kept staring at the moisture I had left on the coffin. It gradually evaporated and vanished before I could decide if it was actually from my lips or tears from my eyes.

When I arrived home I noticed that the door to my parents' bedroom was open. For as long as I could remember it was always kept closed and I was forbidden to enter. I cautiously entered the room and saw a white sheet draped over a tall object next to a dresser. How was I to know about the Jewish custom of covering mirrors in a house of mourning? I hadn't even known there was a mirror in our house. I pulled the sheet away and stared at my reflection. There I was in my black calf laced boots, brown worsted suit, navy blue cap, and black eye patch. I looked more handsome than I ever imagined. I touched my face to make sure it was me, then removed the patch and exposed the folds of flesh surrounding my eye. I had always felt the excess skin but I was surprised at how much there was.

I cupped the skin around the eye, pulled it back, and moved

closer to the mirror just as a burst of sunlight seemed to bounce off the glass and strike me in the eye. Everything blurred. I felt like I was spinning around and would vomit at any moment. Then I fell to the floor. Something very bad is going to happen to me, I thought. I heard someone knocking on the door but learned later that it was my body thrashing about on the hardwood floor. Then I blacked out. It was my first seizure.

After I recovered, Father took me to Dr. Frederick S. Cole, a local physician. As soon as I walked into his office and smelled the sweet aroma of carbolic acid I knew I had been there before, but I couldn't remember when. Apparently Mama had taken me to see Dr. Cole when I was just a baby. My eye didn't look so bad then and he said it would get better with time. Now he bent over, removed my patch, and forced a smile. Something was wrong. His smile was crooked and turned down in the corners. He also kept his mouth closed as if he were hiding bad teeth or something else. He said there were tiny brown nodules, almost like freckles, growing on the iris. When he shined a bright light on them I vomited on the floor and nearly had another seizure.

Dr. Cole said I had a scar on the brain that was causing me to be sensitive to light and triggering the seizures. He asked if I had ever been hit on the head by a baseball, kicked by a horse, or knocked unconscious. I shook my head to each of these, then held my mouth open and waited for him to ask if I had ever been dropped on my head by a witch. He stared at me for a long time, which made me uncomfortable, and I started rocking back and forth in the chair. If he had stared much longer, I would have recited my prayers. Finally, he shook his head sadly and turned to Father.

"It's made the boy feebleminded," he said. "He will not get better at home and should be in a hospital where there are others like him."

Father stared in disbelief.

Dr. Cole opened an oversized book on his desk. "Look," he said. It was the largest book I had ever seen, even bigger than the Sears, Roebuck catalogue and thicker than any volume of the *Encyclopedia Britannica.*

"These are pictures of the hospital in Middletown," he continued as he turned the pages and pointed to several photographs. The brick buildings, the largest and most beautiful I had ever seen, looked like castles in a fairy tale. There was even a photograph of a barn and livestock. It was like a completely self-contained medieval town.

"Here's the hospital room for epileptics where you would stay," he said, pointing to a room crowded with beds touching each other. "And here's the entertainment hall where you can play with other patients."

"I like to read," I said loudly.

Dr. Cole snorted, flipped through several pages, then pointed to another photograph of the biggest library I had ever seen, with hundreds of books. I wanted to lock myself in that room and not come out until all the spines were turned around.

"The boy can't go," Father announced. "He has his own room, a barn, books, and we keep kosher. His mother is gone now and he needs to go to school."

"He needs to be in a hospital," the doctor said. "There are others beside Middletown. Utica has one that's closer. I hear that a Dr. Bernstein has a place in Rome. It's probably kosher." He paused. "Your son needs to be in a hospital," he repeated in a whisper.

"No. He needs to be in school," Father said as he grabbed my hand to leave. He was going to send me to a normal school in Poland, New York. I was hoping they would have a big library.

Before I left I apologized to Dr. Cole for vomiting on his floor. He smiled and told me that carbolic acid would get rid of the stench.

When we arrived home, Father moved the mirror to the shed, announcing that it would no longer be in the house to hurt me. He planned to sell it to a neighbor after the *shiva* period of mourning. You might think that as much as the seizure scared me I was hurt even more by growing up without a real mirror, yet I never felt cheated. I knew that people lived rich and meaningful lives long before Johannes Gutenberg ever put silver backing on a piece of glass. They used the same means I did to catch glimpses of themselves: pools of water, polished metal surfaces, and, most importantly, the reflections in their mother's eyes. Mama's eyes never lied but I knew that mirrors were deceptive. The mirror lied to Snow White's stepmother just as it lies to anyone who interrogates themselves in front of it. As a child, you look and see a young child. Later, when you are older, the mirror still throws back a young child. Mirrors may seem like your best friend yet they will lie to your face. As I prepared to go out into the world and attend school, I resolved to avoid such friends and concentrate on more important things than my physical appearance. Gutenberg had abandoned the manufacture of mirrors and gone on to invent the printing press for people like me so we could find ourselves in books instead. I vowed to live my life like a monk or yeshiva scholar in a cloistered study, free from the trap of the mirror.

3

On an Indian Summer day in September 1912, I left home and set out on a three-mile hike to the Poland School. The trees were flushed with fiery colors reflecting the excitement inside my heart. As I stood on the crest of Buck Hill Road, I paused to gaze at the scene below. Before me lay a small valley divided by three main roads forming a letter "T." Small white houses were loosely scattered along branches of the "T," while more were clustered near the center of the village where the branches crossed. Here and there were small workshops and churches with tall steeples. West Canada Creek ran along the top of the "T," the swift moving water bubbling over large smooth rocks. In the distance I could see a miniature train belching smoke as it moved silently along tracks on the banks. The smoke rose and was quickly transformed into feathery clouds floating in a blue sky.

I started running down the hill only to stumble across a broken sign lying on the side of the road. It read: "WELCOME TO KUYAHOORA VALLEY." I mouthed the strange word. It sounded like the Yiddish expression *kine-ahora* that Mama used when I was a child. I could almost hear her voice: "You are a good scholar, *kine-ahora;*" "You will live to do great things, *kine-ahora;*" "People will remember you, *kine-ahora.*" The expression functioned like the phrase "Thank God," although it literally meant "without the evil eye."

"I'm going to school, Mama," I yelled as I continued running to the schoolhouse below. *"Kine-ahora! Kine-ahora!"*

It took longer than I estimated to reach the school, located on Main Street between the Post Office and the Baptist Church. The building had a deserted and unfriendly appearance. A brisk wind was blowing leaves across the entrance and shutters banged against the windows. I approached and knocked on the door. I waited, then knocked several more times before a man who introduced himself as the principal opened the door and led me upstairs to an unoccupied room.

Mr. Burt M. Robinson, who liked to be called "Professor" by the pupils, whom he called "scholars," explained that Father had told him all about me. He had decided I should be in the sixth grade although most of the other children there were much younger.

"It is important to be regular," the Professor said, scrunching his thick eyebrows together. He looked young but was already very bald, which was probably why he seemed so angry. "Be regular," he repeated.

I responded with a puzzled look.

"Regularity," he said loudly. "Most children miss only a few days each year. We start at nine and end at three-thirty. There is one hour for lunch at noon. Be regular and behave." He grabbed my shoulders and shook me once. "And don't be late again."

I immediately promised to attend all classes on time and behave.

He led me to one of the two classrooms on the lower floor, pausing at the door to stare at my patch. "Miss Beecher uses alphabetical seating," he said. "Will you be able to see the blackboard from the back?"

I didn't know but I nodded so he wouldn't shake me again. He opened the door, whispered briefly to the teacher, then directed me to a wooden seat with an attached desk in the back of the room.

The seats were arranged in four parallel rows of five each. As I walked down the aisle, each pupil stared at my patch but not one turned around as I passed. Instead they all sat straight in their seats, hands clasped on their desks, facing the teacher's large desk in the front. A long blackboard covered the wall behind her. She smiled at me as I sat down and held my hands together. None of the other pupils could see me but I could watch everyone. It was the best seat in the room yet for the remainder of the morning I only watched Miss Beecher. She had flawless skin and dark brown hair which she wore up in the front and long in the back just like Mama. Even from the rear of the room I could see the small brown bone pins holding her hair in place.

At the noon recess, most of the children ran home. A few sat on the hill between the school and the Post Office, where they ate lunches from small sacks. Two of the boys played catch with an apple. I hadn't brought any food so I sat on the front steps determined not to be late for the afternoon session. Nobody bothered me and I tried not to look at the apple.

As we filed out of the classroom at the end of the day, Miss Beecher asked me to stay behind for a talk. When she took the glasses from her nose and moved from behind the desk towards me, a lavender fragrance swirled around her. I inhaled the invisible breeze deeply, silently. She spoke, and the high-collar on her taffeta blouse made a faint rustle as it caressed her neck, bobbing up and down with her Adam's apple. Her voice was soft and caring like a lullaby. I stood motionless, intoxicated by her presence, hearing not a single word. She finally dismissed me with a smile and a pat on my head. Her hand seemed to linger for several seconds before she removed it, leaving my scalp tingling where she had touched. The tingling raced like fire through my body and came to rest in my loins. It was a strange yet totally exciting feeling. My heart was racing. I wanted to ask her to do it again but I was too stunned to speak.

On the way home, I recognized one of the boys from my class walking ahead of me with sort of a shuffle. He turned from Main on to Cold Brook Street and I had to follow since this was the only access to Buck Hill. When he reached the corner, he stopped and turned around, standing directly in my path.

"Say, did Miss Beecher give you hell?" he asked. His voice was surprisingly soft for such a big boy.

I shook my head as I stopped next to him.

"She lives over there." He turned and pointed at a small house with blue trim on the west side of Main. "It's Mr. Jones' boarding house," he added.

I admired the house and the well-kept lawn for a moment.

"What's wrong with your eye?" he asked.

"It's bad. "

He put his hands on his hips. "Show me."

I raised the patch and cupped the skin in order to expose the glassy white orb with its streams of red blood vessels. He adjusted his glasses and leaned closer. His own eyes were a dark gray like a mysterious fog.

"Say, it looks like a croaker," he said in a matter-of-fact tone.

A croaker was one of those oversized marbles that kids used to knock smaller marbles out of a circle. Croakers were killer marbles. I thought it was an apt description since I nearly died the day I saw it myself.

"The light bothers it," I explained as I quickly lowered the patch. We resumed walking up Cold Brook Street together.

"Do people gawk at you?"

I shrugged since I hadn't been around too many strangers.

"You look like a swell pirate," he smiled.

"I'm Noble."

"I'm Jean. I'll call you Croaker. Well, gotta go or my old man will give me an awful time." He headed across the street. "So long, Croaker."

I waved as Jean entered a large house just a few doors from the start of Buck Hill. This street had the nicest residences in Poland and Jean's house was the most handsome of all. His family must have been of considerable wealth to own such a place, I thought. The house was set back a good twenty feet from the sidewalk. A path ran along the side of the house to a small barn in the back. I saw a mean-looking horsewhip next to the open barn door but no horses anywhere.

I stayed awake that night thinking about school, Miss Beecher, and my new friend, Jean. I knew my life was about to change. I was emerging from Mama's cocoon and entering a new world. It was all a bit frightening but I reminded myself that Mama had taught me well. I knew what I was: a Noble Zoken. But I had no idea what I was to become. The thought made me uncomfortable and I reached for the headboard of my bed and ran my fingers over the knotty pine surface, tracing familiar paths I had discovered at an early age. There was comfort in touching the wood and navigating my way to the knothole near the middle of the headboard. Finding that hole centered me. I always knew where I was. I did not need to be big and tall to understand that I was emerging from the cocoon like an insect, fully formed with all the equipment I would ever need. I did not even need two good eyes to see that I was about to fly into the new world, to soar on wings of hope.

I walked with Jean to and from school almost every day. At first I did this because I didn't want to be late again. Jean had been in the Poland School since fourth grade and was one of the most regular pupils, so staying with him would keep me regular, I figured. He was also bright and had earned an average grade of ninety in all subjects in the fifth grade. There was another reason to keep company with Jean, one I am now reluctant to admit: I admired him. He had had so many more experiences in the world and I kept begging him to tell me stories of his adventures. He was like Tom Sawyer and Huckleberry Finn rolled into one, and I played the pirate out to steal his secrets as we rode together on the river boat of our youth.

One rainy morning we were on our way to school and we saw Miss Beecher starting to cross the intersection of Main and Cold Brook Street, heading in the same direction. She was wearing a tan rain coat, rubbers, and a checkered cap with black velvet trim. When she opened her umbrella, her head was hidden except for her long hair which dropped down in the back for about a foot below her cap. We slowed our pace so as to stay far enough behind to be out of earshot. In the misty distance, her slender, diminutive frame made her appear more like a schoolgirl than a teacher. Jean said he would like to see her naked. He told me how he had once played Indian with two little girls in a Bronx park. Since Indians were supposed to be naked, he took off the girls' clothes. I was fascinated by his description of their anatomy, especially their little titties. He said that Miss Beecher had big tits. I tried to imagine what they might look like and, after some thought, agreed that they would be very big.

Jean said that one day he might decide to play Indian with Miss Beecher in the woods and see them for himself. When I laughed, he bristled and told me that he had played games with Miss Lula Davis who had been his teacher in fourth and fifth grade. In the evenings, after school, they would play Parcheesi. I was unfamiliar with the rules for this game and asked if he took off her clothes. Now it was Jean's turn to laugh as he explained that Parcheesi was played by several people who threw dice and moved pieces on a board. He wasn't alone with Miss Davis because there were always other boys present for the game. Besides, she was plain and old whereas Miss Beecher was pretty and young, perhaps very close to our age. There was much hope in his analysis.

I recognized that Jean stood a better chance than I of ever playing Indian with Miss Beecher. After all, he was bigger than I was, even bigger and taller than Miss Beecher. And there was something very grown-up about the way he carried himself. Although he walked with a shuffle, he took long manly strides. He always seemed to know where he was going and was in a hurry to get there. I had to walk very quickly, sometimes skipping, in order to keep up. Whenever I did catch Jean, he would deliberately increase his pace. It seemed important for him to be in front, so I eventually learned to stay a little behind.

One day he led me to a woodshed attached to his house where there was a toilet. There he proceeded to demonstrate how to masturbate. He rubbed himself and made noises as if he was in great pain. The scene reminded me of a cow with its udder caught in a barbed wire fence and I understood why the practice was considered self-abuse. He invited me to try but I was embarrassed. Later, I did try it at home but I couldn't do it. I thought at the time that my failure had something to do with the fact that I was circumcised.

The one thing that I could do at least as well as Jean was read, although he preferred newspaper stories about crimes, or thrillers about war and adventures in far away places, topics I found uninteresting. His favorite books all had similar titles: *The Story of a Bad Boy* by Thomas Aldrich, and a series by George Peck including *Peck's Bad Boy Abroad*, *Peck's Bad Boy and His Pa*, and *Peck's Bad Boy with the Circus*, among other titles. Jean was obsessed by the notion of "bad" and he reveled in telling me shady stories about the bad things people did in real life or fiction. His stories often blurred the distinction between the two.

One morning he rushed out of his house and spoke excitedly about a book he had just finished reading. The book told of a nobleman in Europe, a Count Dracula, who had red eyes and drank the blood of beautiful young girls. Jean was very animated and gestured wildly as he described the terrible crimes of this creature who was finally killed by decapitation and a knife through the heart. Dracula terrified me and I asked if there truly was such a person. Jean glared at me with eyes made red from reading all night and announced it was only a story. When he saw that I was still shaken, he laughed. It was the laugh of a person yawning from lack of sleep and snickering at the same time. It sounded like a wolf howling and it sent chills through my body.

Apple season was upon us and I spent every waking hour when not in school picking and sorting apples in our orchard. I couldn't stop thinking about the vampire Count Dracula. If such people with the appetite of a leech actually existed, one could be living in the very woods around our farm. Perhaps he was attracted to the blood red fruit from our orchard. The thought disturbed me and I began to inspect the apples for unusual bite marks. Whenever I found puncture marks in an apple, I cut it open to make certain there was a worm or insect inside.

At the crack of dawn one morning I went to the orchard to pick a few apples for school. I was startled to see a man squatting next to one of the trees eating the fruit. He had his back turned to me but from his clothes it looked like Roy Finley, a young man who had recently moved from Paine's Hollow, a sleepy hamlet in the southern part of the county, and who was now working on a nearby farm. He was making strange sounds. I stood quietly and watched. I thought he might have fallen asleep because I heard snoring. Suddenly, the snoring turned into short snorts as he swatted and grasped at the air. Then he vomited.

As I shifted my weight from one foot to another, a twig cracked under my shoe. Roy's neck snapped like an alarmed bird and he whirled around and faced me with piercing eyes that appeared almost red in the dawn light. His lips were covered with a froth of saliva. The froth was speckled with bright red blood. I froze.

He bolted to his feet and charged at me. When he was almost upon me he lowered his head and butted my chest like a goat. The impact sent me flying into the air and I landed on my back gasping for breath. He stood over me as his lips jerked back over his teeth in an animal-like snarl. Then he abruptly spun around and staggered off in the direction of the Buck Hill woods. I scrambled to my feet and ran back to the house, too confused and frightened to wake my father.

I set off for school early and waited for Jean on his porch. As soon as he opened the door, it was my turn to tell a wild tale. I whispered a hurried step-by-step account of my encounter as his pupils grew larger. We both knew what it meant: Roy Finley was a vampire. Jean wanted to skip school, get one of his father's bear guns, and go after him. But I warned Jean that there was probably another creature out there who had turned Roy into a vampire in the first place. Who could it be? We began listing possible suspects. Jean had been in many fights and had a long list of people he didn't like or trust. I couldn't name one.

We began to map out a strategy for tracking Roy, who might lead us to the coffin where he slept and to the other creature whom we now believed existed. This became our sole topic of conversation for several days until Jean read in the newspaper that Roy Finley was dead. He had been bitten by a mad dog and died from rabies. He, too, was mad at the end.

"It was a good game while it lasted," Jean said with a nervous laugh after reading the death notice to me.

I never laughed at death and could only wish Mr. Finley's soul well with a silent recitation of a few words from the kaddish. But I was happy to know that his attack upon me was because of rabies; it was not personal. He had no reason to hurt me and people who are violent for no reason are truly mad. Those who have good reason to be violent against others are the real vampires.

I have mentioned that Jean was always in a hurry. Even in school he was always fidgeting. Sometimes he sat in his chair absorbed in studying but his hands were banging the desk like a primitive savage pounding a drum. On several occasions he would be reading a book at his desk and jumping up and down in his seat until Miss Beecher told him not to do it. He also had the annoying habit of tipping over his chair. It happened too many times to be considered an accident. After school, I heard one of the girls in the class call him "loony."

The word didn't bother Jean. He had been called names all his life. He told me that once he ate a mud pie when he was little and some kids made fun of him by calling him loony. He ate another pie just to show them that the name didn't bother him. Jean knew that he wasn't a lunatic. He said that lunatics had to be put in straight jackets to keep still, while he was able to stop as soon as Miss Beecher asked him. Jean explained that he was simply restless and bored in school, not loony. It made sense to me. I would have been bored myself since I knew most of the lessons without studying, but I was learning so much more by watching Jean and everyone else. The class was filled with flesh and blood books and I was determined to remain still in the back of the room while I read them all. Jean had a different ambition. He wanted to be a brakeman on a railroad when he grew up, just like Chester Gillette, the man who had been sent to the electric chair, had been. I decided that Jean's inability to sit still was a good qualification for an occupation where he would be in constant motion. Jean was anxious to run away and see the world like Peck's Bad Boy, stopping his train only when he felt like it. Brakemen like that may be bad and selfish but they are not crazy.

One day on the way home from school we stopped to buy candy at the Poland Union Store in the square at the corner of Main and Cold Brook Street. The store was run by Mr. Joseph Lamb, whose son Lawrence was in our class and was good friends with Jean. We were always treated well in the store and allowed time to feast our eyes on the goodies. This involved considerable effort since the store was very dark even with the overhead gas lights. As we stood in the narrow aisle with other kids and crowded around the glass cases, Jean got into a shoving match with another boy who called him a "wop." This was echoed by others in a chorus of "woppy, woppy." I was appalled but Jean simply shrugged it off.

"I'm not Italian, so it doesn't bother me," he said when we were outside. "Sticks and stones may break my bones, but words will never hurt me."

I agreed. I had not yet learned that words can break your heart but Jean and I were both about to learn about the sticks and stones thrown by Professor Robinson, our principal.

Jean actually threw the first volley in the form of spitballs. First he would chew a small piece of paper to get it wet, then roll it in his fingers until it became a tight wad. He could toss the wads clear across the room at the other kids. Everyone thought it harmless fun, including me. While I never engaged in throwing, I was in awe of Jean's aim, especially when he hit me square in the patch.

Professor Robinson visited our class two or three times a day but usually at noon or after school, so he never saw the wads that occasionally crisscrossed the room when Miss Beecher's back was turned. However he must have received reports from her because in November he barged into the room in the middle of a recitation, throwing open the door with enough force to cause it to rattle against the wall. The pupil who was reciting sat down immediately.

"You must improve your behavior," the Professor began, "without Miss Beecher being required to punish you. There will be no more paper balls thrown around the room. Not one."

He strutted back and forth in front of the class. "Not one, not one, not one," he kept repeating as he looked into each pupil's face, thrusting his finger in the air or pointing at them.

Snickers and muted giggles erupted throughout the class. Everyone seemed to be holding back outright laughter. I failed to understand what was so funny except that the Professor's face was growing beet red. The finger he held up, the middle finger, had a crooked nail with a blackened blood blister. Could this be what was so funny? When he came to me, I held up own middle finger with its discolored tip to show him that I understood the pain of a bruised finger. It was like a secret handshake that united us in the same fraternity. I only wanted him to like me.

"You!" the Professor said loudly, impaling me with a vicious glare. He snarled with clenched teeth not unlike Roy Finley. All that was missing were the red eyes. "Outside," he howled.

There was a collective gasp, then the class fell silent. I marched up the aisle bewildered. There was a sense of dread in the air. Miss Beecher bowed her head slightly and closed her eyes as I walked past her to the door.

Outside in the hall, Professor Robinson shook me vigorously. He spat words of misconduct and respect into my face, then waited for me to say something. When I remained silent, he grabbed my collar and marched me upstairs to an empty recitation room. There he produced a piece of rubber hose and whipped it against my hips. I was dumbfounded: no one had ever hit me before. After the first strike he peered at my face, then struck again. My senses recorded minute details as they burned their way into my brain: the smell of chalk dust in the air, the wooden floor squeaking as I shifted my weight with each blow, the feel of my wool pants pressing against my skin.

A vein swelled in the Professor's neck. His face grew red and so did mine but I refused to cry. I counted four strikes before I was told to sit at a desk in the room until he dismissed me. It hurt to sit but I didn't say a word. I was finally allowed to go home at nightfall, well after school ended.

Jean was waiting for me in the street. He handed me a package of *Zu Zu* gingersnaps and we ate them as we walked home in the dark. He had seen what happened in class and explained the significance of the gesture with the middle finger. I felt stupid but it was the best thing I could have done in the eyes of Jean Gianini. He was a troublemaker in school and now I was, too. It was his fraternity of bad boys I joined that day, not the Professor's.

While Jean confessed that he had been shaken a few times by the Professor, he had yet to endure the initiation by whipping. The whipping taught me to be quiet in school, to never raise my hand, and certainly never to lift a finger, although I knew the answer to every question Miss Beecher asked. The one question I couldn't answer was how Jean would react to a whipping.

One day Jean marked up his desk with ink. Miss Beecher saw it but didn't say a word, at least not to Jean, but the next morning Professor Robinson made one of his rare class-time visits. He strode directly to Jean's desk and ordered him to clean the desk after school. A few weeks later, after Jean continued to mark his desk, as well as tip it over, Miss Beecher told him to report to Professor Robinson after school.

It was a cold and snowy day so I waited for my friend inside the schoolhouse. When I heard the Professor yelling I tiptoed upstairs to listen. The door to one of the recitation rooms was open a crack and I was able to see Jean bent over a desk and the Professor standing behind him with the hose. I could look right into their faces knowing that they could not see me. Spying in this manner gave me a rush of excitement.

"You must not entertain a grudge against her," the Professor said. "Miss Beecher has been reporting your misconduct to me as I requested. She is unable to punish you."

Whack!

The rubber hose flew against Jean's buttocks.
Whack!
"Don't hold this against her," he snarled.
Whack!
Whack!
Jean reached back and tried to protect his rump with his hands.
Whack! Whack! Whack!
The hose hit Jean's bare hands three times in rapid succession. He pulled them away as if they had been stung by a swarm of bees. His face had a blank stare. It was a look of shock and deep hurt, not in the hand but in the heart. As I looked into Jean's eyes fighting back the tears, I felt that I was looking into my own eyes.

Stop, stop, you're going to make him cry, I wanted to scream, but I held my tongue. The Professor stopped and I thought for a moment I myself might actually have screamed. I tiptoed back downstairs and waited for my friend.

Jean held his swollen hands limply at his sides as we walked up Main Street. It was fortunate that Jean wasn't carrying his school books home that day because I don't think he would have been able to hold them. He was noticeably quiet and his shuffle was more pronounced than usual.

I had five pennies, my spending money for the week, so I offered to buy a box of *Zu Zu* snaps as we approached the store at the village square.

"Professor Robinson didn't give me a fair show," Jean said, ignoring my offer.

Me neither, I thought as we continued on to Cold Brook Street.

"The whipping didn't bother me," he announced when we reached his house. "My old man whipped me this morning." He kicked a pile of snow with his boot, then walked to his porch and opened the front door. I noticed that he hesitated for a moment before entering, shaking so hard that small clumps of snow were falling off his pants. Much later I learned that whenever Jean was punished at school, his father would punish him some more.

I awakened hours before dawn the next day and baked an extra large loaf of Mama's black bread. The strong aroma of baking bread was certain to alert Father to my deed so I left half the loaf on the kitchen table under a towel and stuffed the rest inside my shirt to keep it warm before setting out in the frigid darkness. A sticky snow was falling and by the time I arrived at Jean's house, my head, face, and overstuffed torso were covered with snow. I felt like Santa Claus.

Jean's house was still dark when I arrived so I kept running in circles to keep the bread from freezing. A kerosene lamp finally came on in Jean's room upstairs, then others were lit around the house including one in the kitchen downstairs. I moved to the kitchen window and peeked inside. Catherine, Jean's older sister, who we called Moffie, was brushing her teeth at the sink. I felt like Peck's Bad Boy spying on strangers; it was naughty and exciting at the same time. Moffie disappeared from my view for a moment and then I saw Jean run into the kitchen. "You god-damn whore," he yelled. Suddenly, Mr. Charles A. Gianini of New York appeared in his night clothes, grabbed Jean around the neck with one hand and proceeded to slap him across the face several times with the other. When Jean tried to turn away, the slaps landed on the side of his head. The beating eventually stopped and Mr. Gianini left the room.

I moved away from the window and waited on the porch.

"Hello, Croaker," Jean said when he emerged from the house.

His ear was red from the beating and I tried not to gawk. I reached inside my shirt and handed him the bread. He tore off a piece, gave me back the rest, and we ate as we walked to school. The snow-scrapers had not been through the streets yet and we had to plow our way through deep drifts.

"Say, this is good bread," Jean said with his mouth full. "Really good."

I watched him chewing and smiling as he playfully waded through the snowdrifts rather than kicking them. It was then that I first began to realize that life might have been very different for Jean Gianini if only he had a good Mama who baked bread for him.

I continued to spy on Jean's house. I believe I was drawn to this dark activity as much by the thrill of becoming one of Peck's Bad Boy Spies as by the desire to understand the strange happenings. It took many pre-school hours of watching and listening to figure out the mysterious characters who lived in the house of Gianini.

After Jean's mother died, Mr. Gianini had married a woman from Poland, New York. Her name was Florence E. Peterson, and they had three little girls who received all their attention. Jean hated his stepmother and teased the girls to the point of making them cry. Mr. Gianini never actually saw this happen because he generally ignored anything his son did, but if he heard his precious little girls cry he would bolt into the room and give Jean a severe beating. The beatings were not limited to slaps with the open hand; sometimes they were administered with a closed fist. Once I watched in silent horror as Jean's father threw him down, grabbed his head between his hands and beat it against the hardwood floor. Mr. Gianini never seemed to say a word so I never learned the reason, but there must have been grave misconduct to warrant such drastic correction. The nature and extent of Jean's punishments made it clear that he was more of a bad boy than I knew.

As I became more accomplished at my secret craft, and increasingly convinced of my near invisibility, I decided to try spying during daylight hours. One afternoon I left Jean at his house and continued walking up Buck Hill, then doubled back and worked my way through the backyards of houses on Cold Brook Street until I came to the Gianini barn. The barn was a good fifty feet from the house and too far away for effective spying. I crouched behind a rain barrel while I debated the risk of crossing the open space in daylight. *Thwack!* The air fractured with a sound so alien I could not fathom what it was. *Thwack!* This time I located the source as coming from within the barn. I found a slit between two loose boards and peeked inside.

Jean Gianini was standing naked in the middle of the barn. At first I thought Jean was masturbating because he was trembling.

Then I noticed something moving under the sawdust on the ground. It looked like someone was reeling in a fishing line.

"Father, don't," Jean hollered.

A horsewhip flew through the air and snapped against Jean's back, flicking away a tiny piece of skin. I watched the skin float to the ground and become lost in the sawdust. The whip lashed at him again and again. Jean's back was becoming marked with discolored grooves like his school desk. I was too sickened to watch this any longer. I didn't know what Jean did to deserve such punishment but I feared that the penalty for spying would be even more severe so I abandoned my friend and ran home. I have never forgiven myself.

In December Jean and I turned fifteen. He didn't receive a birthday present—he said his old man was too much of a tightwad and a miser—but his father did give him a new pair of long pants for Christmas. I received a new sled for my birthday but told Jean I got it on Christmas so he wouldn't feel bad. We decided to go sledding down the hill near the schoolhouse so I could try out my present. Jean wore his new long pants instead of his usual knickerbockers and took his own sled.

The hill was very steep and had a small U-shaped depression at the bottom that caused a fast-moving sled to become airborne for a short distance. Jean ran rapidly to the edge of the hill and threw himself on the sled. I watched as he descended at great speed, entered the "U" and sailed into the air. He landed on the sled which hit the ground with a jolt, then coasted to a stop at the road. He smiled as he put the sled under his arm and walked back up the hill.

I hesitated and watched him go down several more times as I studied his technique. Finally, I tried it without a running approach. This was successful but I didn't have enough speed to get airborne. Still, it was great fun and my sled performed well over many rides. When we were too exhausted to continue climbing the hill, we decided to build a snowman.

"Let's build a Golem," I said, "to guard against vampires." I told Jean the legend of the rabbi in ancient Prague who made a giant clay statue—the Golem—in order to defend the Hebrew community against a pogrom. The rabbi recited a few magic words and the statute came to life and protected everyone.

Jean liked the idea so we set to work rolling large balls of snow for the body and head. We paid special attention to shaping the face. Jean fashioned arms and a big nose from tree branches while I gave the Golem two large perfectly formed eyes. We stepped back to admire our work.

"Put your patch on him," Jean said.

I refused. The bright sun reflected off the snow would hurt me.

"Aw, come on," he said, grabbing my patch and pulling it down.

I glared at him with my exposed eye, then quickly restored my patch back to its place as I moved backwards. Jean continued to advance, shoving me to the ground. He grumbled to himself, then picked up his sled and attacked the Golem, chipping away large pieces from the body. I asked him to stop but he had a glazed look and I don't think he heard me. I searched my memory for the magic words to bring the Golem to life but I couldn't find them. Then Jean swung his sled at the Golem's head and knocked it clean off. I watched it roll over several times and come to rest with its eyes looking up, questioning me.

The New Year, 1913, began badly for Jean. He had always performed well on the monthly tests at school, sometimes obtaining perfect scores of 100 in history and spelling and averaging 92 in all subjects. Although Jean received help on his tests from the other boys, I had confidence that he could have done just as well on his own if he had only settled down. But in January his grades dropped to an average of 80 with a few 60s on tests despite the help. His constant whispering and talking to the others were distractions not only to him but to the entire class. I knew that corrective action was inevitable but I never dreamed that I would be an agent of his punishment.

One morning in February the Professor pulled me aside before school and asked me to accompany him to the attic. No pupil had ever seen the attic and no one knew what was up there. On stormy days, we could hear the creaking and groaning of the attic floor boards. It was rumored that a monster lived there.

The Professor had to tell me twice before I started climbing the narrow ladder to the attic door. The ladder squeaked as I moved up and pushed the door open. Clouds of dust whirled in the cool air and settled on cobwebs sticking to the edge of the door. I moved to the middle of the cramped attic and surveyed the stacks of dusty boxes, lamps, and extra desks. When the Professor joined me he was forced to stoop under the low ceiling. I knew then that he must have chosen me for this task because I was the shortest pupil in the class. He selected a desk and seat, and together we managed to get it down the ladder and into Miss Beecher's room.

He positioned the desk in a corner next to the chimney and facing a wall. I noticed that he had difficulty fastening it to the floor so I offered to help. He handed me the tools and I quickly secured the desk and seat to the floor. The Professor tried unsuccessfully to move it, then smiled at me for a job well done.

As the pupils filed into the room, the Professor took Jean aside. "Jean, you will have to take this seat next to the wall here in the corner," he began. "I place you here not as a punishment but simply to remove you from the temptation of whispering and talking in an undertone."

Jean shuffled to the corner seat.

"Don't hold a grudge against Miss Beecher," he continued. "This is not her idea. As soon as your behavior improves, we will be glad to give you a seat back in the room."

Jean turned to me, grumbling. He had seen me help the Professor install this instrument of correction. Now in the glare of his eyes I saw the monster from the attic.

The new seat failed to correct Jean's behavior. Although his back remained towards the rest of us, we could see him fidgeting and hear his whispered commentaries on the lessons. During a history lecture on a Civil War battle, Jean bobbed up and down as if his seat was a saddle and slapped his thigh rhythmically as if it was his mount. It was great fun to watch and I laughed along with the others. Even Miss Beecher cracked a smile. During several of my own recitations, I heard Jean make snorting sounds and whisper "Roy Finley's gonna get you," which caused me to stutter and mispronounce my own words, something I almost never did. Finally, after two weeks of such antics, Professor Robinson removed Jean from the class and placed him at a desk in his room upstairs where he could be more closely supervised.

"Miss Beecher feels it would be better for you and her if you were upstairs," the Professor explained as he was taking Jean away. "But don't hold it against her."

I missed my friend from the moment he left. The lessons seemed dull without his theatrical punctuations. It made me feel slightly better to learn that he wasn't having any fun upstairs. Jean said it was torture to be forced to sit absolutely still and study while the Professor scrutinized him. His only reprieve was when he was permitted to return to Miss Beecher's class to give his twenty-minute recitations. I studied him carefully as he spoke, searching for subtle changes. He looked as untidy as ever with those expensive yet disheveled clothes and uncombed hair. But the grins and smirks were gone, replaced by a slightly bowed head, downcast eyes, and a softer than normal voice.

My continuing surveillance at the Gianini house revealed that this new demeanor was only a show for Professor Robinson. Jean was continually whipped by his father for misbehaving at home. Once he had to go for three days with just bread and water. He told me that his old man tied him to a barrel, whipped him, and made him stay there for hours. His father even thrashed him on the sidewalk in full view of neighbors. After he showed me the ghastly bruises on his shoulders and back where he had been beaten with a wooden pole from the clothesline, I brought him a bottle of liniment from our house.

"I guess you are about the best friend I've got," he said as I rubbed the oily mixture on his skin. There was something noticeably wrong with his back besides the bruises. The muscles were stiff and tense. As I applied the liniment I could sense something inside his body getting ready to explode. It was much later that I learned the terrible reason for his tension.

Beyond the range of my surveillance Mr. Gianini had moved his bed into Jean's upstairs bedroom and had been sleeping there for almost a year with the sole purpose of preventing his son from masturbating. The beds were arranged side by side so no movement, however slight, went undetected. Mr. Gianini was an amateur naturalist and bird watcher who noticed every minute behavior. He believed that masturbation was an unnatural act, a vice that led to degeneracy. It was also one of the main reasons for commitment to an insane asylum. I was now an expert in such activity and practiced almost nightly in my own bed. The release helped me sleep and improved my spirits. Although I was doomed to degeneracy, I couldn't stop. But what would become of Jean? He knew of the pleasures he was denied. It must have created tremendous pressure inside him, enough to stiffen his muscles and drive him loony.

On April 1, Jean failed to emerge from his house for school. When he didn't appear on the following day, despite my calling his name at the door, I thought that he must be playing an elaborate April Fool's joke. Of course Jean could have been sick, although everyone attended school whether sick or not. He would have to be deathly ill to skip classes. Perhaps Mr. Gianini finally killed him. It was time for another spy mission.

As I approached his house in the early hours of April 3, Jean bolted from the door and ran down the street to the train station. I ran after him and finally found him sitting on a bench near the tracks. He talked while I tried to catch my breath. The two weeks he had spent in Professor Robinson's room had failed to correct his behavior. The Professor had had a meeting with his father and they had arrived at the conclusion that there was no use in Jean staying in school.

"They gave me the boot," Jean said.

I kept running my hands through my hair and twisting it as he spoke. This was terrible news. I couldn't comprehend losing my best friend—my only friend. I was on the verge of panic. "What are you going to do?" I asked in a halting voice. What am

I going to do? I thought.

Jean explained he was taking the M & M train to Newport, a larger village to the south, to work in the knitting mills where he was going to earn eighty cents a day.

"Are you coming back?" I yelled over the noise of the locomotive as the train chugged into the station.

I couldn't hear his answer as he hopped on a car and waved.

My sadness was obvious at school that day. At the noon recess Miss Beecher took me aside and said she was worried about me. I should not lose interest in my studies simply because Eugene, who never had interest, was no longer present, she told me.

"Jean," I corrected. She always called him Eugene and no one, not even Jean, complained. Now it was making me angry at her and I didn't know why.

Then she did something simply wonderful. She removed an ebonite comb with tiny silver trimmings from her velvet bag and began combing my hair.

"You don't want to be like Eugene and have unruly hair, do you?" she asked.

The sensations that went through me from what she was doing made me ecstatic. "Yes," I said. I was so confused and delirious I was uncertain of what I meant.

4

I finished the school year near the top of my class but at the bottom of my spirits. As the days of a muggy summer lumbered on, my hopes of ever playing again with Jean Gianini were dashed. I didn't see him for weeks. It was almost as if he had fallen into a dark well and disappeared. I went by his house a few times and called his name, hoping he would bob to the surface, but there was no answer. In his backyard I saw the old log and plank we used to ride as a seesaw. Jean was always trying to use his advantage in weight to bounce me into the air. I would fly off the end like a bird, reaching for the sky. Now his end of the plank was empty; mine was stuck in the mud.

Then, just as suddenly as Jean had vanished, he surfaced outside The Hotel Carlton. He told me he had been working in Newport for the past several weeks, leaving each morning on the early train and returning late. Not only did he pay the train fare himself but his father took almost all of his remaining wages.

"The old man swindled me so I quit," Jean explained. "Then he trimmed me."

I had only two pennies but I suggested we chip in for a box of *Zu Zu* snaps and spend the day together.

"*Zu Zu* puts snap and ginger into jaded appetites," we singsonged together, repeating a familiar advertisement.

"Sorry. I've got plans with Peck Newman," Jean smiled.

Frank "Peck" Newman was a local constable who Mr. Gianini employed to watch over Jean, keep him from getting into trouble, and take care of things when he did. I always thought that the nickname came from the peck of troubles Jean gave him. During the previous summer Jean had slipped by Peck's watchdog eye and run away from home. He took a supply of bananas and a can of beans, then hopped a freight train for Herkimer, New York. It rained that first night and Jean was forced to sleep in a coal bin under a bridge. He came home the next day, filthy and feverish, and was promptly given a severe beating. Peck heard Jean hollering and felt so sorry for him that he took him back to Herkimer to see the circus. Now Jean was waiting for his forty-three-year-old friend-for-hire to take him on another trip. This time they were going to Herkimer to see the moving pictures. I had never seen a moving picture.

Peck Newman drove up to the store in Mr. Gianini's car and tipped his fancy hat at us, acting like he owned the shiny black automobile. Jean appeared excited as he jumped into the front seat. He snatched the hat from Peck's head, put it on his own and tipped it at me, then they both had a good laugh. I watched them drive off, the most mismatched friends I could imagine. I was hurt. Two cents was not enough to salvage my friendship with Jean.

I stayed around Russia for the summer helping Father who was glad I could do more work now that I was not in school. I noticed that he would sweat profusely and tire easily, often taking long naps during the middle of the day. I used the opportunity to swim in Zia Nardone's pond with a few of the other kids.

We had free use of the pond since Zia was no longer chasing us away. She had stayed inside her house since 1908 and relied on a helper. In the pre-dawn hours of December 28, 1908, a catastrophic earthquake struck Zia's hometown of Messina in southern Italy. Seismographs picked up the vibrations four thousand miles away in Washington, D.C. It was the deadliest earthquake in European history. Buildings in Villa San Giovanni near the center of destruction collapsed in seconds. Minutes later a tsunami measuring forty feet high swept over the coastline and trapped survivors. This was followed by volcanic eruptions, terrific downpours, hailstorms, lightning bursts, fires, and after-shocks. At the end, typhoid took anyone still alive. All of Zia's relatives along with 150,000 others perished in the apocalypse. Zia had remained in mourning ever since and never recovered from the death of her favorite niece, Angelina, a girl about my age. She had planned to bring Angelina to America to live with her on the farm. I, too, mourned the loss because I would have liked to have had Angelina as a playmate. I didn't learn until much later that Zia blamed my evil eye for the disaster. The day before the quake I was playing with a funny mask that Father had made for my birthday. I was running around near her prop-erty, trying to spook the cows. Zia ran over to me.

"Who are you?" she screamed.

I pulled off the mask and my patch, letting her know it was only me. She spat and said I had grown a big Jew nose just like my father—to her that was a sure sign of my maliciousness. I resisted the temptation to spit back and simply glared. She stumbled and fell, then scrambled to her feet and ran home, cursing in Italian.

Then the quake hit. Zia read about it in the local papers although news of her relatives took months to arrive. Nonethe-less, she remembered that the day I glared at her was the day before the quake in Messina. If there was any doubt about my evil eye, a front-page story in the local paper on a different sub-ject confirmed it. The article claimed that the number of dead in Herkimer County had been steadily increasing since 1897, the year I was born. The last year, 1908, set a new record with 142 dead in the county. In Zia's superstitious mind I was the cause and I had finally acquired the power to avenge her for dropping me on my head as a baby by dropping the walls of Villa San Giovanni on her family. Her reasoning, which she told to neigh-bors, seemed almost logical but I refused to accept the deaths as anything other than coincidence.

Now that I was an accomplished spy I decided to apply my talents to Zia, whose strange ways held a special fascination for me. One night I sneaked onto her property and made my way to the kitchen window which was shimmering with the glow of several candles. I watched at the corner of the window as her gnarled fingers struggled to pour a few drops of olive oil into a bowl filled with water. Zia closed her eyes and mumbled a prayer. I understood neither the words nor the meaning of the ritual and it was then I decided to learn Italian in order to decipher her magical incantations.

I moved to the middle of the window and watched the bowl as the oil slowly spread over the water. She opened her eyes, saw the oil spreading, then looked up. We were staring directly into each other's faces. I saw an old woman with a brow furrowed like a newly ploughed field. Her eyes squinted as though she was in deep pain. The cheeks were deeply cracked with worry lines that the earthquake itself must have opened. The lines held her face and mouth in an expression of utter disgust.

Because I often looked out windows at night I knew exactly what Zia saw: a reflection of the contents of the kitchen and herself. She would also have seen a transparent and barely perceptible image of my face superimposed on her own like a ghost in the mirror.

"*Mal occhio*," she gasped, then threw her arms in the air as if they had just been scorched by the candles.

I dropped down and disappeared like the apparition I had become.

In the following days red ribbons sprouted around the Nardone farm like so many weeds. They were tied to the fence posts, gates, and trees. Her kitchen window was decorated with stripes of red cloth that hung down like bloody icicles. Even the cows wore braids of red wool around their necks. Zia told people that Jews could spread a stench over the land; Jews with evil eyes and big noses like mine were especially infectious. She believed such safeguards were necessary to stop my evil influence, otherwise the cows would get sick, the milk would sour, and the butter would not churn. But rather than scare me, the red pennants waving in the wind only teased me like a matador's cape, inflaming my anger at her ignorance. In a curious way they worked to keep me off her property: I was afraid I might charge like a bull and gore the witch.

One day Peck Newman and Jean drove past my farm on their way to Graves Hollow where Peck kept the horses for the livery stable he operated behind his house on Cold Brook Street. Peck had a reputation for dishonest horse dealing and it was said if you wanted a horse with spots Peck made sure it had spots. Now he was taking Jean up to his farm to see how it was done. They didn't stop but Jean waved from the car. I ran to the road and waved back but they were already on the other side of the hill. Later Jean told me he had great fun at Peck's place and even chased down a stray cow.

A few days later Jean was the one who strayed away from home. His father had pulled him from bed, pushed him against the wall, and pummeled his head. I could only imagine what Jean had been doing to warrant the attack and was not the least surprised to learn he ran away the next morning. This time it was Peck Newman's job to chase down the stray. It took Peck nearly a month driving around the county before he finally located Jean at Flayhaven's hotel in Ilion where he was wiping dishes. I think Peck deliberately took his time so he could drive Mr. Gianini's fancy automobile as long as possible. On the way back to Poland Jean rode in the back, his hand hanging out and beating the side of the automobile like a war drum.

Stray boys like stray cows need to be fenced or roped in order to prevent them from wandering away again. Mr. Gianini settled for ordering Jean to get a job, any job. Jean found one shoveling manure for fifty cents a day. But muckraking was not Jean's idea of a summer vacation so he quit after a few days and went to Herkimer where he jumped a freight train headed to New York City.

He left the train in Albany and wandered around the railroad yard. A yard detective chased Jean and had to shoot his gun three times before he stopped running. Jean was promptly arrested and held for a week until one of Mr. Gianini's henchmen from

Poland could retrieve him. The man arrived and gave Jean a train ticket back to Herkimer which was the equivalent of asking a stray cow to please go home. Jean jumped off the train somewhere near Fort Plain, approximately midway between Schenectady and Herkimer, and disappeared on foot.

In early August, Father and I decided we would attend the County Fair that was to be held in Herkimer in September. There were seventy-five-dollar prizes for the best plate of apples in each category. We planned to enter plates of our very best August Sweet, Early Harvest, and Rome Beauties. There were also prizes for the best breads and I wanted to bake a loaf using one of Mama's recipes, although there wasn't a category for black bread. Still, there were going to be horse races to watch, jellies and cheeses to taste, and handicrafts to admire. And best of all, Father promised to take me to the moving pictures.

As I walked to the Poland Union Store to find the entry blanks for the fair, it was impossible to pass Jean Gianini's house and not think about him.

"Hello, Croaker."

I was lost in a reverie and kept walking.

"Say, where are you going?"

I turned and saw Jean, who was back from his latest adventure. Peck Newman and his father had finally found him working at the same hotel in Ilion.

"They swindled me," Jean said with a smile as he described how they sneaked up and threw him into the automobile. He didn't even have time to collect his wages.

Jean walked with me to the store. Suddenly Mr. Gianini appeared and ordered Jean to go home. Jean muttered a little but obediently lowered his head and shuffled back to his house. I thought the stray boy had finally been corralled until I saw him reach behind his back and extend his middle finger.

Father had a stroke while we were picking apples for the fair. He couldn't move very well so I set the ladder on the ground, placed him on it, then dragged it back to the house where I managed to get him into bed. He complained that his left arm and leg didn't work. I panicked and ran to Zia Nardone's house for help.

I took a shortcut, barging through our patch of giant sunflowers with no concern for the damage I was causing, then ran down the hill to Zia's farm where red flags everywhere waved for me to charge ahead even faster. When I arrived at her door I was huffing and puffing, with tears of sweat dripping from my face.

There were little white cotton balls covering holes in the screen door like fake spider webs. As I reached to knock on the door it flew open so hard some of the cotton balls were knocked loose and tumbled away in the wind. Zia stood on the threshold wearing her black mourning clothes and holding a pitchfork. She looked more like a witch than ever before. Her eyes were squeezed shut.

"Away, away," she yelled, jabbing the pitchfork in my direction.

"Please, my father—" I said, stepping to the side in order to avoid her blind thrusts.

"Away." She lunged forward only to trip over the doorstep, falling to the ground and landing on her side with a thump that sent wisps of dirt into the air.

I continued to plead for my father but Zia neither spoke nor moved. I approached to see if she was all right. A tiny greenish plug of mucous crept slowly from her nostril like a mud turtle peeking from its shell. It withdrew then emerged again, repeating its hide and seek motion with each breath. I waited to see if it would stop, knowing if it did, the witch was dead. After several minutes she coughed and sucked the snot back into her nose.

I left her there and ran home as quickly as possible. As I retraced my steps I saw that several of the sunflowers had dropped their petals and seeds in the wake of my panicked passage, leaving only bare and dying stalks.

I did not return to school that year but stayed home to take care of Father and gather the fall harvest. Meanwhile Jean's father decided to take care of him once and for all. In official papers, Mr. Charles A. Gianini of New York said he had had enough of "that incorrigible boy" and charged him with juvenile delinquency. Jean was committed to the custody of St. Vincent's Industrial School in Utica for six months. Mr. Gianini gave Jean the impression that St. Vincent's was Miss Beecher's idea. The kids called it a reform school, but the only real changes from the Poland School were the Catholic curriculum and a reformed method of corporal punishment utilizing the strap instead of the Professor's rubber hose.

Jean viewed the change as a new adventure and didn't protest as Peck Newman and Mr. Gianini took him to the massive three-story building on the corner of John and Elizabeth Streets in Utica. Mr. Gianini was hopeful Jean would reform. But he failed to realize that inside the forbidding parochial walls was a grand dormitory housing dozens of incorrigible delinquent boys. The opportunity to learn from them was unlimited. Peck was the one who was worried because he was now deprived of his extra income. One of the kids from school told me that when Mr. Gianini dropped Peck off at his house on the corner of Cold Brook Street and Main, he actually patted the automobile goodbye.

On February 6, 1914, Mr. Gianini asked Peck to once again drive the car to St. Vincent's in order to bring Jean home. Jean was subdued during the ride, saying only that he didn't like the school because he was always being punished for no reason. Frequent beatings with a strap had marked his entire body including the palms of his hands. The marks made on the inside had not yet risen to the surface.

In order to keep Jean busy and out of trouble, Peck gave him a job in Graves Hollow piling wood for fifteen cents a hour. Jean stayed at that job for all of two and one-half hours. This was followed by a succession of other odd jobs around the valley including shoveling snow, sawing wood, driving a wagon, and hauling manure. Jean kept quitting and moving from job to job every few days. The straps of Catholicism had failed to hold him down. Even Mr. Gianini seemed to give up and stopped beating him. The bad boy was back, more restless, more agitated, and more uncorrected than ever.

Later in February Miss Beecher moved into Mr. James Dayton Countryman's boarding house on Cold Brook Street. It was a large white colonial house just a few doors from Jean's house on the opposite side of the street. Miss Beecher had never been far from his thoughts and now she was practically living next door. I was jealous. Jean could look out his window or stand on the porch and catch a glimpse of our beautiful teacher. I have tried to imagine how this affected him. It had to have been unsettling. She was going back and forth to school each day and he was not. She was living next to him but probably acted like he didn't exist. She would have seemed as distant and uninviting as school. Watching her from his bedroom window, where his frustration was never permitted relief, he must have gone loony.

I learned that as Jean shuffled from job to job, he ran into acquaintances from the Poland School. The chance encounters reminded him of why he was no longer a scholar. He couldn't help but blurt out what was on his mind. When he met Morris Howe coming out of the schoolhouse one day, Jean mentioned that Miss Beecher didn't like him and that he wanted to get even with her. Later, Jean told Estus Compo that Miss Beecher had sent him away to reform school and he would kill her some day. Still later he told Lawrence Lamb he would do it before spring.

Then Jean came to visit me at home. When I opened the door he was smoking a tobacco cigarette and offered me a puff, grinning mischievously. We had once smoked cornsilk together and I didn't enjoy it so I declined. We talked about my father for a few minutes, then Jean's dark eyes seemed to glaze over.

"I want to break into the Union Store and get the money there," he said. "I need it so I can skip out in a few days. Will you go with me?"

I shook my head.

"Does your old man have any tools for the job?" he asked, eying the toolshed next to the barn.

I didn't want to lie so I changed the subject and suggested we go inside the house and get something to eat. He sat at the kitchen table while I prepared the food.

"Miss Beecher did me dirt," he said. "She was the one who sent me away to reform school."

I handed him a plate of cheese and bread.

"Nobody likes me but you, Croaker," he said as he tore off a piece of bread.

I nodded, keeping my mouth full so I wouldn't have to speak. As he described his plan to take Miss Beecher up Buck Hill, I thought he was telling another story that blurred the boundaries between real life and fantasy. He said he had been encouraging her to come to his house, which he told her was a new one up on Buck Hill, in order to speak with his father about coming back to school.

"When I get her up there, I will Indian her, maybe rape her." He leaned forward on his chair. I could smell the manure on him from his current job cleaning stables. "Will you go along and help me?" he whispered.

Jean always whispered when he wanted to emphasize a particularly horrifying point in a story he was inventing. It sounded like another vampire-type story only this time Jean wanted to make-believe he was the vampire. It was only a fantasy, I thought, but I shook my head anyway.

He told me the names of his other friends he had asked to help but they all refused. I was his best friend, he pleaded. I had to help. But I shook my head again, this time more in disbelief than refusal. His eyes narrowed. "I'm going to kill her when I get the chance, with or without you. Do you have a gun I could use?"

I stared and said nothing.

Suddenly he reached over and pulled my patch down. "Let me borrow it," he said.

I glared angrily at him and put the patch back in place.

Jean abruptly stood and walked out. I later heard that on the way back to Poland he ran into Leon Coonradt. "I will do something that the people of Poland will be sorry for," Jean announced.

On the morning of March 16, 1914, Father died. Since the

stroke seven months before, his body had been dying. It had become a mere shell that was slowly thickening, squeezing the insides until there was no room for him to live. First his left side went, then another stroke paralyzed his right side and stole his speech. He retained some awareness, his eyes following me around the room as I fed and bathed him. When I read to him he often squinted at humorous passages or blinked rapidly at sad ones. He had the partial use of his right hand but it was more like a doll's hand, disconnected from the orientation of the face and eyes. Yet he still had dignity. His eyes never asked for pity nor reflected pain although he sometimes stared at me with a resigned, terrible look. He remained a Zoken until the end when I found him lying in bed, clutching a picture of Mama against his bosom with his good hand. I realized that I had never actually seen my parents holding each other, but I couldn't imagine a more tender embrace.

I prepared a simple pine coffin the way Father had taught me, then placed Mama's picture on his chest before nailing the lid. When it was done, I walked around the coffin several times to admire my work. There was one duty remaining. I grasped the nail of my middle finger with a pair of pliers, took a deep breath, and pulled slowly. The nail began to rip from its underlying bed, stretching tiny tendrils of tissue past their breaking points. My entire body tensed and stiffened as I continued to pull. I felt pain spark along nerves I never knew existed. The entire finger was on fire. I opened my mouth and screamed *"Kriah"* at the top of my lungs as the nail came out, dangling from the bloody teeth of the pliers. I sank to the floor, panting, staring at my throbbing finger. I had my father's hand now—a man's hand.

"Po-Do will do you," Uncle Sam said with a smile as he grabbed a tin of *Peau-Doux* Styptic Powder from his bag. He unscrewed the gold cap, sprinkled the powder on a dampened towel, and held it against my raw finger tip which had continued to bleed for a week. I started to pull away but he held my finger in a tight grip. It stung worse than a bee yet I could only laugh as he made a funny face, wagging a tobacco-stained tongue against his bushy mustache.

Uncle Sam always made me laugh. He was a Russian Jew who came from the same village as my parents but he wasn't a real uncle. My parents had met him in New York where he was working as a barber on Hester Street. They became good friends and traveled north together but Uncle Sam got off the train in Herkimer where he found work in a local barbershop. He visited us often and I cannot remember a single holiday meal when he was not at our table. He always brought me a toy or an interesting present. I still have a seashell he said came from a beach on the Atlantic Ocean. I have never seen an ocean but when I put the shell to my ear I can hear a noise that I'm told is the roar of the waves. It is an ominous, almost canonical sound, and I think the shell is mourning for the snail who once lived there.

Uncle Sam had arrived after the *shiva* week of mourning, too late to help with Father's burial which tradition demanded be done within twenty-four hours after death. But he did help me get the farm ready for sale and arranged for me to live with him in Herkimer. We packed my clothes and loaded his wagon with the only belongings I wanted to keep: my books and bed; my father's tools, prayer books, *tallis* prayer shawl and *tefillin* phylacteries; Mama's silver wine cup, and a black sweater she knitted for me which I can still wear.

On Friday afternoon, March 27, I walked down Buck Hill Road to say goodbye to Jean. I promised Uncle Sam I would return by sundown to light the Sabbath candles.

The walk into Kuyahoora Valley had once been full of excitement and thanksgiving. Now, in the approaching twilight, it was oddly disquieting. My parents were dead, our farm was no longer, and I was about to lose my best friend. Maybe it was my fault, my evil eye. There was a force more powerful than I that was directing my life with utter indifference. I turned to face the sun to protest directly to God.

"See what you have done!" I screamed, lifting my patch.

The next thing I remember is kneeling on the side of the Buck Hill Road and vomiting. It was after dark and the air was misty. My head hurt. I struggled to my feet and staggered back to my house. I didn't think I had made it to Jean's to say goodbye.

Uncle Sam was standing vigil on the porch and rushed to help me inside where I noticed that the Sabbath candles had burned down most of the way. I realized that I must have had a massive seizure and lost all memory of the past several hours. My hair was matted with blood from where I probably had fallen. Uncle Sam tried to tend to me but I didn't want to be nursed. In the nauseating aftermath of my seizure everything sickened me. I wanted to leave for Herkimer immediately.

"It's *Shabbes*," Uncle Sam said. It was not appropriate for an observant Jew to ride in a wagon until after sundown on Saturday. However, he was only thinking of me because he always worked on the Sabbath which was the busiest day of the week in the barbershop. "You should rest and take care of yourself," he added.

"Why should I? God doesn't care," I yelled, surprised at what I was saying.

In the middle of the night we drove down Buck Hill Road through a landscape of dread. The willow trees stood like menacing shadows in the darkness of the new moon, the twisted branches reaching out and threatening to hold me in their stiff embrace. An owl called plaintively in the distance. The light mist mixed with a thick fog and conjured unbidden memories. Uncle Sam cracked the whip on his horse and it was as if I heard Jean hollering in the barn. The wagon hit a bump and I remembered the Professor shaking me by the shoulders. A box fell out of the wagon and I recalled the Golem's head rolling away, eyes glaring at me. Uncle Sam stopped the wagon so I could retrieve the box. As I climbed down one of the large iron wheels, I slipped and fell into a puddle. Now I was covered with slush and mud, soiled by the land.

5

"BRUTAL MURDER OF POLAND TEACHER"

The bold headline on the front page of the Saturday, March 28, paper stunned me like the bright light of a seizure. There was the roar of a thousand sea shells in my brain. I was no longer in my room behind Uncle Sam's barbershop but inside a waking dream.

It was one of those bad dreams wherein you are helpless to change what is happening. I sat there as some invisible force scrolled the second headline: "**BODY OF LYDDIA BEECHER FOUND LYING IN WILLOWS ALONG THE ROADSIDE— HER FACE BADLY CHOPPED WITH A KNIFE AND WRENCH—HER HANDS RAISED TO PROTECT HER FROM SAVAGE BLOWS.**" This cannot be true, I thought. Yes, of course, they misspelled her name, thereby betraying the hoax. I was forced to read a third headline: "**CLAUDE GANNINI CONFESSES CRIME.**" There was no such person. It must be a dreamlike distortion of my memory of Jean's visit to my house only a few days earlier.

A smaller fourth headline that followed was a dead giveaway that the story was false. After all, even the death of a president or a declaration of war was granted only one or two headlines. I read the awkward headline with amusement: "**TELLS WHERE**

TO FIND THE WEAPONS HE USED—THE OFFICERS UNEARTH A WRENCH AND A KNIFE." If this was a true story there should have been a revolver which Jean always said would be his weapon of choice. And what happened to the clothesline that Jean told me he was going to use to tie up Miss Beecher before he did the "Indian" to her? I now suspected that Jean had invented the entire story as an early April Fool's joke and told it to an incredibly naive reporter, purposely changing his name and dreaming up gruesome details. All that was missing was Count Dracula.

I threw the newspaper across the room and began unpacking my belongings. But before the paper settled on the floor I ran and snatched it back, then glanced over the actual text of the article. I picked out several more errors including "Elida Beecher," "Eugene Gannini," and "Charles Gainnini."

"See, see," I said as I pointed at each mistake. It appeared safe to read the entire fabricated story from start to finish.

Early this morning, the story said, Henry Fitch, a farmer I knew, was driving his milk wagon from Russia down Buck Hill. He had just entered the area where the road leads through the thick willows when his mare was suddenly spooked. Henry managed to quiet the horse, then noticed a ten-foot length of clothesline coiled like a snake in the road. There was a large patch of blood next to the rope.

I reared up from my bed where I had been sitting. "No, no, no!" I snorted as I paced around my room. The clothesline snake had the bite of reality. I realized then that the story must be true and my teacher really murdered, but two deaths in as many weeks was almost too much to bear. I was breathing so rapidly that I was forced to lie down and rest for fear that I might give myself a seizure. My hand automatically stretched back to the headboard and touched the rough wood. As my fingers probed the familiar contours of the knothole that had always comforted me and told me where I was, I felt lost in the hollow of my heart. After reciting a few prayers I was able to calm down enough to resume reading.

There were other objects found on the road including Miss Beecher's black velvet cap and her broken comb that had once gently stroked my hair. Nearby was a large clump of her dark brown hair. I feared that Jean had scalped her, as well as doing the Indian, but I learned later that it was only a switch she wore. This upset me because I always thought she had long hair like Mama. People were turning out to be very different from what I had once believed.

Henry Fitch followed the path of blood down a slope to a snow-covered field where Miss Beecher's body was lying face down covered by a raincoat. She appeared to be sleeping, her body as stiff as a nearby apple tree that marked the spot. The paper said that she had been turned over after death and placed in that position under the tree. Whoever did this was not a cold-blooded killer but must have cared deeply for the teacher. Under the raincoat her red dress was drawn up to expose her bare legs clothed only in black socks and patent leather shoes. I had watched the tips of those shoes peek out from under her dresses as she walked in front of the class and often wondered about the style of ladies shoes she wore. Mama always wore high ones that laced. Now I read that Miss Beecher wore high top button shoes. For me the mystery was over but Jean had always wanted to see more, especially her breasts. He wanted to get near enough to touch them. The knife closed the distance better than the gun. I couldn't help but think about what Jean must have felt as the knife pricked her flesh and her warm blood bathed his hand. The thought was disturbing.

It was painful to read of the many bruises and cuts he made on her body so I merely skimmed the sentences, mentally marking their places so I could return to them when I was more composed. For now it was enough to know she was actually and undeniably dead. My heart was strangely aching.

Mr. Gianini told a reporter that Jean had come home and gone to bed. "That boy is an incorrigible," he said. "He has made us lots of trouble. But I know he is innocent of this crime." Presumably one does not sleep after committing such a heinous deed. By such logic I was a guilty party because now I was sure I couldn't sleep despite my fatigue from traveling all night and setting up my room. I stared at the high ceiling over my bed, images reeling in my brain. I remembered Miss Beecher combing my messy hair while calling Jean unruly. I saw her turn her back on Jean, refusing to help while Jean was removed from her class and beaten by the Professor. Having a teacher turn against you is like losing your mother all over again.

My thoughts were racing as I busied myself with examining my new surroundings and arranging my belongings. The room itself was a large storage area for the barbershop and it had many shelves, a closet, a toilet and sink. A single bare light bulb hung from a cord in the middle of the room. There was a door leading to the outside alley behind the building and another door which opened into the shop itself. My bed was nestled against the only wall with a window, although the window was small, frosted, and too high for me to clean, let alone see through. Uncle Sam, who lived in a small apartment upstairs where I would be eating my meals, had given me a wooden table and two wooden chairs with yellow upholstery on one seat and red on the other. He was hoping I would do my studies at the table until I returned to school in Herkimer when the new term started in the fall. One of the chairs had a broken leg and I decided to fix it. I opened the chest containing Father's tools and began sorting them. I counted everything several times. There was no doubt about it: one of the wrenches was missing.

I wanted to take the next train back to Poland to get the wrench, which I assumed was left in Father's toolshed, but I didn't want to have to go by the crime scene. The article in the newspaper said that reporters were now swarming over the entire area. One of the local papers, *The Herkimer Citizen*, boasted they had over one hundred correspondents—one hundred spies—spread out across the county to investigate the tragedy. I knew that many of them simply picked up their party line telephones and eavesdropped on conversations between county officials. Others went to the murder scene, looked at the evidence in the road, and traipsed through the field to gawk at the bloody body. Their initial eye-witness dispatches were already included in that first article. I read their accounts with the same horror and fascination I had experienced when reading Jean's copy of *Dracula*.

Despite the chopped and distorted appearance of the face, Miss Beecher was recognizable to everyone. The undertaker removed the body from the crime scene because it was raining. I learned later that before the rain washed away most of the remaining evidence, one of the kids from the Poland School picked up a souvenir from the road and put it in his pocket.

The villagers told reporters that Jean Gianini had probably committed the murder. His obsession with Miss Beecher was well known to me but I was surprised to read that others knew of it. The two had been seen together many times in the past weeks: on the street, near the school, and at the Post Office only yesterday. Her roommate, Ethel Clark, reported that Miss Beecher had no gentleman friends and Jean was the only one who ever came calling for her. He would visit her after supper and the three of them would talk. Jean told them he didn't like his home and hated his father. He spoke of getting away from Poland some day, of going to the Great White Way in New York, of acting in moving pictures. I don't know what Miss Beecher made of such dreams but judging from his "performances" in the classroom, it was easy to see he was a natural actor who might very well end up in the moving pictures.

The roommate told reporters that Jean was always trying to get Miss Beecher to see his father about returning to school. Jean was so importunate that Miss Beecher had confided that she couldn't put him off any longer and would probably go with him. On the night of the murder, she was last seen walking with Jean from the Post Office toward his house. Some people in the village gossiped to reporters that they were secret lovers and she was pregnant with his child. A few said he mistook her kindness and caring attitude for a romantic interest and he raped her. Whatever it was, I was jealous of such intimacy. I never spoke to her outside the classroom. I never called upon her like a gentleman. I never told her of my dreams and desires. Yet, I, too, was also a secret lover.

The paper printed all the details about Jean's capture and arrest. County Sheriff William Hamilton Stitt arrived on the train from Herkimer with the coroner and an army of reporters in tow. At the murder scene the sheriff found a button in the snow and held it up for all to see. The villagers told the sheriff it probably belonged to Jean Gianini. Word went out that he was wanted but Mr. Gianini's henchmen were already searching for a runaway boy—not a murderer—and they found him walking down the train tracks near a local market. Peck Newman picked Jean up at the market and drove him away. Jean later said that he thought Peck was taking him to the circus again. Instead they ended up at the home of Squire Moore, the local Justice of the Peace.

When Jean walked inside, his father was waiting in the sitting room packed with reporters and other people. Everyone could see that Jean's clothes looked like they had been torn by a barbed wire fence, and he was wearing mismatched rubbers but no shoes or leggings. He kept making swallowing sounds in his throat, something I had seen him do when he was expecting a beating from his father. The sheriff ushered Jean and his father into the parlor and closed the folding doors. He told reporters he grilled Jean for two hours but Jean refused to answer any questions. I know that Jean was more afraid of his father than the sheriff and would never admit to any serious wrongdoing in his father's presence. When the sheriff pointed to Jean's jacket, which had a tear and a button missing as well as a row of red spots along the right sleeve and shoulder, Jean explained that he didn't keep track of all the buttons on his clothes and the red stuff was paint from the market. Since there was no way to test for blood and there was indeed a fresh coat of red paint on the market counter, the sheriff was unable to get anything from Jean and let Deputy Sheriff John Nellis question him. Nellis kicked Mr. Gianini out of the room and locked the folding doors. When the doors opened again Nellis had a confession in his hand and bragged to reporters about how he had obtained it. He made Jean strip naked and stand in the cold, then promised him he would get no more than five or ten years if he talked. Jean confessed.

As I read Jean's detailed description of the murder, I tried to imagine what Miss Beecher had thought before dying. As she and Jean climbed the hill and entered that dark section where the road leads through the willow groves, she no doubt grew uneasy. She didn't see any house or lights and refused to go further. She turned around to go down the hill while Jean stepped around her back. When the first blows struck from behind, she probably felt deceived, swindled. On the ground she turned as if to get up. The knife jabbed at her to stay down. At first the jabs were hesitant but then they took on a relentless, fiendish rhythm. When her raised hands could do nothing to stop the attack, she realized she was finished. When he dragged her by the feet across the road, drawing bloody tracks through a field of virgin snow, her dress moved up her legs, exposing her thighs. She was embarrassed which was a silly thought because by now she knew she was dying. I'm sure Jean saw the dress ride up and thought about touching her. He had all he could do to keep himself from pulling her dress off and seeing her totally naked like an Indian, then opening her legs and climbing into her right there. Her body made a strange sound, as if to protest his plan, and this scared him away.

I shook my head to rid it of this imagined scene and continued reading the newspaper story. Deputy Nellis told reporters that after confessing, Jean bragged: "You wouldn't think any one could do a job as quick as that. I wanted revenge and I knew I had it." It sounded just like something Jean would have said. I could even picture him grinning. "They will talk of insanity," Jean added, "but I'm no more insane than you. I am content and happy."

How could he be content and happy? There was no way Jean was so insensitive. There had to be more to it than this. I suspected that there would be many more newspaper stories in the coming days. One of the advantages of living in back of Uncle Sam's barbershop was that he subscribed to all the local newspapers and had charged me with the responsibility for cleaning the shop every night and throwing away the old papers. I decided I would collect all the articles about the murder. I carefully cut out that first article and saved it in a wooden box that had once contained the huge stoneware spittoon which now rested on the floor of the shop.

I returned to unpacking my books while listening to the customers in the shop talk about the murder. By peeking through a crack in the door I was able see and hear everything. I was happy to be back in the spy business. To investigate the murder of your teacher by your best friend is one of the most solemn missions a spy could ever undertake.

"Look at that mob moving down the street," said Uncle Sam. I couldn't see the mob from the crack in the door but I could certainly hear them yelling.

"There's going to be a lynching," said a customer.

"There ought to be," said another customer. "He's a pervert and a goddamn murderer."

The crowd was getting louder. Jean and the sheriff were scheduled to arrive in Herkimer on the 5:10 P.M. train. At 5:00 the shop emptied as everyone, including Uncle Sam, rushed out to greet the train. I left my room and went to the front window to watch.

In a few minutes I saw Jean and Sheriff Stitt running up Main Street toward the safety of the County Jail opposite the Herkimer County Court House. No one could have accused Jean of shuffling that day as he and the sheriff easily outran a mob of several hundred. They stopped in front of the barbershop to catch their breath. The sheriff twirled his white handlebar mustache as he eyed the mob which had stopped its pursuit about a block away and now gawked, uncertain as to what to do. A photographer ran up to Jean with his camera. "Turn your head, you goddamn murderer," he yelled.

Jean turned away from the camera and faced the window. He was bent over and panting so hard his entire upper body heaved, almost as if he was rocking back and forth in prayer, then he looked up and saw me. His panting turned to giant sobs that continued to rock his body. He was trembling. My skin was all prickly and I, too, started shaking. I stared into his gray eyes. They were frightened eyes, little boy eyes, my eyes. Suddenly, I felt like I was falling into the glass, falling down a rabbit hole. I found myself looking out through his eyes, feeling his fright and, yes, his shame. Tears streamed down his face and his lips quivered, mouthing regrets in a secret language only best friends understood. I felt like crying, too, but I couldn't. I watched my tears escape through Jean's eyes.

I wanted to comfort him, to lullaby him. I longed to smile for him but I could no more smile than cry so I took my index fingers and pushed up the corners of my mouth into a smile. It felt grotesque, like the rabid snarl it must have resembled. But Jean stopped his sobbing. Tears continued to well in his eyes but now a smile crept hesitantly across his face. It was a genuine, warm smile, the kind he had when he was eating a piece of Mama's black bread. He nodded. Then he put his hand over his mouth and shook his head. I didn't understand the gesture and yelled through the glass for an explanation. It was too late. Jean had turned away and resumed his run with the sheriff.

I ran outside and joined the mob that followed them to the County Jail. The turnkey, a big burly man known only as Decker — although no one knew if this was his first or last name — stood at the entrance and blocked the crowd from surging forward. Decker looked as rough and solid as the limestone blocks of the ancient Grecian-styled jail. Jean turned to the crowd and grinned, then disappeared inside.

On Sunday an autopsy was conducted in Poland. All the newspapers reported it and published a picture of Miss Beecher, showing her in one of my favorite dresses, with a beatific smile. The edges of the photo were brushed so that they faded into a cloud-like background. It looked like a picture taken in heaven. The papers reported that the autopsy had shown that she might have lived for thirty minutes after the attack but there was no evidence showing an outrage on her. The autopsy was performed by the coroner, who was assisted by a surgeon from

Utica and my old physician, Dr. Cole. I remembered that he had a light touch when he examined my eye and I hoped that he had been just as gentle with Miss Beecher. I reread the description of her wounds from Saturday's paper and tried to imagine Cole's examination.

I touched my eye as Dr. Cole had done and pretended my fingers were grazing Miss Beecher's more perfect skin as she lay naked on the undertaker's table. My fingers moved like a butterfly over my-her forehead, across her cheeks and neck, here and there slipping into deep valleys cut in her body, exploring her with the same kindness she had always shown me. Her body was pretty and, as the surgeon later said, very well developed. I looked at her beautiful face. She was asleep, eyes closed, lips slightly parted. I touched them for fear they would speak and break the spell. My fingers moved over her so delicately that even if she were awake she would have mistaken the touch for a summer breeze. My hands found the wounds on the back of her head and I covered them with her hair, allowing my fingers to become entangled in their curls for a moment. I stepped back to look at all of her, my hands lingering on top of her head. "*Ziskeit*," I whispered, "my sweet thing." My voice shattered the reverie as her image vanished in a cloud. I carefully clipped the photo from the paper and placed it at the very bottom of the wooden box under the other articles for fear it might some day rise up to haunt me.

A more complete account of the autopsy was published the following day. I read that the doctors inserted measuring sticks and instruments deep inside each wound, enlarging them even further. Why? Couldn't they see she was already dead, cut to pieces? There was a small cut on her left ring finger. They enlarged it, cutting right down to the bone so they could find a tiny blot clot. Was this necessary? Her skull was crushed so the surgeon removed the scalp and found a large clot of blood. Wasn't it obvious? The skull was opened and the brain examined. Put it back, I wanted to shout. They tore open the back and exposed the spinal cord. God in heaven, stop it. Then, horror of horrors, the surgeon stepped forward and made an incision from the upper part of the breast bone down to the pubic bone and opened her up, turning her inside out. I ran to the sink and vomited, my entire body heaving and sighing.

She hadn't been outraged but what they did to her was a medical outrage. It was gross, indignant, violent. They raped her in a way that neither Jean Gianini nor Dracula himself could conceive. When they were done with their violation they held her uterus aloft in their blood soaked gloves and proclaimed to the world that she had not been violated. I prayed and pounded my chest for the once lovely maiden who was now unable to cry for help. I believed that men who desecrate the dead were no better than those who butcher the living, even under the guise of medicine. I think it was then that I began to entertain bad thoughts about doctors.

An angry crowd milled around the jail hoping to catch a glimpse of the first boy in America to kill his teacher. Most people wanted to lynch Jean for doing such an unheard-of crime. I hid in a near-by alley and listened as they yelled and cursed for the sheriff to give up his prisoner. Turnkey Decker stood guard like a giant Golem outside the jail door. Above the entrance, wrought into the iron works, were two oversized crossed skeleton keys, a stark symbol of the power of the jailer over the jailed. Some said Decker had a tattoo of the keys on his arm, the stigmata of a binding faith. To all those seeking entry Decker spoke the only word anyone ever heard him utter: "No," his sonorous voice buttressing the very walls of the jail. No passage was given to anyone but the prisoner's father and lawyer.

Then I watched as the Reverend William A. Beecher, Miss Beecher's father, walked up to the door and politely asked for the privilege of seeing Jean and talking to him. Decker appeared baffled by the request from this meek little man peering up at him with sparkling blue eyes and a pleasing smile. He scratched his face, not knowing what to do.

"I am the girl's father," the Reverend added, his eyes tearing.

"I humbly beseech you."

Decker opened the door and the Reverend entered. If a Presbyterian minister could get in so easily, why not a religiously observant Jew? I rehearsed what I was going to say for many minutes, then, after the crowd thinned, walked over to Decker clutching my cap in my hand. The mass of his shadow seemed to press down on me.

"I am the girl's father," I said. "I humbly beseech you."

"No," Decker said.

I gulped and realized that not only was I talking to the man's waist but I had said the wrong thing.

"I am the girl's pupil," I corrected, looking up at the giant. "I humbly beseech you."

"No," he yelled.

"I am the lad's friend," I said. "I humbly beseech you."

"No! Now go away!" he yelled even louder, smacking his fist into an open palm.

I ran back into the alley. At least I had gotten him to say something other than "no." It was a minor achievement.

As I waited for the Reverend to exit, I tried to imagine the scene inside Jean's cell. I had heard that even at midday the cells were darker than twilight. I could picture the Reverend extending his hand to a slender youth who grasped it. Both hands trembled but neither let go, two shadows hanging on to the little light left in their lives. The Reverend probably asked him to be a good boy and repent. Jean probably said nothing.

Eventually the Reverend exited the jail and immediately made his way down Main Street to the train station. I watched as a large man wearing a checkered lumberman overshirt rushed up and handed him a note, than ran off. The Reverend looked at the note then tossed it away as he continued walking. I ran across the street and grabbed the crumpled paper. I opened it and read the neatly penned words: "THE COURTS ARE SLOW. LAW IS MOCKERY. SAY THE WORD. ONE HUNDRED MEN STAND READY TO BREAK THE JAIL AND TEAR THE BRUTE LIMB FROM LIMB BEFORE HE BLAMES ANOTHER." Then I did what any good spy who was on a mission to save his best friend would do—I ate the note.

Before the Reverend left Herkimer he granted a reporter a brief interview that appeared in the evening paper:

"Was your visit satisfactory?" the reporter asked.

"Hardly as I could have wished."

"Did the boy express regret?"

"No. But I am quite sure of one thing; that boy had an accomplice."

"An accomplice in the murder?"

"I am sure of it."

"Who?"

"I cannot reveal what was said to a minister in confidence. There was another. They took the girl to where she was killed. Look sharp and you'll find the one."

In the following days the news about the accomplice was in all the papers. Everyone in the barbershop was trying to guess who it could be although few knew anyone in Poland.

"You know the people in Poland," Uncle Sam said as he was cutting my hair after he closed the shop in the evening. "Who do you think it was?"

I had removed my patch for the haircut and was keeping my eyes closed so as to avoid the mirror. The question caused my eyes to spring open. Fortunately, Uncle Sam had known enough to keep my chair facing away from the mirror so I only saw the open door to my room and my little bed nestled against the wall. The question made me want to crawl into bed and touch the headboard to make the nervousness in my stomach go away. Something told me that the notion of an accomplice was the missing piece from Jean's murder story that was so troubling to me. I didn't believe Jean would have acted without help. There had to be an accomplice. I felt like an accomplice of sorts because Jean had asked me to help him. Yet I knew he had asked other kids before me. Did he ask anyone else after I refused? Did someone finally agree? Roy Finley, mad from rabies, might have helped if he were still alive, but who else could attack Miss

Beecher with such beastly rage? The kids at school were basically good scholars and never did anything more mischievous than
throw the occasional spitball. One boy shot a crippled horse that
no one could save, but any caring person would have done the
same. Jean Gianini was the only bad boy I knew.

"No ideas, huh?" Uncle Sam asked when I didn't answer.

I shrugged.

"Try to keep still," he said as he continued trimming my sideburns. He was much more skilled than Father, who was the only
other person who had cut my hair. He also talked more. Father
was a man of few words but Uncle Sam had an opinion about
everything, especially politics, and didn't hesitate to tell you. He
was against the federal income tax which had just been introduced but he liked President Wilson and thought he could keep
us out of the Balkan War. Reading was important to him and
besides the daily papers, he enjoyed reading poetry. He said
poets knew how to use words better than reporters or politicians. His favorite was a new poet I had never heard of at the
time—Robert Frost. Uncle Sam said President Wilson should
read Frost's new book because he knew all about what really
mattered in the world. Besides poetry, Uncle Sam thought zip-
pers were the greatest inventions and *Zu Zu*'s were the greatest
snacks. I couldn't help but love the man, especially as he was
massaging my scalp with a delightful tonic. After combing my
hair, he slapped a little witch hazel on my face.

"The flowers of the witch hazel wither," he said, quoting
Frost. He felt a few whiskers on my face and promised he would
give me my first shave next time. "It is customary to pay the barber," he said as I jumped down from the chair. Before I could tell
him I had no money, he reached into his pocket and gave me a
whole dollar. "Today I'm paying you for all your work. Each
week I'll give you a dollar and save another for your schooling."
He bent down and kissed me very close to my left eye. "You're
a good boy, Noble." I could detect the anise scent of his mustache wax. The smell was vaguely reminiscent of the healing
syrup Mama had used. I kissed him back. That night I cleaned

the barbershop as I did every night. The shop had a long mirror along one wall and I was careful to keep the lights off so as not to catch an accidental glimpse of my reflection. I quickly learned how to sweep in the dark and Uncle Sam never complained about my work. My secret was to sweep the floor several times and to clean the sinks and counters in the same meticulous manner. Sometimes the moonlight would shine through the front windows of the shop and bathe the interior with a pale glow. The moonlight never bothered me or caused a seizure so I used these times to perform a more thorough dusting of the jars and bottles on the counters. When I finished my work I liked to go outside without my patch to watch the moon as it made its slow, sad exit in the sky. That night as I watched the moon pass over the jail I felt like howling.

6

Two people knew the identity of the accomplice and neither would tell. Jean Gianini said he wouldn't snitch and the Reverend Beecher said he couldn't. In their own way each had taken a vow of silence.

Everyone who knew Jean, including myself, wanted to believe that he could never have done such a thing alone. I had spied on Jean many times and knew that he was never bad when he was by himself. I never saw him do anything wrong unless people were watching. He acted bad in the classroom and clowned around for others but he never threw a spitball when alone. He always needed an audience. The notion of him killing with an accomplice, even one who only watched, made sense. His family believed that the accomplice was not only an eyewitness but the instigator and primary killer as well; they believed the accomplice had to be caught so Jean might go free. I prayed they were right. Jean's relatives in New York City raised funds and hired the Burns Detective Agency to help. Detectives were immediately dispatched to follow all leads, identify all suspects, then catch the dastardly accomplice who had turned Mr. Gianini's beloved son into a ruthless killer.

A reporter for the *New York Sunday Tribune* made a special trip to the Reverend Beecher's home in Sennett, near Auburn, in the hopes of getting him to tell more. If he didn't identify the accomplice, the reporter told him, he might be seen as withholding evidence. He could be charged as an accessory. The Reverend remained stubborn. "The boy has told me some things about how he murdered my daughter which he has told no one else, and which may fairly be regarded as confidential," he said. "Unless he chooses to tell publicly all he knows, I shall not violate his confidence. I have only bitter pity in my heart for him. Christ teaches me to love him."

How was that possible? After all, the Reverend had already lost his brother and two sisters in the last year. Now his daughter was gone. I knew the pain and anger of such losses. Yet I could not be comforted by reading his words of love and forgiveness. Jean himself was not sorry and showed no remorse. Christian love was not likely to quiet the lynch mobs still roaming around the jail or untie the knots circling my stomach like a noose.

"How is it possible for you to feel pity for Jean Gianini?" the reporter asked the Reverend, echoing my own incredulity.

The Reverend responded with his indictment of the real culprits: "The boy is no different and no worse than boys right here in Sennett, and boys in every village and city in the country whose physical health is weakened by cigarette smoking and other vices and whose imaginations are inflamed by motion pictures of crime and by cheap novels. As I looked at the boy, I saw behind him these influences, which I have always fought and am still fighting, and I hold them, not him, chiefly responsible."

Jean may have borrowed a few ideas from stories of Peck's Bad Boy, although there was much more violence and killing in the Reverend's "good book" or any number of the classics. I had never seen a motion picture so it was hard to evaluate the impact it might have had on Jean, but I imagined that it was no different than the fantasies and make-believe games we once shared. Yet the Reverend mentioned "other vices" and there was one that was causing me considerable worry: Jean and I were masturbators. My favorite masturbation fantasy was to imagine Miss Beecher in various stages of undress as she combed my hair. Jean would think about her breasts but he didn't have the privilege of masturbating to the fantasy since his eagle-eyed father was always watching. I suspected that his sexual frustration was the force driving Jean to take her, life and all.

I was very angry at Jean. He had betrayed me. The betrayal ran deeper than the betrayal of our friendship; it was the betrayal of our fraternity, our brotherhood. I tried to imagine what I would have done if I had happened upon him bludgeoning Miss Beecher on Buck Hill. I saw my hands grabbing the knife, slaying Jean, and feeling strangely satisfied. The fantasy frightened me. I was like Cain who slew his brother Abel. The rabbinic literature held that Cain had an evil eye, and thus the evil eye was responsible for the first murder in the history of humanity. I didn't believe I would actually "Cain" Jean, unless I really had an evil eye which of course I didn't want to believe. Instead, I directed my anger at the accomplice. Damn him for taking away my friend and my teacher. The accomplice was the evil one. He had to be found and punished. Perhaps Jean would identify the accomplice for his best friend. I decided to call upon all my skills as a spy to find a way to see Jean, *kine-ahora*.

I would have preferred to wait for the dark cover of a new moon before venturing outside the barbershop but I was so disturbed I could no longer sleep or eat. My hunger for answers from Jean drove me recklessly into the night during a near full moon. I stayed in the alley behind the shop for several minutes, listening and sniffing the air for the telltale signs of voices or tobacco smoke until I satisfied myself the street was empty. Keeping close to the sides of buildings, I made my way up Main Street to Court Street where the Herkimer County Court House, County Jail, Dutch Reformed Church, and an impressive brick mansion occupied the four corners of the intersection. Only hours earlier this intersection had been filled with an angry mob calling for a lynching of my friend. Now there was only the wind whistling over the empty street of our friendship.

The mansion attracted me, not for the architectural elegance of its tall towers and steeples, but because the overall size cast huge shadows on the sidewalk in which I could hide while planning my assault on the jail situated on the diagonal corner. I dashed to the front entrance of the mansion and huddled against the massive mahogany doors. I knew this was the home of Dr. A. Walter Suiter, a local physician who had insinuated himself into the defense team after convincing Mr. Gianini to retain him to observe the autopsy. At the time I had never heard of anyone using a letter for their first name. It seemed silly. I also knew that Dr. Suiter was a silly man who refused to sleep in his own house; he actually lived with his sister around the corner and used the mansion only as an office to see patients. No one knew why he refused to live in the richly ornamented building, but it was rumored that he had built the house for his bride-to-be who ran off with the contractor. Silently I thanked the contractor for inadvertently providing me with a safe hiding place.

As I studied the jail, my hand automatically rubbed the surface of the wooden doors. I felt unusual shapes in the wood and turned to see two large carved gryphons. The gryphon was a fabulous monster with the head and wings of an eagle and the lower body of a lion. In Greek mythology, the gryphon was the embodiment of Nemesis, the goddess of retribution. Dante portrayed it as a satanic figure entrapping human souls. The smooth carved lines on Dr. Suiter's gryphons suggested a softer and less threatening beast. I preferred to think of the friendly gryphon who accompanied Alice in Wonderland and led her to that bizarre trial about the stolen tarts.

I turned back to the jail and tried to muster the courage to run across the wide street. In my mind, I could hear the Wonderland Gryphon: "Drive on, old fellow! Don't be all day about it!" I knew I couldn't wait forever. If Jean got the electric chair, I'd never have the chance to speak with him. "They never execute nobody you know," said the Gryphon. "Come on."

I ran to the jail and crouched next to the limestone wall, trying to make myself even smaller than I was. There was only one light shining though a top window. The windows were covered with heavy metal screens to prevent outsiders from passing anything through the bars to the prisoners. I didn't know if the light was on in Jean's cell, yet of the eighteen inmates in the jail at the time he was the only one suspected of murder. It seemed reasonable that the jailers would want to keep a light on to watch him.

There was a row of elm trees next to the jail and I decided to climb the tree opposite the window with the light. I was an excellent climber of apple trees but unpracticed with elms. They had long narrow trunks and no lower branches to step on. I wrapped my arms and legs around the trunk, hugging the slippery bark as tightly as possible, then slowly squirmed my way upward. Midway to the window I stopped to rest. I looked at the moon and suddenly felt sorry for Jean, locked in such a forbidding fortress, denied such simple freedoms as looking at the moon. His must have been a terrible sorrow.

"He hasn't got no sorrow, you know," said the Gryphon. "Come on!"

I moved up as a gust of wind shook the tree and cooled my skin. When I was even with the window, I wiggled around so my face was closer to the jail. I could see the metal bars on the window and beyond that a solid gray wall. A shadow moved somewhere inside but I couldn't tell if it was Jean or someone else.

"It's Croaker," I said loudly.

"Hey!" a man answered. The voice came from the sidewalk below. I glanced down but saw no one. I quickly slid down the tree and jumped the last five feet to the ground.

"Run," screamed the Gryphon.

I ran.

"Hey, stop," the man yelled.

I glanced back at the voice while continuing to run and I ran directly into another elm, hitting my head. Tiny stars flickered in the air. I quickly covered my patchless eye and turned to face a tall, skinny man who had a very pointed chin and was holding a broom.

"If you're trying to see the murderer, he's in the back. You can't get there." He came closer to me. "Are you hurt?"

"My eye is hurt," I said as I took a step backwards.

"Your nose is bleeding."

I moved my hand to my nose and felt blood dripping onto my jacket.

"You really did hurt your eye," he said.

I covered it again and used my other hand to hold my nose. I moved back a few more steps.

"I'm the sweeper," he said as he turned away and began sweeping the sidewalk near the jail. "I sweep at night and do it right. Then in the day I hit the hay."

I stopped and watched the way he swept the leaves and dirt from the high sidewalk into the unpaved road. He gripped the broom low with his left hand so his arm cradled around it. His entire forearm pushed while his right hand gripped near the top of the broom and pulled. It was an unusual technique but very effective and one I would eventually copy.

"Are you going to the trial?" he asked without looking up at me. Good sweepers never take their eyes away from their work.

"No," I said. The word came out as a high pitched squeak since I was still holding my nose.

"The trial will be fair, then he must sit in the chair."

I watched as the sweeper moved across the street to the courthouse sidewalk. I turned and headed home. There were several spots of blood on my jacket and I didn't know how I would explain them.

"It's all about as curious as can be," said the Gryphon. "Come on! The trial's beginning."

The following morning the defense team began assembling, shadowed by reporters who covered their every move. In addition to local Herkimer attorney Charles B. Hane, Mr. Gianini spared no expense in retaining the best talent in the state. "It is my duty," he told the press, "to spend every cent I have to insure the boy a trial that will do him justice." He wired John F. McIntyre in New York who arrived with his partner, David C. Hirsch. McIntyre was a prominent attorney known for his pleasant and affable style. He had been a prosecutor in New York for nine years before switching sides and becoming a criminal defense attorney with an international reputation for winning most of his cases. McIntyre had actually planned to retire but Mr. Gianini's money changed his mind. He was on the next train to Herkimer. The picture of him in the paper resembled an oversized bulldog in a topcoat and derby, desperately looking around for someone to pet him.

McIntyre's oratorical skills were legendary. He barked his lengthy arguments so loudly that the walls of justice and all those inside literally shook, including McIntyre himself, the rolls of fat around his collar shaking and changing colors with the heat of his tirades. It was rumored that he was forced to almost yell because he was hard of hearing but it got the attention of witnesses and jurors alike. It frightened, cajoled, and persuaded without ever biting. Newspapermen loved him for the style if not the substance of his courtroom theatrics and they wrote him starring roles in every case.

As a prosecutor McIntyre had obtained convictions in 580 of 614 murder trials. As a defense attorney he earned huge fees to protect clients from such fates. His most recent murder case had been defending a Lieutenant Becker of the New York City Police Department. Despite the fact that corrupt Tammany politicians paid McIntyre a small fortune to win, Becker was convicted, then granted a new trial which had just begun. McIntyre did not have the strength to continue. He withdrew from the case, considered retirement, then took on the defense of Jean Gianini. Now Becker, Gianini, and McIntyre were sharing headlines every day.

Everyone in Herkimer was impressed with the choice of McIntyre, even Uncle Sam, who was not easily impressed. "It's like driving a Maxwell touring car into a horse and buggy town," Uncle Sam said. "He's going to run over everybody."

McIntyre claimed to have known the Gianini family for a long time. "It is my personal friendship for the boy's father that brings me into the case," he announced to reporters waiting for him in the hallway of the courthouse. "I knew the lad's mother. She was a very sweet and refined woman yet she lost her mind.

There were times she suffered from homicidal mania. She was insane when Jean was born."

"What is your impression of Jean?" a reporter asked.

"I am convinced the boy is a victim of hereditary insanity. There is no question he is not in his right senses. He is unable to exercise the power of concentration. His talk is incoherent, rambling; he jumps from one topic to another," McIntyre said while jumping from one topic to another. "He has marks about the ears and eyes and the shape of his head is characteristic of persons of unsound mind. Why, just look at him; his features are not normal. His head has a dent just about where the bump of self-esteem is said to lie. His ears protrude. He exhibits a nonchalance and a profound indifference toward the homicide and its possible results for him. There is a void in his face—something is lacking."

"Is it likely, then, that insanity will be the defense?" the reporter asked.

"I believe so," McIntyre said. "I cannot characterize the precise form of his mental disability but it is undoubtedly some form of imbecility or idiocy—the distinction is a fine one. He is not only a defective, but a degenerate, totally irresponsible for his actions. I've watched him look in the mirror and laugh. He is unable to see what is happening to him."

I didn't know how my own overall appearance was perceived by others. Did I exhibit the same void that McIntyre saw in Jean? Did I have a bump of self-esteem? It was at times like this when I longed to look in a mirror. Sometimes I wished there was a new mirror I could use, one that never looked back at anyone, one that would never hurt me.

At breakfast the following morning I asked Uncle Sam where the bump of self-esteem was located. He wasn't sure and told me to look it up in the library. Although I was reluctant to go out during the day, especially knowing that the Burns detectives were out there looking for suspicious characters and a boy wearing a patch would be highly suspicious, the Herkimer Free Library was almost directly across the street from the barbershop.

When the librarian opened the door, I bolted across the street and was the first and only person inside. She helped me find a book on phrenology that she said was very popular and I was fortunate it had not been borrowed. I could find my self-esteem in the book, she quipped. I took the book to a corner table in an empty reading room where I could raise my patch and remain undisturbed.

Phrenology is the study of the skull to determine a person's character and mental capacity. It was clear from McIntyre's assessment of Jean that he was a believer in the science, although the more I read, the less scientific and more superstitious it seemed. Phrenology is based on the assumption that mental faculties are located in "organs" on the surface of the brain and that these can be detected by merely looking at the hills and valleys of the skull. At the time I thought this was some type of astrology of the mind, a harmless amusement not to be taken seriously.

I read that the bump of self-esteem was located on the back of the skull at an angle of forty-five degrees. An underdeveloped bump of self-esteem caused a lack of self-confidence. I immediately patted the back of my skull but could detect neither a bump nor a dent like Jean's. I certainly didn't have an overdeveloped bump, which supposedly caused egotism and arrogance. Then I remembered the photograph of McIntyre in the newspaper showing his derby tipping forward. I recognized that an over-developed bump of self-esteem on the back of his skull could explain the tilt. I felt my head again, carefully palpating the entire surface. It was perfectly smooth. In phrenological terms, it was as if I was a mannequin and not even alive. I could not accept this and decided that you could not do phrenology on yourself. I finished the book, gawked for a moment at the thousands of books on the library shelves, then ran back to the barbershop.

The village became very crowded that day and I was glad to be back in the seclusion of my room. Witnesses were arriving from all over the county to testify before a special Grand Jury considering the case against Jean Gianini. While there were at least a dozen other prisoners in jail waiting for their own Grand

Jury to convene, the district attorney moved Jean's case to the top of the list. Newspapermen from around the state poured into the village and took every available hotel room and barber chair. The entire village was excited and enraged. Although the Grand Jury proceedings were secret, almost all the witnesses had been interviewed by the papers. Most of the facts, not the least of which was Jean's confession, had been front-page news and the number one topic of conversation in the barbershop for days. The barber chair seemed to free people's tongues from any inhibitions. Customers suggested an array of ghastly tortures to make Jean pay for his heinous crime. Not one of Jean's body parts was immune to their imagination. One person wanted to beat Jean senseless with a monkey wrench, then pull him apart with it, beginning with his male organ. Listening to the talk in the barbershop made me feel like I was watching Jean getting horse whipped in the barn all over again. And, again, I felt helpless to stop it.

Everyone, including the defense team, knew that an indictment was inevitable. McIntyre announced to the press that the defense would not dispute any of the alleged facts in the case. Instead, it would present evidence about Jean's mental condition. Of course, everything could change if an accomplice was found.

District Attorney Farrell told the papers he didn't believe there was an accomplice. Every available clue had been examined and he was convinced that Jean alone was responsible. Yet no one knew what evidence had been taken as souvenirs, washed away by rain, or obscured by the butchery of the autopsy. No one knew about Jean's visit to my house. No one knew about me...or even cared.

"I don't care if Jean Gianini had help; he still committed murder," said a customer as Uncle Sam was cutting his hair.

When I heard Jean's name I rushed to the crack in the door and watched the man in the chair. Charles D. Thomas, whom friends called Charlie Tom, was the most capable and respected trial lawyer in the county. His office was on North Main Street, only a few blocks from the barbershop, and he was always dropping by for a trim whether he needed it or not. He enjoyed the banter with the courthouse regulars and village politicians who frequented the shop. I studied his skull as Uncle Sam moved the chair around. It was an odd-shaped head with a forehead butting over the eyebrows but I couldn't see any bumps or dents. However, as Uncle Sam clipped the sides, the protrusion of his ears became apparent.

"Besides, there is no evidence that Jean Gianini had help in conceiving and carrying out his plot for the destruction of a human life," Charlie Tom said.

"You sound like that prosecutor Farrell," Uncle Sam said. He certainly didn't sound like the same attorney who had vigorously defended Chester Gillette only a few years earlier.

Charlie Tom looked in the mirror, smiled, then announced that he had just been offered the job of special prosecutor to go after Jean Gianini. District Attorney Farrell, who was only twenty-three and inexperienced, felt that Charlie Tom, forty-four, was more qualified to face John F. McIntyre, the defense attorney, who was fifty-four. Charlie Tom was eager to avenge his defeat in the Gillette trial and accepted the job of going after the first pupil to kill a teacher. Since he had been a grade school teacher before becoming a lawyer, he also saw it as an opportunity to avenge teachers everywhere.

"Are you also going after the accomplice?" Uncle Sam asked.

"We'll let the Burns detectives do that and let the defense pay for it. I hear they're in Poland interviewing the boys who said that Jean Gianini told them about his plan. The only ones they found so far are those who came forward after the murder and talked to reporters. Jean still refuses to tell who actually helped him but William Burns has the largest agency in the world. He always gets his man, or in this case, his boy."

"A regular Sherlock Holmes," Uncle Sam said. They both laughed.

Charlie Tom put on his coat and studied himself in the mirror while Uncle Sam brushed him off. His hair was now so short that his head appeared dome-shaped, a sign of honesty, integrity, and truth. Any student of phrenology would know it was a good haircut for a trial lawyer, but I was sure McIntyre's overdeveloped bump of self-esteem would not permit him to be intimidated by the looks of this man despite his bow-tie, fancy suit, and fresh haircut. I knew there would be much butting and bumping of those odd-shaped heads in the coming days. Charlie Tom didn't seem worried. Before leaving the shop he put a plug of tobacco in his mouth, chewed it a few times, then spit in the direction of the spittoon several feet away. It was a perfect shot.

The Grand Jury finished its deliberations in two days and Jean Gianini was brought from the jail to the courthouse to hear the decision. I watched from a nearby alley. Jean was dressed in a perfectly tailored light brown suit, a cap to match, and a dark red-striped tie. His hair was combed for a change and he wasn't wearing his glasses, which made him look younger than sixteen. Obviously, a lot of money was spent on his appearance but the entire effect was ruined by a pair of ugly jailhouse slippers that flopped around on his feet. He took Sheriff Stitt's arm and moved through a horde of spectators standing on the jail walkway. Suddenly two photographers jumped in front of Jean, who held a new white handkerchief to his face. He took extra long strides to quickly cross the street. As he approached the courthouse, Jean may have recognized that he was about to enter a building that resembled the Poland schoolhouse. Both had a colonial appearance and large bell tower, although the school was a small white structure, the courthouse a giant red monster. Jean walked fearlessly right into its mouth.

I was afraid to abandon the safety of the alley and had to wait for reports from my fellow spies, the newspapermen, who followed Jean to the courtroom on the second floor. The evening papers described the court as packed with pretty young girls who tried, without success, to pass notes to Jean. He looked around and made eye contact with several girls, sucking in his breath and curling his lips each time. He blushed. One newspaper reported that this indicated he was nervous. The girls obviously had different interpretations as they giggled and whispered with each other. Another paper described Jean's eyes as beady, darting, and blinking like a reptile's rather than a human being's. The girls smiled coquettishly, winking back at him.

Jean stepped inside the thick wooden railing separating him from the spectators, removed his cap, and took a seat beside Sheriff Stitt. Almost immediately Justice Irving Rosell Devendorf took the bench. I studied his picture in the newspaper. His black robe contrasted sharply with his white hair, neatly parted in the middle. It was an excellent haircut for a fair-minded justice. His light skin was offset by dark eyebrows that cast shadows over deeply recessed eyes. This created the appearance of a mask and it was easy to see the resemblance to a raccoon. Raccoons are bright and cute and it's hard not to like them. Everyone liked the jurist and admired his superior intelligence and skill.

Justice Devendorf had been the district attorney in Herkimer for six years before becoming a county judge, then Supreme Court Justice. He was courteous and fair, and his decisions were always respected by higher courts, but he had sharp claws like a raccoon and did not tolerate misbehavior inside or outside his court. I read that he once arrested and fined Bat Masterson for fictitious reporting on the Gillette murder trial which he had presided over in the very same courtroom a few years earlier. Until now, the Gillette murder had been called Herkimer County's crime of the century and Justice Devendorf could see from all the press crowding the courtroom that the Gianini case might become an even bigger story. He started the proceedings with a militaristic pace, polled the Grand Jury, received their indictments, then excused them with thanks.

District Attorney Farrell called the name of the defendant, Jean Gianini, who did not come forward until nudged by the sheriff. He was formally charged with murder in the first degree. The proceedings were adjourned and Jean was taken back to his cell, slippers flopping and handkerchief waving in front of his face.

The trial was scheduled for May 4, which gave McIntyre and

his team less than a month to put together a winning defense or else Jean was certain to die in the electric chair. Everyone thought the trial would be as short as the Grand Jury proceedings, and the punishment just as swift. The idea of a long sanity trial was hard to accept by everyone, including me. Jean seemed as sane as I did. Yet sanity—since it would result in a death sentence— had never before sounded like such a gloomy word.

The following night, as I was cleaning the shop windows, I saw the street sweeper walking down the sidewalk with the broom on his shoulder. I quickly slipped on my patch and ran out to join him.

"I see your eye is still hurt," he said, looking at my patch.

I nodded.

"I'm going up to the jail. You can tag along if you like."

We walked up Main Street past the Palmer House hotel where the defense lawyers were staying. Lights were on in several rooms. "The lawyers are probably figuring a way to break Gianini out of jail," he said with a laugh.

"Is that possible?" I asked.

"A few years back six men escaped by sawing the bars on their windows but Gianini is in an inside cell in the north end," he said, pointing to the area as we approached the jail. "It's a cell within a cell. He'd be dead before he sawed through all that iron." He took the broom from his shoulder and began sweeping the sidewalk.

I was reluctant to ask how he had acquired such an intimate knowledge of the jail layout so I simply watched him work as he made his way along the high wall surrounding the rear yard of the jail.

"What's in the yard?" I asked.

"The ghost of Roxy Druse," he said, stopping to jiggle his hands in the air with a wide-eyed look. He told me that he watched as Roxalana Druse was hanged in the yard for the axe murder of her husband. She stood under the dangling noose wearing a thin black satin dress, apparently insensitive to the intense winter cold. Her arms were strapped, a black cap was put on her face, and the noose was tightened, crushing the roses pinned to the top of her bodice. The sheriff gave a signal and a large iron counterweight was dropped, causing the noose to jerk violently upward. Her entire frail body leaped into the air as the handkerchief she had been holding floated slowly to the ground. It took her fifteen minutes to die.

"Hanging!" the sweeper shouted. "Now that's what Gianini deserves."

"What about the accomplice?" I asked.

He stopped sweeping and looked at me. "That's Gianini's only hope," he smiled. He began to recite:

"Jean sat in a cell all by himself,
Refusing to say who gave him some help.
After a while he decided to snitch,
The accomplice for freedom he offered to switch."

I went back to my room and crawled into bed. My sleep was haunted by images of a jail yard hanging. Jean was standing on the gallows, the noose around his neck. The counterweight dropped and my body jerked awake. I was sweating and couldn't get back to sleep. I didn't think I would ever sleep again.

During the following sleepless weeks before the trial began, I took frequent walks around the village in the middle of the night. I discovered that Dr. A. Walter Suiter, the physician who had been hired as part of Jean's defense team, was another soul not sleeping very well. The light in his study was frequently on late at night and sometimes I could see him pacing the floor. I didn't think he was haunted by the ghost of Roxy Druse, although, as I later learned, she certainly had good cause to torment him from the hereafter. Suiter had provided the cornerstone of the case against her. In order to prove that she had murdered her husband William, who she claimed had simply gone to New York City, the district attorney hired Dr. Suiter to do the "medical detective" work. There was no body to be found, only a pile of powdery ash in her parlor stove. Suiter sifted through the ash with fine mesh, filtering out tiny bone particles which his chemical tests determined were from a human skeleton. Next, he burned several cadavers in her stove and determined that a body the size of William Druse could be completely incinerated in only eight hours. It was not scientifically convincing but it was good enough to convict Roxy. The sweeper told me that Suiter was with her at the gallows, looking at his pocket watch and waiting impatiently for her to stop struggling and wailing so he could declare her dead of asphyxiation. Immediately after this he announced the birth of his new career as a pioneer in forensic science.

Now Dr. Suiter was burning the midnight oil and probably hoping for another headline in the history of forensic science. The prosecution had already retained two alienists who were veterans of high profile celebrity cases. Everyone was anticipating that they would be pitched against Dr. Suiter in rebuttal. It was being billed in the papers as one of the biggest battles of experts to ever take place in a murder trial. I understood why Dr. Suiter couldn't sleep. He referred to himself as a chemist, a microscopic technologist, and a general physician. Since he was not an alienist, he needed to find mental help in a hurry.

The local newspapers were already comparing the upcoming murder trial of Jean Gianini with the infamous 1907 murder trial of Harry Thaw, the first so-called "trial of the century." Both murders appeared premeditated, deliberate, and motivated by revenge, yet Thaw was found not guilty by reason of insanity. Suiter and the defense attorneys were studying the Thaw case to see how it was handled.

Harry Kendall Thaw, the heir to a forty million dollar Pittsburgh railroad fortune, had approached architect Stanford White during the New York opening of a musical in the rooftop theater at Madison Square Garden, a building White had designed, and shot him three times. "You deserve this," Thaw cried, "You ruined my wife." Years earlier White had given show girl Evelyn Nesbit, whom Thaw eventually married, a glass of spiked champagne, then had taken her virginity while she was unconscious. Thaw wanted revenge—and he had it.

At the trial, Thaw's attorney invented a new term and said his client suffered from "dementia Americana," a form of insanity that convinces an American male that whoever violates the sanctity of his home or the purity of his wife forfeits the protection of the laws. He argued that when Thaw saw White he was overcome by a "brainstorm," resulting in temporary insanity. The argument partially worked as it resulted in a hung jury and another trial. In the second trial, in 1908, the defense hired nearly all the eminent alienists in the world with the idea of using a few and keeping the rest away from the prosecution. Doctors, friends, and family testified that Thaw had been irrational all his life. The murder was portrayed as an inevitable outcome of his progressive irrationality. It worked and Thaw was acquitted and sent to the asylum at Matteawan.

I could almost read Dr. Suiter's thoughts as I watched him pacing in front of his bookshelves one night. He must have realized that the way to get Jean out of jail and into Matteawan, thus sparing his life, would be an insanity defense but with a new label like they had used in the Thaw trial. Perhaps he could also find a novel scientific test like he had used on Roxy Druse's ashes. This would definitely impress the jury. I was not surprised when I later learned that Dr. Suiter obtained the list of experts used in the Thaw case and started contacting them. He also contacted a few of the more modern alienists who were advocating novel ideas about feeblemindedness. They used a new language that few had ever heard spoken outside of medical circles, let alone inside courts of law, and their terms were defined with a test which supposedly measured intelligence. Pioneer Suiter liked the notion of using new terms and tests to filter the ashes of the brain. He was not just preparing for a battle of experts, but for a war of words.

The alienists began arriving in Herkimer. I had hoped they would stop by the barbershop where I might be able to get a good look at the shape of their heads, but they never stayed in the village for long. The prosecution experts were in and out of the village before they needed a shave, let alone a haircut. The defense experts didn't stay very long either and their examinations at the jail were as brief as thirty minutes. The longest jail visit was only a little over two hours, in contrast to the days alienists had spent examining Harry Thaw. Yet it was long enough for Dr. Suiter to see what he wanted, and he told the defense attorney, John McIntyre, that Jean Gianini was definitely an imbecile. Word was leaked to the press that the defense would ask for acquittal on the grounds of imbecility.

"It won't work," said Charlie Tom, who would be prosecuting Jean. Charlie Tom was getting a shave and yet another trim from Uncle Sam. "It didn't get Scott off in Chenango County and it won't work here. People are too angry." He explained that, in 1908, William Scott took his mother-in-law to a woods on Chenango Lake near Norwich, New York, and shot her. The defense was that Scott was an imbecile, although the only really stupid thing he did was to show the sheriff where the body was because he believed he should then be allowed to go free. Evidence was presented showing that he was an imbecile, but the jury said Scott still knew the nature and quality of his act and that the act was wrong. They found him guilty.

"You got to be more than an imbecile to get away with killing your mother-in-law," said a customer in the barbershop, awaiting his turn. "You need an accomplice to do it for you."

"You don't need an accomplice. The best way to get rid of your mother-in-law is never to get married in the first place," Uncle Sam quipped.

Everyone in the shop roared with laughter except Charlie Tom. Despite his confidence that he could obtain a conviction for a confessed killer who was obviously sane, he disagreed with the district attorney about the existence of an accomplice. Charlie Tom now believed that there was an accomplice, a boy who might even be the real killer Jean was protecting, and that he had to be brought to justice before he killed again. "I here pledge to you that on my honor as a prosecutor and a former school teacher," Charlie Tom said, "I will see that both the boy and the accomplice get the chair." He announced that he had hired his own detective from Boston to search for the accomplice. The Boston detective had already arrived in Poland and begun work.

The county was now crawling with detectives as well as reporters. They were looking for Jean's acquaintances who had known about the plan to kill Miss Beecher. I preferred not to be found and questioned. The likelihood of being ordered to testify against others, especially my best friend, was an unpleasantness I did not wish to face. While I had never said goodbye to anyone in Poland, and no one knew where I had moved, I still chose to stay in my room. It didn't seem safe to go outside except on the darkest of nights. Even then, I usually kept to the alley behind the shop and simply gazed at the stars.

As a child I thought that the stars had once been fireflies that died and went to heaven. If I could be any insect in the world I would have liked to be a firefly. But the indifferent God who ruled the universe allowed me to metamorphize into a dragonfly with a huge monstrous eye. When dragonflies died they came back as the black nothingness of space. I didn't want to be nothing so I tried to convince myself that God wouldn't care about my bad eye. He would judge me by my devotion to him. I decided to make the alley my temple where I could recite my prayers in the dark so God could hear my words echoing against the walls without having to look at me.

One night during a new moon I felt a seizure coming on while I was chanting my prayers in the alley. I had goose bumps and shivered uncontrollably. I wandered around the village that night—no, it was more like floating—and ended up at the jail. Even in the pitch-darkness, the building seemed to glow and shimmer as if it belonged to an otherworldly realm. I thought I heard Jean screaming just as my seizure hit. All I remembered was Jean's screams. They turned into a nerve-racking saw cutting away at my brain. When I recovered I vomited, then rushed back to the barbershop, surprised that it was almost daybreak.

At noon the following day, Friday, May 1, turnkey Decker noticed that the metal screen over a rear window in the jail was loose. He reported this to the sheriff, who went to investigate and discovered that two of the bars on the window had been sawed nearly off, both at the top and bottom. Someone had been trying to help a prisoner escape. The bars were promptly repaired and the sheriff dutifully confiscated the table knives from the prisoners because he believed they could have been used as saws. If I had wanted to saw through the bars I would have chosen my father's steel saw which I kept with his other tools in a chest in my room. When I opened the chest to check on them, I was surprised to see that the saw was right there on top of the other tools. I had the vague feeling I might have used it recently but I couldn't remember.

Nobody paid much attention to this incident, which was buried on an inside page of the local paper next to an advertisement for a traveling circus coming to a neighboring city. The front-page news was still the trial of Jean Gianini which was to begin at ten o'clock Monday morning. A bigger circus was coming to Herkimer. Like dueling ringmasters, Special Prosecutor Charlie Tom and defense attorney McIntyre would be shouting to get the crowd's attention. In one side ring would be the prosecution alienists tossing their words about Jean's actions in premeditated and deliberate ways. The defense alienists would be in the other side ring juggling their words about Jean's behavior in the most insane patterns. And in the center ring, ladies of the court and gentlemen of the jury, behold a creature who looks like a boy and acts like a crazed beast. You decide what word to call him.

What did words matter? Miss Beecher was still dead. How could any word do more than death had already accomplished?

That night, after I lit the Sabbath candles with Uncle Sam and cleaned the shop, I went into the alley for my evening meditation. The air was still and quiet; the moon was in its first quarter. It was hard to believe that I had been in Herkimer for less than three moons, even harder to imagine where I had been before then. My life had been totally eclipsed by the murder of my teacher and the trial of my friend. The apple farm seemed like a dream. Somewhere up above, but never far from me, Mama was looking down. "Do good deeds so people will remember you," she was saying.

I went back into the shop, grabbed my broom, and made my way to the courthouse. I waited in the moonshadows until the sweeper appeared with his broom, then approached him and began sweeping the sidewalk. He looked at me, smiled, and together we worked, our sweeping filling the silent night with that rare harmony of strangers becoming friends.

"Are you going to the trial?" he asked as we turned the corner from Main Street to Court Street and moved to the side of the courthouse.

"No," I said. "Are you?"

"Of course."

I stopped sweeping and stared at the monstrous building as I tried to imagine what it was like inside.

"Want to go in?" he asked, reading my mind.

Before I could answer he entered a side door and motioned for me to follow. We descended a series of stairs and ended up in a large room off the basement. He lit a small lamp. This room had been set aside for the exclusive use of court reporters on the Gianini trial, he told me. The strong smell of tobacco suggested someone had been working late. The room was now deserted and I could see a large table filled with piles of paper, another with one of those new Remington typewriters, and a dictaphone machine.

I took a few steps toward the machine and immediately felt something soft being crushed under my shoes. The floor was covered with tiny shavings of black wax. According to the sweeper, these were the remains of the Gianini Grand Jury proceedings and arraignment. Five people had been assigned to work in this room to turn out the transcripts. One stenographer would take down the proceedings in the courtroom for an hour, then would be relieved by another. The stenographer would bring his written pages here where he would read them into the dictaphone. The machine made a wax record which a typist would listen to as she prepared the transcript and two blue carbon copies. After the wax record was transcribed it would go into a shaver which peeled away the recording and prepared it for use again. I approached the machine, picked up the earpiece, and held it to my ear. It would have been wonderful to hear a record of the trial, better still to hear it live.

We made our way back to the street where I stopped to gaze longingly at the building. The sweeper asked if I would like to return with him on Monday morning to see the trial. I was afraid of standing out in the courtroom, of being watched, of the detectives. But I only said that the daylight bothered my eye even with the patch.

"I can fix that," he smiled.

"I'm afraid," I confessed. "People will gawk."

"You can hide by my side." He assured me that no one bothered him when he sat in the rear of the gallery during Jean's arraignment.

"Can we hide like spies so no one will know we are there?"

He laughed. "No one can ever see a sweeper like you or me."

While I was undressing for bed that night I noticed a piece of the Gianini wax record stuck to my shoe. Somehow I knew I would never get it completely off.

7

"The trial to determine the fate of Jean Gianini is now on," announced Sheriff Stitt as Justice Devendorf entered the Supreme Court of Herkimer County. The justice strode to the bench wearing a flowing black robe and looked at the courtroom clock which read 10:02 A.M. The trial was only two minutes late but already off to a bad start. The court crier hadn't shown up so the sheriff substituted, mangling the opening words. District Attorney Farrell and Special Prosecutor Charlie Tom had not yet arrived but that didn't stop the regimental Devendorf from marching forward with the case of the People of the State of New York versus Jean Gianini.

I was sitting in the last row of the courtroom gallery next to the sweeper, who had given me a pair of sunglasses to wear over my patch. The glasses had wire frames and large round lenses with a dark amber tint. There were small leather protective flaps on the sides near the temples. He said they were driving goggles and the flaps helped cut the wind and sun. I discovered they also cut my fear and I felt as concealed as I had when spying on Jean in Poland. I could have been mistaken for just another young boy in the courtroom. In a sense I felt like I was back in school, sitting in the rear of the room with a clear view of everyone. I could see Jean's head with the unruly brown hair. I relaxed and studied the sweeper for the first time in daylight. His cheeks were so inflamed with acne they appeared as if they had been sanded and painted red. I understood why he preferred a night job. Despite the difference in our height and age, we were much alike. He turned to me and smiled while blinking both eyes, his pointed chin jutting forward as he rose like a jack-in-the-box to squeeze next to me as others sat down. I enjoyed the little pantomime. I was no longer sitting in the back of the room alone. A new friend had popped into my life.

The second floor courtroom was the same one in which Justice Devendorf had presided over the Gillette trial. The room held nearly one thousand spectators in pew-like benches on the main floor and in a gallery in back. The side walls were lined with tall windows that ran almost to the ceiling some twenty-four feet above. Several gas lights hung from the ceiling.

The spectators were separated from a carpeted area in front by a wooden railing with ornate posts that curved around in a half moon. The railing was so thick it resembled the gunwale of a ship. The justice sat at a long table on a raised platform at the front edge of the moon under three large oil paintings of those who had preceded him. To the right of the justice's table was the stenographer's desk and a chair for the witness.

The small jury box on the extreme right was raised a few inches off the floor on a shaky platform and, when filled with twelve grown men, I imagined it might resemble a rowboat in danger of capsizing. In front of the jury box was a very long narrow table. The prosecution would sit at the front end nearest the jury with the defense at the other end. On the left side was another long table for the press.

The court clerk called the names of the prospective jurors. Twelve jurors would be selected from an initial panel of 150 who crowded into the courtroom. It was expected to take most of the week before a dozen were found who were acceptable to both sides.

Jean Gianini, sitting between his attorneys, gazed vacantly out the window as the names of the talesmen were called. When Justice Devendorf asked for those desiring to be excused to come forward, it seemed like the entire courtroom rose to be heard. Jean turned to look. I suspected that our former class clown was entertaining a fleeting impulse to stand as well. Thirty men were systematically excused for illness, age, or other reasons. Jean cracked a smile when one man reported in a quivering voice that he was unable to serve because he had not fully recovered from accidentally blowing himself up with dynamite.

It was 11:25 A.M. when the two prosecutors arrived and took their places, then formally moved for Jean Gianini to be tried on the indictment. McIntyre stood and introduced attorney John P. McEvoy from Little Falls, New York, who was seated with the defense and would be assisting. There were now four defense attorneys. "The defendant is ready," McIntyre said. Jean adjusted his glasses and grinned. Newspaper reporters at the press table saw the grin and interpreted the expression as one of disdain and disgust for the proceedings, but it told me that Jean was happy to be back in a classroom setting and the center of attention once again. I wondered how long it would be before he tried to tip over his chair and create a scene.

The first talesman to be called for questioning was a locomotive engineer from Frankfort, New York. Knowing Jean, I'm certain he was making little train whistle noises under his breath. The engineer was asked how many children he had, but McIntyre couldn't hear the answer and asked him to repeat it. When he was asked their ages, the engineer acted as if he didn't hear the question. After a few more exchanges, it was clear that the engineer was more deaf than McIntyre but he was neither against capital punishment nor the insanity defense so both sides permitted him to be seated as a temporary juror.

The questioning continued with many being challenged and excused for having formulated strong opinions against the defendant. But who hadn't? The newspapers said it was impossible to shop, ride a trolley, or get a haircut anywhere in the county and not hear talk of lynching Jean Gianini for the gruesome killing. Not surprisingly, many people seemed eager to be on the jury.

By the end of the day only three jurors had been temporarily accepted. The tedious task of jury selection continued throughout the following days. After the first panel was exhausted, another panel of forty was summoned. Jean appeared bored much of the time. He chewed gum vigorously and toyed with his fingers, examining each one in great detail. So did the press. They reported that some of his fingers were discolored by the cigarettes he smoked incessantly in an anteroom during recesses. The reporters wrote about the flaring of his nostrils as he exhaled streams of smoke. McIntyre called this another example of the degenerate mind and the reporters hastily agreed.

Inside the courtroom Jean would often allow his head to drop, first to his chest then almost to his knees. I knew he was tired because he did this at school whenever he had been up late reading his bad boy books. He would doze in this position which was more comfortable and less noticeable than allowing his head to rest on the desk. The press reported that Jean was "dopey," a label which made about as much sense as when the kids in Poland called him "woppy."

In the evening I pored over the newspapers in my room and tried to amuse myself with the printing errors. I chuckled when I read that the expensive insanity defense being constructed with Mr. Gianini's considerable wealth was going to fall like the "Roman Umpire." I read that judges and lawyers from across the country came to watch the trial. I was surprised that Justice Devendorf invited the visiting judges to sit on the bench with him. Themis, the Goddess of Justice who set the example for all officers of the court, may have worn a blindfold but it certainly did not cover the bump of self-esteem. Indeed, McIntyre, who had the biggest bump of all, invited friends such as H. DeWight Luce, who had been the defense lawyer for Roxy Druse, to sit at the counsel table.

There were moments of relative amusement during the week of jury selection. As jurors were finally accepted and seated, they were confined to the Palmer House under the watchful guard of two deputies. Several jurors developed severe stomach disorders after drinking the local water, something I had experienced when I first moved to the village. From time to time, strange organic sounds could be heard erupting from the jury box, but the jurors sat stone-faced, pretending they were all hard of smelling as well as of hearing.

The juror whose selection surprised me the most was Bronson Plattner, who managed a feed store. Jean and his sister Moffie used to visit Plattner so often that they called him "Pa." Plattner, a kindly old man, was married and had five children, seven if you counted Jean and Moffie. His own oldest daughter was a school teacher about Miss Beecher's age so he must have been shaken by the murder. Yet he had always been protective toward Jean and had even arranged a job for him when he returned from St. Vincent's Industrial School.

The final juror was expected to be seated on Monday, May 11, and trial testimony was to begin immediately. Everyone had been preparing for days. The court hired an extra stenographer. The sheriff called in extra deputies from around the county. Hotels put on more staff and even Uncle Sam had hired another barber, Tony, from the south side of Herkimer.

Tony was a thin young Italian man with shiny black hair that appeared to be pasted on his round head. He had a habit of touching people when he spoke, his hands lightly grazing their shoulders or arms. Sometimes he would jab them with a finger, punctuating a particular point in his conversation. The customers in the shop didn't seem to mind, but I was nervous watching Tony poking them while his hands were holding a razor or scissors. There was something sinister about the way he peered into their faces as if he wanted to see a look of terror in their eyes.

I had never met anyone who complained so much about being bitten by things as Tony. He had a blister on his foot that he claimed was from a shoe bite. His shirt collar was always biting him on the back of the neck and he would show you the rash to prove it. I don't know why Tony's clothes bit him so much, but one day he made me so mad that I wanted to bite him myself. It was Sunday morning, May 10, and the shop was closed but Tony had opened it to give a friend a shave. Suddenly, he barged into my room to retrieve some supplies. Uncle Sam always had the courtesy to knock but Tony didn't. He treated me as an out-of-sight elf who existed only to clean the shop at night. The one time he spoke directly to me was to order me to wash out the spittoon instead of simply dumping it outside as Uncle Sam let me do. Now I was all too visible as I stood in the middle of the room reciting my morning prayers, the leather thongs of the *tefillin* wrapped around my arm and forehead, my *tallis* draped over my head and shoulders.

Tony scrunched his face into an expression of disgust as he walked behind me and grabbed a few items from a shelf. As he walked back he kicked me hard enough to move me forward a few inches, then he left. The kick was so sudden and astounding that it actually didn't register for several minutes and I continued with my prayers. Only when I was putting the *tefillin* and *tallis* back into their small velvet bags did I begin to tremble with the recognition of what had transpired. I tried to tell myself that I was at fault for standing in Tony's way but I was unconvinced by this. There was something more behind the kick. Whatever it was, it was making me very angry.

I was still seething with anger when I went into the alley that night to pray again. It was not a good night for the faithful. Although it was a full moon, there was not a single ray of light in the sky. A heavy rain was falling. I looked to the heavens and started chanting a prayer of atonement for committing the sin of anger. I could not see the stars and had no idea if God was listening. The rain fell into my mouth as my prayers flew back out like spit. I allowed myself to add some prayers of my own, yelling and spitting until I was completely soaked.

An article in the morning paper told of a strong earthquake the previous night near the base of Mount Etna in Sicily. More than a dozen villages had been destroyed. The death toll climbed to over 150, and thousands more were stricken with terror. It happened again, I thought, as I remembered the Messina earthquake that had killed Zia Nardone's family. I wondered if Tony had any relatives in the area near Mount Etna but I knew better than to ask. Besides, I was feeling better now. It was strange, but there was no longer any anger in my heart. It was almost as if the quake had shaken all the bitter spittle from my body.

By three o'clock on Monday, the twelfth juror was finally seated. After a brief recess, Charlie Tom rose to give the opening address for the prosecution. He announced that the defendant was responsible for the death of Lida Beecher by such means as constitutes murder in the first degree. He pointed to maps and photographs of Poland and the crime scene as he told the jury what "I understand," "I assume," or "I think" happened. His manner was so humdrum and unemotional he could have been describing a boring business trip rather than a vicious killing. And it was so disorganized, one had to wonder if he had paid any attention to either the business or the trip.

He mentioned a few facts not widely known. "The boy disclosed what is not necessary for the People to establish—motive. He said that Miss Beecher had humiliated him while she was his teacher, and while he was away from home at St. Vincent's Industrial School at Utica he made up his mind that when he got out he would get even with her. Not only that, gentlemen, but for some days previous to the murder, the defendant had made known his purpose to three of his young associates, and the purpose was to rape, to disfigure, to kill, to get even."

Charlie Tom pointed to the defendant. "The defense will say this boy is insane but we will show that no matter how mentally disturbed he was—as well he might be to design, plan, and execute a cold-blooded murder—he was not in such condition of mind as not to know the nature and quality of his act, as not to know the act was wrong. Although he was under twenty-one, he merits punishment of the law even if he was different or odd."

McIntyre waived his own opening address until the start of the defense's case. Court was adjourned for the day. Everyone was talking about the certainty of conviction as they left the courthouse. Some were making bets on the outcome.

I had never seen a trial before and I was surprised that spectators were taking sides as if it were a baseball game. I didn't feel like cheering for either team. I wanted my friend and my teacher back and neither side could promise me that. I certainly didn't want to see Jean put to death for his crime as the prosecution and most spectators wanted. And the defense theory that Jean was insane or an imbecile was an idea I could not get used to. The possibility that Jean might be protecting another—the accomplice who might have been the real killer—was easier to accept. But finding that accomplice seemed as unlikely as raising Miss Beecher from the dead. Yet I had no choice but to try. I began by studying the faces of those who were calling for Jean's quick execution. I searched the crowd for a face filled with both guilt and relief—the face of someone who was happy to see Jean take all the blame for his own crime.

I was glad I arrived early the following day to get a seat. Crowds surged against the courthouse doors, unable to gain admittance to the packed courtroom. The street-vendors hanging around the courthouse did a brisk business selling "Jean's favorite" chewing gum to the men and boys denied entry. The young girls who couldn't get in to gawk at Jean in person had to settle for buying copies of his photograph that were clipped from the local papers.

At McIntyre's request, the counsel table had been moved nearer the witness chair so he could hear better. But the noise from the crowd outside drowned out any small improvement from the arrangement. Jean was assigned a new seat next to Deputy Sheriff Hinman at the corner of the table. I think the justice had seen some of Jean's facial expressions, perhaps even overheard his muttering, and was trying to control his behavior just as any school principal would do with an incorrigible pupil.

The first few rows were packed with the group of young girls who had attended daily since the start of jury selection. Behind the girls was a large contingent of boys about Jean's age who were gawking at everyone. Mrs. Devendorf attended and stared at Mrs. McIntyre and Mrs. Hirsch, who were dressed in the latest New York City fashions. Mrs. Gianini, Jean's stepmother, was also dressed in fine clothes; she took a chair next to her husband just behind the defense lawyers. And sprinkled among the spectators in the main room and gallery were the many witnesses who were waiting to be called. I studied the kids from Poland who were going to testify about Jean's plan. They seemed nervous and I scrutinized their faces for signs that they might have done more than just talk with Jean.

The first witness presented maps and photographs of the crime scene. When the People next called Mrs. Beecher to the witness stand, I couldn't understand why they would want to put the mother of the slain teacher on display. Then I learned that the Mrs. Beecher on that stand was actually Ethel Clark, who had been Miss Beecher's roommate at the boarding house. A few weeks after the murder Ethel had quietly married Miss Beecher's brother Willis. Although it might have appeared to have been inappropriate timing, I didn't blame Willis for a moment. Ethel Clark was even more beautiful than Miss Beecher. When I saw her I wanted to marry her myself. Her features were similar to my teacher's and she had Mama's eyes. She was a little shorter than Miss Beecher and I think we would have made a better couple. People said it was wrong for Willis to marry her so soon after the funeral, but I knew there was nothing wrong with trying to hang on to your sister or your mother to keep from drowning in sorrow. Willis, who was in the Navy and served as personal yeoman to Admiral Fletcher on the steamship *Tennessee*, knew all about the importance of staying afloat in troubled waters. If war came and something happened to Willis, who was due to ship out soon, I wondered if there was a chance that Ethel and I could end up clinging to each other. I enjoyed thinking about such a possibility and secretly wished for a big war.

Mrs. Beecher, or Ethel Clark as I preferred to think of her, told the Court about the many times Jean had come across the street to visit with her and Miss Beecher at the Countryman boarding house. When Jean learned that Ethel was from the Rochester area he asked about the State Prison at Auburn and how inmates were housed.

"He wanted to know what the sentence was, whether they had an electric chair, or whether they hanged people," Ethel said.

"Sentence for what?" Charlie Tom, the special prosecutor, asked.

"I cannot recall a specific word but Miss Beecher and I both laughed at him."

The word didn't matter when Charlie Tom began parading the evidence in front of the witness and asking her to identify each exhibit. First came Miss Beecher's umbrella. The initials "L.B." were scratched on the wooden handle. Charlie Tom opened it with a showman's flourish and placed it on a table at the front of the courtroom. Then came the checkered cap with the little black velvet rim. This was placed on the table just under the umbrella. The switch of hair was introduced and placed below the cap. Her barrette was placed on the switch. Ethel identified Miss Beecher's nose glasses and Charlie Tom took pains to place them below the switch, just where the nose should be. He studied the arrangement, then adjusted the glasses so that they were peering directly at the jury. It didn't take a great imagination to see the outline of Miss Beecher's body taking shape. I longed to get a closer look and touch everything.

The tan raincoat was handed to the witness, who identified it as Miss Beecher's. It was spread on the table below the other items. When Charlie Tom reached into the bag under his table and pulled out the blood-stained red dress, McIntyre charged out of his seat like a mad bulldog. "If Your Honor please. I don't see the real necessity of their proving the garments and other things that were worn by Miss Beecher on the night that she lost her life because the defendant does not now say that she did not lose her life or that she wore certain garments. If Your Honor please, it is because I fear that there might be some things offered and observed by the jury—gruesome in their nature—which may unconsciously bias and prejudice the jury."

"I think, Mr. McIntyre, I will leave it to the district attorney to proceed in the manner which he claims proper and best," the justice said. Besides, everyone including the justice was now curious as to what else was inside Charlie Tom's bag. Knowing Jean's love of the macabre, he was probably hoping there were a few remains from the autopsy yet to come. Specimens had been shown to the Grand Jury, and even the press was hoping for a look at them in trial.

"To that I respectfully except, if Your Honor please," McIntyre said as he sat down. His objection only caused the jury to focus more on the ghost of Lida Beecher now resting on the exhibit table.

Charlie Tom laid the red dress on top of the spread raincoat. The dress was serge with long sleeves, a white frill around the neck, and a white vest with little black buttons. He gently buttoned the vest so everyone could see the rusty splashes of blood that covered the front. I found myself agreeing with McIntyre's objection. The exhibit table was filled with bias and prejudice. I could easily imagine the empty outfit rising up and shaking an angry umbrella at Jean.

During cross-examination McIntyre asked Ethel why she and Miss Beecher had been laughing at Jean.

"Because it impressed us that he seemed to be planning on going to prison. Miss Beecher laughed at him and I joined her."

"How's that?" McIntyre asked, cupping his ear. He always asked witnesses one or two worded questions whenever he didn't hear their previous answer.

"Like this," Ethel said. She looked at Jean and proceeded to laugh. It was a cold, mocking laugh that silenced the court like a gavel. Jean's face reddened as though it had been slapped.

It is not nice to be laughed at by someone you want to marry. It just kills you inside.

A languid rain fell over the village during the next two days as District Attorney Farrell and Special Prosecutor Charlie Tom examinined witnesses who told how Miss Beecher came to be the ghost that now haunted the garments on the exhibit table. These witnesses included the kids from Poland with whom Jean had discussed his plan for revenge, the people who saw him walk up Buck Hill with her, and those who saw him come down alone. The rope, the coat and button, the knife, and the monkey wrench were displayed for all to see. The jury was told that the wounds on the body suggested the use of the wrench and knife. Jean had carried the wrench in his coat for two weeks. "I have use for it," Jean had told a boy who saw the sixteen-inch, two-pound tool sticking out of his right side pocket. The day before the killing, Jean took his father's knife and sharpened the three-inch blade to a razor edge.

As each witness testified, I tried to picture that person as the killer accomplice. Gertrude Trask, the last person to see Miss Beecher alive, made the prettiest picture. Gertrude was an attractive sixteen-year-old girl who lived across the street from Jean and was the closest thing he had to a real girl friend. They often played together and, until I came along, walked to the Poland School together. Jean was always teasing Gertrude, poking her and making her laugh. I could tell she had a fancy for him. She smiled demurely at him as she testified that on the night of March 27 she met Jean at the Post Office and walked with him along Cold Brook Street. She said Jean had tugged playfully at her hat, pulling it down over her face. They had a good laugh. Then Miss Beecher came along and Jean left to walk with his teacher. Gertrude frowned when she told how she watched the two disappear in the shadows of Buck Hill. She sounded jealous of Miss Beecher. Perhaps she was jealous and angry enough to kill. While everyone assumed that the accomplice was a boy, I knew that good-looking teenage girls are not immune to murderous rages. Mary Druse, Roxy's pretty teenage daughter, stood by and watched as her mother killed her father with the axe, then joined in and helped chop up the body. Gertrude Trask stood and watched Jean and Miss Beecher go up the hill. I could easily imagine her following, even helping. When she left the stand, she exchanged smiles with Jean. I was suspicious of those smiles and hoped that the detectives were watching.

I was also suspicious of Claude Barhydt, a newspaper boy in Poland who testified that he saw Jean and Miss Beecher walking towards Buck Hill with Gertrude trailing behind. Claude was delivering the evening papers to houses along the same route. About thirty minutes later someone saw a boy running down Buck Hill and told a reporter it was Jean. Another person saw a boy running down the hill and said it looked like Claude. The first newspaper story had identified the murderer as "Claude Gannini." Perhaps this was not the silly printing error I originally thought but a confused identification of both the killer and accomplice leaving the scene. I hoped that the detectives would read between the lines and know enough to verify Claude's whereabouts during the murder itself.

On Thursday, May 14, the rain stopped and sunshine flooded the courtroom, yet a gloom hung over the defense end of the counsel table. Defense attorney McIntyre's usual beaming smile was replaced by a worried frown. He hid behind huge tortoise-shell glasses and consulted frequently with his colleagues in what looked like a prayer huddle. Everyone sensed the seriousness of the coming testimony. Three hundred people jammed the steps of the courthouse, unable to gain entry and unwilling to leave for fear of missing even the few words that escaped through the doors. This was the day the prosecution was going to put on their star witness.

Deputy Sheriff Nellis was called to relate his parlor conversation with the defendant. McIntyre jumped to his feet, shaking his head. He knew that Jean had described the murder in that conversation and he had to keep it out.

"Now if Your Honor please," McIntyre began. "We object that the conversation is inadmissable and incompetent in view of the way in which the statement was obtained from the defendant. He was denied the right of counsel. Counsel was in the house at the time and the witness on the stand knew it. The witness did not see that the accused was afforded the benefit of counsel in this case and he excluded all from the room in which the boy was taken. He permitted no one to have access to him. And taking into consideration the tender years of this boy, the statement was obtained by fear and fright and by threats made by the witness. He was placed naked in the ice-cold air and lied to. And the statement was obtained contrary to and in violation of his constitutional rights."

I found myself agreeing. Jean was practically tortured into confessing.

"Objection overruled."

McIntyre shook his jowls and I shook mine. "We object on the additional grounds that the conversation was reduced in writing by the witness as a summary," he said, "and it is neither the spoken words nor written words of the defendant which would be the only proper evidence. The statement was not voluntarily signed and the defendant was not judicially informed of his rights."

The justice scowled. "Objection overruled."

McIntyre faced away from the bench and let out his breath like a deflating balloon. But he would not be subdued. Every time Nellis opened his mouth, McIntyre tried to close it by objecting to both the conversation and the confession. Each time the objection was overruled but each time the jury heard how a boy of tender years was locked in a room, stripped, and coerced into giving a statement. McIntyre also objected to the exhibits and wanted the knife and wrench to be declared inadmissable. He was overruled each time.

Finally District Attorney Farrell prepared to read the confession. Mr. Charles A. Gianini of New York turned away and looked out the window, probably wishing he had never left New York City. The jurors moved forward in their chairs, their faces stern and jaws squarely set. The tension in the courtroom was palpable as Farrell read the confession:

"State of New York, County of Herkimer. Jean Gianini being duly sworn deposes and says he resides in the village of Poland and is sixteen years old. Deponent further says 'I went to school with Lida Beecher and had trouble with her and wanted to get revenge. I met her above the hotel and walked up the street with her, up beyond the stone quarry. She had been a coming to see my folks about school and was a coming up to see them last night and I told her they lived up the hill and when we got up there on the left side of the road I hit her with a monkey wrench that I got out of my father's barn. I had the wrench in my pocket when I went up. After I had hit her about three times with the wrench I hit her with a knife several times to be sure to finish her and then I took her over in the lot. I dragged her by the foot and then I went home and got there about seven-thirty. The knife I stabbed her with was one that belonged to my father and I took it home and put it in the pantry drawer. I left the wrench somewhere near where I hit her. When I hit her first she did not scream but moaned. She said she thought it was quite a ways and she did not see any house. I was not afraid when I got home. I was just as happy as I ever was and didn't think anything about it as I thought I had revenge. I make this statement voluntarily and under no force or threats and knowing the same may be used against me. Jean Gianini.' Subscribed and sworn to before me this twenty-eighth day of March, 1914. Squire Fred H. Moore, Justice of the Peace, Town of Russia."

When Farrell finished, I was able to see that there were many wet eyes in the room. Gertrude Trask, who was sitting near me in the gallery, smiled. She turned around and caught me staring at her. Her smile turned into a smirk.

During cross-examination of Deputy Nellis, McIntyre was again unsuccessful in getting the confession thrown out. When he interrogated the next witness, Sheriff Stitt, McIntyre tried to show how Jean had made completely different statements than those said under duress to Nellis.

McIntyre approached the sheriff, rubbing his hands together. "Now Sheriff Stitt, you had your first conversation with the defendant about three o'clock in the afternoon of March 28 in Poland, did you not?" McIntyre asked.

"I think you are mistaken," the sheriff said.

"What is it sir, what was the hour?"

"Between twelve and one."

"Did you ask him at that hour to tell you the truth?"

"His father was also there and he told Jean to tell the truth."

"Now then, did he tell you at that time that he hadn't committed the deed?"

"Yes. Jean said he didn't do it."

"Did you charge him with telling a lie?"

"Yes, sir."

"Well, will you tell me now, Sheriff, when you accused him of telling a lie, how did you know he was telling a lie?"

"My own suspicion."

"So he was suffering from untruthfulness, was he not?"

"Yes, sir. He lied."

"Now, while suffering from the mental disturbance of untruthfulness did he then meet with Deputy Nellis and say that he had done the crime?"

"Yes, sir."

"If he was suffering from untruthfulness, how do you know which story was the lie, the one told under honor to his father and you or the one told under duress to Deputy Nellis?" McIntyre smiled as his cheeks puffed out like an overfilled balloon.

"I asked him."

McIntyre looked as surprised as everyone else in the courtroom. "You asked him?"

"Yes, sir. On the following morning I went upstairs to the cell where he was and I said 'Jean, why didn't you tell me the truth yesterday?' He said 'Well, I wanted to tell you the truth but my father was there. I told him a story earlier and I didn't want to say anything different from that because he would not like it. I want to tell you the truth now.' He then told me how he got the girl to go up Buck Hill and how he killed her in almost the exact words he used with John, I mean Deputy Nellis. He said he was happy she was dead."

"Now Sheriff, how do you know this untruthful boy who lied to you before was not telling a tall tale and that the only person he ever told the God's truth to was his father?"

"At the boy's request I brought Mr. Gianini up to see him. The boy wanted to tell his father the truth. I stood there and heard the conversation. Mr. Gianini said 'I do not want to hear it, I can't stand it. But son, answer me one question: Did you do it?' The boy dropped his eyes to the floor and nodded twice. Mr. Gianini said 'Look me in the eye and tell me you did it.' Jean raised his eyes and said 'Yes.' Then Mr. Gianini said 'God help us.'"

McIntyre leaned on the counsel table, rubbing his brow which was now wrinkled like a collapsed balloon.

8

G od help McIntyre," Uncle Sam said with a chuckle as he read the evening paper at supper that night. The big city lawyer had been beaten badly in court by his own bungled cross-examination of the local small-town witnesses. All his efforts to kick out the signed confession only resulted in the discovery of two more confessions given by Jean: the one to Sheriff Stitt and the one to Mr. Gianini.

People were fuming when they learned that Jean had told the sheriff he was happy that Miss Beecher was dead. After court adjourned I watched the crowd shake their fists and curse as he was taken back to the jail under heavy escort. Willis Beecher, the brother of Miss Beecher, was in the crowd, his face flushed with anger as he glared at the confessed killer of his sister. While some spoke of lynching Jean, I could imagine yeoman Willis wanting to keelhaul him under his ship before hanging him from the yard.

"At least the boy stopped lying about it," Uncle Sam said after reading the front-page confession that was printed in bold Gothic type surrounded by tiny stars.

"Then why did he plead not guilty?" I asked as I cut a piece of rare beefsteak and swirled it in gravy.

"Sylvester told him to."

Uncle Sam was referring to Deputy Sheriff Sylvester Wilson,

one of the regulars in the barbershop who was also a guard at the jail. Sylvester had advised him to plead not guilty when he was arraigned. Jean didn't want to and said, "That would be a lie; I had help but I killed the girl."

"Sylvester wanted to take credit for persuading him so that there would be a lengthy trial," Uncle Sam explained, "but I suspect his lawyers also instructed him to plead not guilty. I know it bothered the boy a lot. Sylvester said the boy didn't sleep well after the arraignment. He kept muttering 'croak her'."

I thought I heard my nickname. My fork froze midway between the plate and my mouth. "Wha-What did he say?"

"Sylvester said it sounded like 'croak her' or 'croaked her,' as if he was trying to say 'I croaked her.' He was probably having bad dreams about the murder. The boy's got some shame which is good but not good enough to bring back the dead. Noble, are you feeling all right?"

I wasn't. I dropped the fork on my plate. Gravy splashed on my sleeve. Uncle Sam leaned across the table and put a hand on my forehead.

"You're sweating like a horse. You better go downstairs and lie down. I'll sweep the shop tonight."

In my room I soaked a handkerchief in the sink and tied it around my forehead just as Mama did whenever I was sick. Once my parents and I were stricken with a bad fever and we all put wet handkerchiefs on our heads. Mama called us her "lovely band of Indians."

Now I feared I might be feverish again. I felt miserable and crawled into bed without undressing. Pictures whirled in my head so fast I couldn't make sense of them. I didn't know if they were thoughts or dreams. They seemed as vivid as yesterday's memories. I saw someone playing Indian with Miss Beecher on Buck Hill. A handkerchief was tied around her head, then pulled down over her eyes. She looked as beautiful and statuesque as the blindfolded Goddess of Justice. The blindfold came off the goddess. A single word was uttered: "Croaker." I saw a knife cutting rare beefsteak. Everything went red, then black. I woke in the morning with the feeling that I had done something awful.

That afternoon, after thirty-five witnesses in five days, the People rested. I didn't care how many witnesses or confessions they had. The only witness I needed to hear from was Jean himself. There would never be any rest or a decent night's sleep for me without talking directly to my friend. I didn't think Jean would take the stand when the defense case started the next day, but I remained hopeful he'd talk to me if we had the chance.

The chance came that night. Sylvester asked Uncle Sam to come to the jail and give Jean a haircut. The defense wanted him to look as young and clean-cut as possible. They were willing to pay a handsome fee for the service. I asked Uncle Sam if I could go along. Jean and I had been friends in Poland, I explained. It would cheer him up. It would be a *mitzvah*, a good deed. I would clean the shop as soon as we returned.

Uncle Sam was surprised I hadn't mentioned that I knew Jean before. He agreed that I could go as his assistant. I think he felt a little guilty accepting the generous sum of money for the haircut so at least he could bring one of Jean's friends to visit and feel like he was doing something extra in return.

I had avoided Jean in court and I don't think he ever knew I was there, hiding in the back of the gallery behind a thousand people. Now that I was finally going to confront him, something told me that I should not reveal my attendance to him. I didn't think he would want me to hear all the nasty things they were saying about him. He would probably prefer to tell me his own story. Hopefully that story would include the identity of the accomplice, the one who might be able to save my friend. Since that day I had seen Jean through the shop window on his way to jail I felt closer than ever to him. His eyes cried for me that day. Tonight I hoped his lips would speak and say something to make sense of the terrible thoughts I was having.

Uncle Sam gave me one of the white jackets he wore in the shop so I would look like an official assistant. The jacket fit me like an oversized coat, the collar covering most of my neck and the sleeves hiding my hands. I rolled up the sleeves but there was nothing I could do about the length; the jacket dropped well below my knees. Uncle Sam said I looked like a flour sack with little feet. He laughed several times.

We walked to the jail and I had to move with tiny steps to avoid tripping on the jacket. This caused Uncle Sam to laugh even more. It was infectious and I couldn't stop laughing. I was carrying a box with the scissors, comb, whisk, and bottles of tonics and talcum powder. On the top of the box I had placed several folded hair cloths and towels. When we arrived at the jail I raised the box so the pile of linens hid my face and patch. Sylvester, the Deputy Sheriff, opened the door. Uncle Sam introduced me as his assistant and nephew. He called me *Zak*, meaning sack.

"Glad to meet you," Sylvester said.

I was biting down on the towels in front of my face to keep from laughing and could only muster a muffled noise.

"He only speaks Russian," Uncle Sam explained, doing his best not to laugh.

Sylvester led the way through a maze of narrow passageways to the rear cellblock, which consisted of two tiers of cells surrounded by an iron catwalk. The air was dank and smelled of human sweat. The plaintive voices of prisoners calling out bounced around like dying echoes. The walls of the jail were made from limestone, two feet thick, which made the cells inside as dark as caves. The only light came from small heavily barred windows in walls outside the catwalk. A small staircase led to a third level, the most isolated of all. The smells were not as bad here. Jean's cell, a seven-foot by five-foot by seven-foot steel tomb, was in the north end, the darkest area. It contained a small cot and nothing else. Chester Gillette had slept in this same cell, and for all the dirt and waste, parts of him might still have resided in the corners. Gillette had been allowed to use an adjacent cell as a storeroom for clothing and so had Jean. A larger outer cage, approximately twelve feet by eight feet, contained a toilet, a sink, and an area for meeting with visitors. Sylvester opened the two-hundred-pound door to the outer cage where

Jean was waiting for us on a stool.

"Holler when you're done, Sam," Sylvester said as he locked us inside and disappeared down the hall.

I set the box down and faced Jean. He bolted from the stool, ran over, and hugged me. I didn't know what to do, especially with Uncle Sam present, so I just stood there like a barber pole and let him embrace me. I had never been hugged by anyone other than my parents and I had forgotten what it felt like but I didn't think it was supposed to tickle. I started to giggle and then realized that Jean was poking and tickling me. He stepped back, grinning.

"How are you?" I asked.

"I feel okay. I'm getting good care and the food is good. Mrs. Stitt made cherry pie tonight." He pointed to some leftover crust on a plate in the sink.

I introduced Uncle Sam who immediately asked Jean to sit, then spread a hair cloth around him and started combing.

"My old man wants it short," Jean said.

"How short?" Uncle Sam asked.

"Real short and neat so I won't need to comb it," Jean said. He looked at me. "They want me to take the stand and snitch on the accomplice so they can blame him but I won't do it." It was something he had already said to the press.

"Do you want me to keep the part?" Uncle Sam asked.

"I don't care."

"What do you like?"

"I'd like another piece of cherry pie or some *Zu Zu's*." He smiled at me.

"*Zu Zu* puts snap and ginger into jaded appetites," we sing-songed together as if we were in another time and place.

"I'll bring some next time," I promised.

We stared at each other while Uncle Sam started cutting.

"You look skinny," Jean said. "I hope you're taking care of yourself."

I was touched by his concern. "It's the jacket. It's too big," I said.

"He looks like a flour sack with feet," Uncle Sam said.

Uncle Sam and I laughed but Jean was silent, looking down at the floor with glassy eyes. I noticed that a few cut hairs were sticking to tears on his cheeks. He appeared scared, like a little boy getting his first haircut, or getting his first trimming by a principal. Gone was the defiant grin of the bad boy. Here was the terrified face of a child, who had been rejected by an angry world and thrown into an iron crib. It was almost as if the clumps of hair falling on the cloth were draining his strength and rendering him defenseless. I think that if I had asked him any question, any question at all, he would have answered honestly. I believe he would even have snitched to me despite Uncle Sam's presence. Yet I could not do such a thing. At that moment I only wanted my old friend back, my old life back.

"Have you visited with Harry?" I asked. Jean and I used to call our penises "Harry."

Jean grinned. Slowly the hair cloth around him started to move. I saw that he had placed his arm between his legs and was slowly raising it like a tent pole. "Nope," he snickered.

"Try to keep still," Uncle Sam said. "I'm almost finished." Happily, he didn't understand our private joke. Jean and I laughed.

The haircut was over and Uncle Sam started to clean up. Jean asked me if I wanted some pie. I nodded, assuming he could get more from Sylvester. Instead he grabbed the plate from the sink and began throwing pieces of crust at me like they were so many spitballs. I grabbed a few and threw them back at him. Soon we were engaged in a food fight, laughing and playing much to Uncle Sam's amusement.

"Want to see my cell?" Jean asked when it was over.

I nodded and he showed me the small area where he slept. He pointed with great excitement to Chester Gillette's name scratched on the floor. I was more impressed with the copy of *Moby Dick* resting on his cot.

Jean climbed on to the iron door of his cell, pumping his legs and trying to get the door to swing. "Come on," he said. I jumped on the other side and together we managed to swing the heavy door back and forth several times. In the dizziness of the moment I stared at Jean through the bars, unsure which side I was on.

"Sylvester!" Uncle Sam yelled. "We're ready to go."

Before we left, Jean hugged me again. "I'm afraid," he whispered. I hugged him back.

In court the next day I admired Jean's new haircut from the back of the gallery. There was not a single unruly hair. The short cut made him look younger but his ears stood out more. Defense attorney Charles Hane stood, adjusted his bow tie, and began the opening address. He had none of the theatrical gestures used by McIntyre or Special Prosecutor Charlie Tom but he spoke in a beautiful flowing voice.

"If the court please, and gentlemen of the jury," Hane said, "we are here, myself and my associates around this counsel table, aiding in the defense of this boy. We are mindful of the great calamity that came down upon the Beecher family and the great misfortune that befell this girl. Lida Beecher was a beautiful girl of a beautiful Christian character and it is a great misfortune to everyone who knew her, to all the people of the village of Poland, that she came to so untimely a death. It is indeed a sad story that has been told. But we have a duty to perform here, and we shall continue through this case and until its end on behalf of this defendant for we believe that above all, the greatest misfortune has befallen the Gianini family, and this boy, the greatest calamity of them all. It becomes necessary, gentlemen of the jury, to drag from the closet, to tell the secrets, the family secrets, which Mr. Gianini has known and which after the events of March 27 he knew he had to tell so you would know the cause of this calamity."

Reporters at the press table picked up their pens and wrote furiously as Hane revealed the "secret" story of the mother's melancholia and alcoholism as well as the father's ancestry.

"Mr. Gianini's grandfather was born in that part of Switzerland where cretinism, a form of imbecility, is present," Hane said. "It is what is known as endemic, it arises from the soil, and thousands of people are afflicted with this trouble and this disease. And the experts shall tell you about this most important feature of the boy's heritage. He is a great-grandchild of this soil, an imbecilic child. Imbecilic children are selfish, mischievous, cruel, untruthful, devoid of ordinary affection for parents and friends. They are perverse creatures of morbid impulses. They thieve. They are inclined toward incendiarism. They have homicidal tendencies."

Jean grinned as Hane pointed to him. "The evening of the homicide this boy ate heartily and even asked for a second piece of cake. His behavior upon that occasion was no different than at any other evening meal. My friends, if he understood the nature and quality of the act he was about to commit, how could he sit at the table and eat so deliberately as he would at any other time? How could he ask for another piece of cake? And after the homicide he retired for the night and slept as peacefully as a child that knew no trouble, that knew no responsibility whatever. Can you, my friends, conceive that a man who perpetrated such an act could have slept like a child if his brain was enthroned with reason? And the next morning he had his breakfast before he started to run away down the railroad tracks. An imbecile always thinks first of his stomach before anything else. His act and his conduct in no way indicate that he comprehended or understood the seriousness of the offence or its consequence."

"Then why did he run away?" the sweeper whispered into my ear.

Hane's next remarks seemed to address the question. "The experts tested this defendant and found he has the mental development of a ten-year-old although he is sixteen. He is defective. The experts will classify him as a high-grade imbecile and assign him to that class which is prone to exhibit characteristics not unlike those of paranoiac insanity. He was suffering from the paranoiac fantasy of an imagined hurt that his teacher caused. He was laboring under a defect of reason when he struck the girl, striking and striking as if possessed of a demon. It was the act of a maniac who has no reason. He could not help himself. He is an imbecile.

"It is said that we have at least 25,000 imbeciles and weak-minded people in the State of New York. We are breeding imbeciles. Any one of them is likely to commit some act of violence. In the time of ancient Sparta mentally weak boys were put to death, but we don't do that in this country. Now, my friends, we are not saying that this boy be let out on the public street. We don't want him let out. We want to see him incarcerated in some institution where he may be cared for and where he can not perpetrate such an act again."

Hane folded his notes and looked at the jury. "I know you will not inflict the penalty of death on this boy because of the intemperate habit of his ancestors. He should not be held responsible for that. He is an imbecile and it's not his fault. Now, gentlemen, we believe you will do your duty."

The first witnesses called by the defense were the doctors who had taken care of Sarah Gianini during her pregnancies. They described her as depressed, smelling of liquor at times, and dressed in a slovenly manner. She was nervous so they prescribed bromides to quiet her and help her sleep.

Was that all there was? Jean's mother was depressed, drank liquor, and was dressed in a slovenly manner. This was hardly the proof of hereditary insanity that the defense claimed, although I had always felt that Jean was a sloppy dresser and never washed around his neck. Next on the stand was the impeccably dressed Charles A. Gianini of New York. His neck was very clean.

Mr. Gianini was uncertain about the date of his marriage to Sarah McVey or her age at the time. In fact, he seemed uncertain about almost everything.

"Before your marriage to Sarah McVey, will you tell the jury her appearance?" McIntyre asked.

"Very bright, interesting, well dressed, well kept, and I might say an intelligent lady. Very fond of pleasures such as society and dancing."

"How about music?"

"Very fond of music, and a very good piano player."

"Now, after your marriage, what did you notice?"

"That all changed. Her desire to dress well had gone. She wore an apron around the house. Sometimes just a petticoat and a wrapper. She became slouchy. Instead of being bright, she was dull. Instead of being intelligent, she seemed to have lost her intelligence and cleverness."

Mr. Gianini did not know the birth dates of any of his children or even how old little Charlie had been when he died.

"After the birth of the boy Charles, what did you see?" McIntyre asked.

"She never played the piano after that."

McIntyre looked like he was feigning surprise. "Not at all?"

"Not for me. She never played for me again."

"What else did you notice?"

"All interest was lost in me," Mr. Gianini whined. "She took an aversion to me. She would sit and mope, wouldn't help me, wouldn't converse with me."

"Did she converse with others?"

"Yes." There were murmurs among the spectators. Mr. Gianini coughed. "To a very small extent," he added.

"Now I want you to tell us what would happen when you tried to talk to her?"

"I could see she tried to avoid me, wouldn't listen to me. My words were wasted on her. I knew enough that she would rather I was away than there."

"Had you done anything to invite that contempt or dislike?"

"Absolutely nothing," Mr. Gianini said, adjusting his tie.

"Did you notice anything else?"

"Yes, that she had lost all love for me."

"Now what did she do that made you feel as though she had lost love for you?"

Mr. Gianini continued with his previous answer as if lost in remembrance. "I tried to convince her that she was wrong. I talked to her and told her I loved her. She wouldn't respond. She acted as if she didn't understand."

"What made you feel she had lost love for you?" McIntyre asked again. "Did she ever tell you that she didn't love you?"

"No."

"Well then how on earth did you know she didn't?"

Mr. Gianini blushed. "For the reason that she shunned me... shunned her obligation."

McIntyre blushed as well. "Yes, well, now what else did you notice?"

"I noticed at the time, five or six months after the birth of Charles, that she took to drink."

"After the birth of the second child, Catherine, what did you notice?"

"That the condition continued. Her morose, melancholic condition, and her drunken condition."

"How often did you see her under the influence of liquor?"

"At least once a month."

The courtroom buzzed with comments. "Is that all?" asked the sweeper. "Ain't a lot," said someone else. The justice banged his gavel until everyone was quiet.

"Between the birth of the second and third child, that is to say the defendant, did that condition continue?" McIntyre asked.

"Yes. It was the same. She drank and the same conditions prevailed."

Mr. Gianini did not know too much about Jean's early years because Jean had been raised by a series of nurses. However, he remembered the sounds Jean made as a child.

"Tell us what sort of sounds he made?" McIntyre asked.

"Why, they were yells."

"What?" McIntyre asked, cupping his ear.

"He was very boisterous, loud," yelled Mr. Gianini.

"Well, what did the yells sound like?"

Mr. Gianini cleared his throat, drew a deep breath that caused his vest to tighten across his chest, and let out one of the strangest sounds I ever heard. The sound came out as a stream of noises alternating between a yell in a normal voice and one in a falsetto. Everyone was stunned. The stenographer froze. The justice twitched. I have never heard a yodel but I've been told that is what it sounded like. It was a crazy sound and one most difficult to duplicate, although Mr. Gianini must have inherited the ability from his Swiss ancestors. It was a fine display of his own Swiss hereditary insanity rather than his son's. The yells I heard Jean make when we played were much softer and more appropriate than his old man's outburst.

Aside from the yelling, Mr. Gianini did not hear Jean talk until he was about six. But since Jean was raised by nurses and had only been returned to his father at that age, I don't think he was around much to hear anything. Even when Mr. Gianini regained custody, he spent most of his time running his furniture business or traveling and collecting antiques. During this period, he turned Jean over to the care of a housekeeper, then friends, then placed him in the Lady Cliff Academy. He paid such little attention to Jean he didn't seem to notice that Lady Cliff was only for girls, although the school agreed to keep the boy after Mr. Gianini offered a large donation.

"When he was at Lady Cliff, did you see him often?" McIntyre asked.

Mr. Gianini shifted uncomfortably in the witness chair. "Occasionally."

"Now, when you saw him in Lady Cliff, how did he appear?"

"Usually appeared pretty dirty."

"Well, is there anything else that you noticed?"

"No."

Mr. Gianini finally married Florence Peterson and brought Jean to live with them in the Bronx.

"During that time did he go to school?" McIntyre asked.

"Yes, he went to school."

"Do you know how he did in school?"

"No."

"Do you know from your own knowledge how he acted in school?"

"No."

"What else about him did you notice during this time?"

"That he was dirty."

"What else during that period in the Bronx did you observe?"

"He lied once."

"About what?"

"I gave him a penny to buy a piece of candy. He said a boy had taken it from him and I gave him another. He came back and said he lost it and wished to have another so I gave him another penny. Later I looked in his pockets and saw that he had many pieces of candy. I threatened him that if he didn't tell me the truth I would give him a good whipping. Then he admitted he had lied to me."

"How often were there occurrences of that kind?"

"I couldn't tell you."

"What else did you notice about Jean in the Bronx during those years?"

"I can't recall any more."

Mr. Gianini didn't seem to recall much of Jean's life in Poland, either. He testified about taking Jean fishing once at a stream for a full hour.

"Jean was bareheaded and barelegged. The flies were biting very fiercely that summer. I felt them myself. He came back with his face and neck bloody, his legs bloody from the bites of the flies. He denied the flies bothered him. He was irrational."

McIntyre's next questions implied that you had to be an imbecile to want to fish when flies were biting and you were bareheaded and barelegged. After all, Mr. Gianini said he would never do that. He probably wore his suit and derby.

In addition to the confrontation with the flies, Mr. Gianini told about Jean's "irrational" fights and quarrels with other children in Poland. He described one incident involving me.

"I was walking down Main Street and I saw Jean quarreling with two little children," Mr. Gianini said. "I was on the opposite side and I stopped and watched. I told him to go home and he stopped and wanted to argue with me. He wanted to explain or tell me something but I wouldn't listen. I said 'Go on,' and he did. I didn't know them. They were very small children."

I remembered that day very well. I was there talking with Jean and another boy. I guess we both appeared small compared to Jean. Actually, we were arguing about how to divide the cost of a five-penny box of *Zu Zu* snaps among the three of us. Mr. Gianini stormed across the street and screamed at Jean, his eyes filled with a wild look he must have copied from his first wife. He glared at Jean, totally ignoring me. I had been to his house many times to wait for Jean to walk to school. It hurt me that Mr. Gianini didn't know I existed. It must have hurt much more to be the son he didn't know.

When court resumed at 9:30 A.M. on Saturday the justice ordered all women and girls to be excluded. The defense had informed him that there would be a line of examination they should not hear. Mr. Gianini took the witness chair again. He deliberately avoided making eye contact with Jean.

"Mr. Gianini," McIntyre began, "did you ever observe any vices in your son?"

"Yes, sir."

"Mas-tur-ba-tion?" McIntyre spoke the word slowly, enunciating each syllable.

Masturbation. The word swept through the courtroom like a giant brush painting scarlet letters on the cheeks of young and old. People moved uncomfortably in their seats. Jean stopped chewing his gum, his face flushed with anger. A few men nervously stroked their beards. I thought the sweeper's face was a tad more red, if that was possible. Without warning McIntyre had introduced a forbidden word into the trial. Everybody knew masturbation was a vice that led to degeneracy. There was no need to mention the word itself. One spoke with euphemisms such as self-pollution, self-abuse, defilement, vice, even evil would do. It was best to cover one's mouth rather than utter the word masturbation. The newspapers refused to print it. Even the highly educated Charles A. Gianini of New York avoided the word in answering McIntyre's questions. At first, he refused to answer at all.

"Was it mas-tur-ba-tion?" McIntyre repeated with obvious relish.

"Yes, sir."

"Did it impress you as rational or irrational?"

"Irrational."

"What did you do when you discovered that he was masturbating?"

"I warned him, told him what might be the consequence of such actions. I told him that if he repeated the same I would punish him."

"Did you go in the same room in which he slept?"

"Yes, sir."

"And did you sleep in that room?"

"Yes, sir."

"For what purpose?"

"To watch him."

"For what period of time would you say of your own knowledge that he was guilty of masturbation?"

"From early 1912 until the spring or summer of 1913, when he left home."

"What did he say to you about masturbation?" McIntyre asked. I felt like raising my hand and answering but I didn't.

"He admitted that he did it frequently."

"Frequently?"

"Yes, sir."

McIntyre paused for a moment to study his notes and let the testimony sink in to the jury. I watched Jean start chewing his gum again. He toyed with it with his fingers, stretching it out and rolling it into a ball. I allowed myself to get carried away in a reverie. I imagined Jean preparing to toss the wad of gum. He took careful aim and threw it directly into his old man's mouth, choking him and bringing the embarrassing testimony to a halt. McIntyre immediately objected by wadding up a piece of legal paper and lobbing it at Jean. In rebuttal, the prosecutor hastily tore up his own notes, chewed the pages into wads and fired them at McIntyre. The defense team retaliated with a barrage of wads torn from their own papers. Reporters at the press table were getting hit by stray wads. The stenographer ducked under his table. Finally the justice shredded his law books with his teeth and spat wads of rules and codes at everybody with raccoonlike precision. By the time it all ended, the jury box was sinking in an ocean of spitballs.

When I recovered from my reverie, McIntyre had changed the subject of his questioning. He didn't need to dwell on masturbation, for with that single forbidden word he had reminded the jury, as well as all the young boys like myself sitting in the courtroom, that there was a higher power that could explain and thereby forgive Jean Gianini for being a degenerate killer. That higher power was a silent expert witness who did not need to be called to the stand, for his testimony was already part of the collective morality, ruling our daily thoughts and actions. The voice of that higher power had been recorded for all time. All of us had heard the teachings or at least read them. All of us were true believers in the words of Sylvanus Stall, Doctor of Divinity.

McIntyre had carefully selected eleven jurors with young sons, knowing full well that most were familiar with the Reverend Dr. Stall's ideas. They might not have recognized Stall's name but they held his truths to be as self-evident as any in the Scriptures. Most had undoubtedly given their sons copies of Stall's book *What A Young Boy Ought to Know*. The book was almost as widely read as the Bible and had been translated into nearly as many languages. It had been written in 1897, the year of Jean's birth and mine, which I now know was not a coincidence, for I believe our destinies were inextricably bound to the book's message.

I had heard that message on the day I heard a phonograph for the first time. Jean and I went to our schoolmate Nicholas' house to listen. He showed us a wooden packing crate containing twenty-four black Edison record cylinders, a gift from his father who was nervously watching from an adjoining room. He picked a cylinder at random and put it in the phonograph. "My dear friend Harry," Stall began in a high-pitched scratchy voice. It was a very clever introduction. Stall was not talking to us but to someone else and we were permitted to eavesdrop. It was just like spying and it made us feel safe from personal embarrassment.

"Poor Harry is going to catch an awful time," Jean said as we sat on the floor by the phonograph and listened with rapt attention.

"No boy can toy with the exposed portions of his reproductive system without finally suffering very serious consequences," Stall began. "In the beginning it may seem to a boy a trifling matter, and yet from the very first his conscience will tell him that he is doing something that is very wrong. It is on this account that a boy who yields to such an evil temptation will seek a secluded, solitary place, and it is because of this fact that it is called the 'solitary vice.' Because the entire being of the one who indulges in this practice is debased and polluted by his own personal act, it is also called 'self-pollution.' It is also called 'Onanism' because for a similar offense, nearly four thousand years ago, God punished Onan with death. This sin is also known by another name and is called 'mas-tur-ba-tion,' a word which is made from two Latin words which mean 'to pollute by the hand.'"

Each of these definitions told me something new about the vile character of this sin. I was familiar with the story of Onan from Genesis but I never realized what it really meant. And I didn't know about the Latin etymology. I was learning things from the Reverend Dr. Stall that Miss Beecher could never teach me.

Nicholas had changed cylinders and we listened as Stall spoke with a sense of urgency. He described how the pleasurable emotion of masturbation ended in a spasm of nerves that damaged the entire nervous system beyond all hope of recovery. "The health gradually declines," he said. "The eyes lose their luster. The skin becomes sallow. The muscles become flabby. There is an unnatural languor. The hands become cold and clammy. The boy sits in a stooping position, becomes hollow-chested, and the entire body, instead of enlarging into a strong manly frame, becomes wasted. Many signs give promise of early decline and death. The mind is suffering. The boy is gradually losing his power to comprehend and retain his lessons. His memory fails him. His mind begins to lack grasp and grip. Gradually he loses his place and sinks to the bottom of his class.

The boy seeks to avoid meeting people, pulls his cap down so as to hide his eyes, and goes about with a shy and guilty bearing."

We didn't listen to any other cylinders that night, but Nicholas let me borrow the book that came with them. I still had it among my books and knew I should return it if I ever saw him again.

Now as I turned my attention back to the trial, I watched Jean stooped over in his chair, looking hollow-chested with sallow skin and lusterless eyes. When the morning recess was called, he quickly put on his cap and pulled it down over his eyes as he shuffled out. His grin showed that his mind lacked grasp and grip. Everyone on the jury could now see that masturbation had turned him into an imbecile. It was becoming clear that McIntyre—whose bright eyes and heavy frame suggested that he never masturbated—was setting the stage for the defense alienists to testify about Jean's irrationality, evidenced mostly by self-pollution, as the cause of the murder.

When cross-examination began after the recess, Special Prosecutor Charlie Tom managed to get Mr. Gianini to admit that Jean had stopped masturbation and all other irrational behavior from the time he came home from St. Vincent's until the night of the murder. It was a skillful cross-examination but the jurors did not seem to be listening. I imagined that the omnipresent Reverend Dr. Stall was covering their ears.

Charlie Tom then asked about the beatings Mr. Gianini gave Jean. Mr. Gianini mentioned one instance when he corrected Jean after he made his little sisters cry.

"What did you do?"

"I gave him a good whipping, a beating."

"With your hand alone?"

"At that time, yes, sir."

"Where did you hit him?"

I could see McIntyre getting read to jump and bark.

"I don't know. I couldn't say."

"Did you cuff him about the face and head?"

"I think so."

"And how many times did you strike him?"

"I couldn't say."

"Did he cry?"

"Yes, sir. He hollered."

McIntyre pushed his chair away from the counsel table.

"Did his hollering in response to this punishment that you gave him impress you as rational or irrational?" Charlie Tom asked.

McIntyre finally stood, gesturing frantically toward the justice. "We object to that, if Your Honor please. I don't think that he has the right to inquire into the punishment that is administered by a father to a child. It has nothing to do with this case."

It had everything to do with this case, I thought. His father was the irrational one.

"Objection overruled."

"What is the answer, Mr. Gianini?" Charlie Tom asked.

"His hollering didn't impress me either way."

McIntyre pursed his lips. In so many words Jean's old man had just told everyone he didn't care about his son.

It was now late Saturday afternoon and the justice adjourned the court until Monday morning. "Gentlemen of the jury," the justice said. "It again becomes my duty to admonish you with reference to your duties during the adjournment hours. And you are not to discuss the case among yourselves, or form any opinion, until the case is finally submitted to you."

As we left the courthouse I saw Jean's older sister, Moffie, in the crowd on the street. She had just arrived from New York City where she was now living with her grandmother. Moffie was looking very grown up and was stylishly dressed except for a funny sailor hat. The hat didn't make sense until I realized she kept looking at yeoman Willis Beecher with an idiotic smile. I entertained the possibility that she was flirting with him. I secretly hoped he might run away with her and leave Ethel for me. When juror Bronson Plattner appeared, Moffie ran to him, tears streaming down her face. "Pa," she cried, throwing her arms around the man who had been so fatherly to her and Jean. He kissed her cheek and told her he would see to it that everything would be all right. In defiance of the court's admonition, I had just witnessed an opinion being formed.

That night I dreamed I returned to the courtroom and looked at the exhibit table. Miss Beecher was lying there in her red dress. I struggled to approach her, but something was holding me back. It was as if the floor had turned to molasses and I was sinking. I keep pushing my body forward through the sticky mess. When I woke, I realized I had ejaculated during my dream and polluted myself.

Although I had stopped masturbating days ago, vowing to never use my hands in that way, my body seemed capable of polluting itself without assistance. I looked through the storage shelves in my room and found a wooden tube, about the size and shape of a small cigar, that had once held pills or powder. I removed the wooden top and shook a few white flakes into the sink, then rinsed it out. My penis fit snugly inside with very little pain and absolutely no sensation of arousal. I was confident that this would cure me of future accidents. I proudly dubbed it my "vice grip" and vowed to wear it in bed every night. It was an act of prevention, not punishment, and it was no different than putting on a cap to keep the flies from biting me while fishing. I knew that for me to have done otherwise would have been irrational.

I returned to court on Monday to hear the rest of Mr. Gianini's cross-examination. The women and girls were allowed back into the courtroom. Just before Mr. Gianini was called to the witness box, four defense alienists entered the courtroom and took seats behind the lawyers. They were dressed alike, carrying identical black notebooks, and all sat rigidly, like well-disciplined choir boys, eyes riveted on the witness box. The press had identified them as Carlos Frederik MacDonald of New York, Henry Herbert Goddard of New Jersey, Charles Bernstein of Rome, New York, and Herkimer's one and only A. Walter Suiter.

"What methods of punishment did you adopt with Jean in Poland?" Charlie Tom asked.

"One form of punishment was to make him study his lessons," Mr. Gianini said.

"Yes?"

"Go to his catechism for one thing."

"Yes?"

"And I would whip him."

Charlie Tom smiled. "How?"

"Well, with my hand."

"Anything else?"

"No, sir; not as I know of."

"Did you say that you did not?"

"I say so."

"Do you remember ever striking him with a pole?"

"No, sir; not that I know of."

"Will you swear you did not?" Charlie Tom asked.

"I will not swear that I didn't, but that I don't remember."

"With reference to whipping, did you ever punish him in the barn?"

McIntyre waved his arms. "I object to it, if Your Honor please. And we will object to all this line of cross-examination respecting the corporal punishment administered by the father to this child. I submit it has nothing to do with the issue involved in the indictment."

I bit my tongue to keep from joining in the objection, not because it had nothing to do with the issue, but because I did not wish to revisit the horror of that whipping.

"Objection overruled."

"Yes, I did," Mr. Gianini answered.

"And how did you punish him in there?"

"I think I used a whip."

"A horsewhip?"

"I think it was."

"Where did you strike him with the horsewhip?"

"Same objection," McIntyre said.

"Overruled."

"I couldn't tell you," Mr. Gianini said.

"Did you strike him several times?"

"Might have been."

"Was he clothed when you whipped him?"

"I couldn't tell you."

"Do you remember what he had done that in your opinion merited the horsewhipping?"

"I don't remember."

"Did you ever take his head between your hands and pound it on the floor?"

"I have no recollection."

"Do you say that you didn't?"

"I can't say."

"Is there anything about his actions when you were punishing him in Poland that impressed you at the time as rational or irrational?"

"Sometimes before being touched he would start hollering 'Father, don't.' That fact impressed me as irrational."

"Then you think that being apprehensive of punishment and hollering before he was actually whipped was irrational?"

"Yes, sir."

"And you proceeded to punish him, didn't you?"

"Yes, sir."

"Mr. Gianini, isn't it true you gave him a severe whipping before he left home in April 1913?"

"He probably got a whipping."

"Yes, and who gave it to him?"

"I gave it to him. I had many of those myself and I didn't run away from home," Mr. Gianini snapped.

"Now, I didn't ask you that—I had some myself—now what did you whip him for?"

"He was whipped for tormenting his sisters at that time, making them cry."

"Did you horsewhip him at that time?"

"That time I slapped him with my fist, I mean my hands."

"As a matter of fact you not only slapped him with your open hand but you struck him with your clenched fist, didn't you?"

"I didn't say that."

"Answer the question, yes or no?"

"I don't say one way or the other. I have a recollection of giving him a good beating."

"Did you horsewhip him or strike him with anything so that it left marks on his arm or shoulder?"

"I couldn't tell you."

"Have you no recollection of the incident?"

"He got a whipping for a number of previous acts he had done. It was an accumulation for a series of tormenting acts."

"And it was a series of accumulating anger on your part, was it not?"

"Partly."

"Was it the following day he ran away?"

"I can't say. I wasn't home."

"Now Mr. Gianini, that beating that you gave him was severe and extreme, wasn't it?"

"It wasn't extreme. I have had worse myself."

"Was it excessive?"

"The acts were deserving of it. It was a good beating, as I told you."

"It was such a good beating that it satisfied you, did it not?"

"Yes."

"So the beating made you feel good?"

"Yes."

"No more questions. That is all, Mr. Gianini."

The courtroom was deathly silent as Mr. Gianini left the witness chair. Jean was visibly shaking and making those swallowing movements in his throat. So was I.

9

During the noon recess one of the defense alienists, Dr. Carlos MacDonald, came into the barbershop for a quick trim. Uncle Sam greeted him graciously, apologized for being busy with another customer, and directed him to Tony's chair. I was disappointed because Tony had a habit of keeping his customers facing the mirror and rarely turned them around, so I couldn't get a good look. I think he did this on purpose—not that he knew I was spying but as a way to force them to watch as he poked and jabbed them with the scissors or razor clutched perilously in his hands, waiting for signs of fear in their eyes. It was a sadistic game and I suspected that as a child he had enjoyed torturing insects and small animals.

Today Tony met his match. As the alienist sat down, Tony quickly swiveled the chair around so that he was facing the mirror. Tony smiled and began snipping, jabbering, and jabbing away. A certain glaze came over the alienist's eyes. They didn't blink and didn't move, like the eyes of a fish when you pull it out of the water.

I had observed many people looking into the barbershop mirror and had studied them out of both curiosity and envy. No one looked in the mirror with indifference. Men looked in the mirror and scrutinized their body's physical features. They examined their shaved faces, checked to see if their hair was combed properly, and even investigated their teeth. The women who occasionally came into the shop with their sons used the mirror differently. They seemed to explore the mirror searching for what they were inside. I watched as they examined themselves from every angle, stepping close, stepping back, stepping close again in a dance of interrogation. When they left they often twirled in front of the mirror as they put on their coats, then nodded to themselves in the glass as if to say goodbye to someone only they could see.

The alienist in the mirror remained starkly uninvolved. He appeared totally focused on Tony, not on his own reflection. The glaze that came over his eyes turned them into a magical mirror capable of absorbing all light and reflecting it back without changing it or adding anything of itself. If you looked into those eyes you would see only yourself. It was like looking at the eyes of the fish you just hooked and seeing only the horror of what you had done. It was a most remarkable feat and I wished I was able to do it myself.

Tony jabbered about the trial. "Hanging is too good for that murderer. They should cut him up in little pieces like he did to that girl." Tony clicked his scissors several times in the air in front of the man's face. "Do it nice and slow for the half hour it took her to die," he said with a hint of glee.

The alienist stared at him as a fish might eye a fisherman.

"They got the electric chair now," said the customer sitting in Uncle Sam's chair. He started to add something else but Uncle Sam whispered in his ear and he stopped with a forced cough.

"Yeah," Tony said. "I read all about it. They say it's like being burned alive. The electrodes have these little sharp prongs that cut into your skin. There are sparks and smoke and all sorts of yelling and twitching. That would be good for Gianini if it wasn't too fast."

When the trim was over the alienist stood, grabbed the whisk away from Tony, and brushed his own clothes. "You don't know what you're talking about," the alienist said with a deep professorial tone. "The electric chair is quick and painless. There is, however, a rather offensive odor." He sniffed the air a couple of times. "I don't think you would notice it." He looked at Tony with those cold fish eyes, handed him the brush and some money, then walked out of the shop.

Uncle Sam laughed. "Tony," he said, "that was the man who invented the electric chair." Everyone in the shop joined the laughter, including me.

Tony bolted to my door and threw it open. I was standing in the doorway. He had never seen me without my patch and he stiffened as if momentarily electrified, then turned and walked back to his chair. The man who was always being bitten by his clothes had now suffered an eye-bite. It was a very pleasing moment for me.

When I returned to the courtroom, the alienist from the barbershop, Dr. MacDonald, took the witness stand for the defense. McIntyre guided him through his qualifications and established that he was the most famous alienist in America and president of the American Medico-Psychological Association. He had testified in many trials and examined many murderers, including Leon Czolgosz, the assassin of President McKinley.

My later research into MacDonald's background revealed that he had participated in a series of barbaric experiments with animals at Thomas Edison's laboratories in Menlo Park, New Jersey. On the afternoon of March 12, 1889, he and his colleagues led four dogs, four calves, and a horse to a wooden structure in the rear of the lab. Several young boys about Jean's age, who procured the animals, were permitted to watch. The dogs were the first to go. One by one they were lured into the structure where a brass electrode was placed on a hind leg and another electrode on either the chest, neck, or head. The electrodes were soaked in salt water, a dynamo was cranked, and light bulbs lit up indicating the show was ready to begin. Everyone stood back as a switch was closed and instantaneously the dog's limbs stiffened. After ten seconds the switch was opened and the dog dropped in a dead heap. The calves took a little more time and coaxing; one kept crying when it was her turn. The horse, a mare named Daisy, affectionately nudged the technician as he attached the electrodes to her front legs. Daisy held on for twenty-five interminable seconds before her heart stopped and the air left her lungs with a heavy sigh. As repulsive as the experiment was, I could imagine that if Jean was in the group of boys watching he would have led them in a macabre chorus of "Old MacDonald Had a Farm," marking each throw of the switch with a loud "Ee i ee i oh."

The animal experiments led MacDonald and a electrician at Sing Sing prison to build the electric chair. The first human execution went badly—someone placed the electrode on the spine instead of the head—and the prisoner sat sizzling and wheezing in the chair for eight minutes before it was over. Death in the electric chair seemed brutal but MacDonald argued it was an important advance for higher civilization. Improvements were made and more chairs were eventually put to use.

So now MacDonald was in the odd position of sitting in the witness chair trying to save someone from that other chair he had invented. He seemed to be trying awfully hard. During the recitation of his qualifications, he volunteered that he "built" the Matteawan asylum when he actually only worked there. He appeared to be having trouble with his memory for other events as well. At first he said he saw 3,000 patients a year. Then the number grew to 25,000 every six months for seven years. Then he said the total was 75,000 or 100,000 over forty-three years. His arithmetic seemed no better than his memory.

The alienist couldn't remember many details about his interview of Jean, whom he had seen in jail only a few weeks earlier, so McIntyre reminded him by reading a stenographer's transcript of the examination. Jean had been expecting a visit from the jail photographer and was surprised by MacDonald's appearance, yet he handled himself as well as he did on any of the surprise tests we had in school. He answered all the questions about his life in New York and Poland, recited his entire medical history, and provided the names of every doctor he had ever seen. When MacDonald asked if other doctors had examined him in jail, Jean gave their names, addresses, and even the telephone number for one of them. All this he did from memory without the aid of a stenographer's record. I was very proud of my friend's performance.

MacDonald reported that his physical examination of Jean revealed the stigmata of degeneracy. The head was disproportionate. One ear stood out at a different angle from the other. There was a scar near one eyebrow. His tongue was long and pointed. The arch of his palate was high and narrow. His gait was shambling. His hands were cold and clammy.

"What diagnosis did you arrive at?" McIntyre finally asked.

"The defendant is suffering from a mental deficiency which I would characterize as imbecility."

"What is imbecility?"

"Imbecility is an arrest of mental development from some accident or a combination of heredity and accident."

"He cannot develop now to full manhood?"

"No, sir. He is arrested."

McIntyre then read a long hypothetical question that took over twenty-five minutes. It was a lecture, an argument to the jury on the defense version of Jean's lifelong descent into imbecility. He ended with a question: "Assuming all of this is true, at the time of the killing of Lida Beecher on the twenty-seventh day of March 1914, can you state whether he was an imbecile or not?"

Charlie Tom objected vehemently because the hypothetical contained many facts that had not been presented in evidence, but the justice overruled. After listening for twenty-five minutes, I think he wanted to hear the answer as did everyone else in the courtroom.

"Give us your opinion, Doctor," McIntyre said.

"I would say that in my opinion, assuming the statements contained in the hypothetical question to be true, and in applying the same with my examination of the defendant as here stated, that he is and was suffering from a condition of mental defect or mental weakness known as imbecility."

"Now, Doctor, assuming all the facts as recited in the hypothetical question, do you think in this case, from your experience of mental and nervous diseases, from your knowledge of imbeciles, in your opinion was Jean Gianini, at the time of the killing of Lida Beecher, in such a mental condition as to know the nature and quality of the act he was committing, or that the act was wrong?"

"In my opinion he did not know the nature and quality of what he was doing, and did not know that it was wrong."

McIntyre had cleverly incorporated the language of the law which would be provided to the jury as part of their instructions in reaching a verdict. In essence, he had managed to have the most famous alienist in America tell the jury what that verdict ought to be.

Now the special prosecutor, Charlie Tom, was standing still in front of the courtroom, pausing before beginning his cross-examination. He had never faced an expert witness of MacDonald's reputation, I later learned. So first he admitted that he was unprepared and asked for a continuance. But McIntyre said his witness had a train to catch and pressured the justice to keep things moving. Then he did his best to stop Charlie Tom dead in his tracks by objecting to almost every question. MacDonald was an equally stubborn witness and refused to answer most questions, saying that he couldn't give a yes or no answer as the prosecutor requested. Even when the justice ordered him to answer yes or no, he got red behind the gills but still refused.

Charlie Tom was clearly annoyed with the witness. He took the monkey wrench from the exhibit table and approached him, brandishing the weapon high in the air. MacDonald's beady fish eyes followed the movements as if the wrench were a grotesque fish hook bobbing above him. Several jurors gasped.

McIntyre was on his feet again. "I object," he barked. "The exhibits have already been shown once and Your Honor will readily recognize how revolting and gasping it is here. There's my learned opponent, tall and athletic appearing, with a wrench in hand, a sinister expression on his face, and apparently fit to cope with one of Napoleon's armies and—"

"*Aouuuuuuu.*" Charlie Tom howled like a big wolf at the little bulldog lawyer. McIntyre backed away, shaking a finger. People in the courtroom chuckled.

"Objection overruled," the justice smiled.

"Did the stenographer get Mr. Thomas' wolf howl?" McIntyre asked.

"In answering the hypothetical, Doctor, did you consider these weapons?" Charlie Tom asked.

"I assumed that it was true that he had those weapons."

"What did you consider was his object and purpose in striking that girl with these weapons?"

"I would be unwilling to express an opinion on any isolated fact in this case. My opinion is based on the whole history of the case."

So Charlie Tom gave MacDonald the whole history of the case in the form of his own hypothetical question which took longer to read than the defense's question due to all the courtroom wrangling. McIntyre repeatedly objected to the way in which Charlie Tom would remove objects from the exhibit table to display to the witness. Charlie Tom objected to the way McIntyre was objecting. The justice objected to one of the statements in the hypothetical question. Attorney Hirsch corrected Charlie Tom. District Attorney Farrell corrected Hirsch. The justice was so confused he took a recess. Then Charlie Tom finished reading the hypothetical and McIntyre objected to everything. It was almost impossible for Dr. MacDonald to remember all the facts that he was being asked to assume were true. He asked for the question to be read again. Then he refused to answer.

"If the court please," McIntyre said, "I don't want to object any more, but the doctor has got to make his train."

"Doctor, beat it," Charlie Tom sneered at the big fish who was getting away.

The evening paper reported that the prosecution was already in trouble. The rumor was that one of their own alienists had concluded that Jean was not mentally responsible and, of course, would not be called by the People. McIntyre told reporters that he was trying to persuade that alienist to testify for the defense.

"McIntyre's buying a bunch of experts, but I don't think the jury is buying it," the sweeper said that night during one of our regular discussions about the trial.

"Do you think the other experts will call him an 'i-em-bee-sill'?" I felt like an idiot trying to pronounce the word but I had never tried saying it before.

"Imbecile," he gently corrected with a smile. "Sure. Calling people names is the alienist game. A name can save him from the chair and that's what they're getting paid to do. McIntyre will try to get anyone, even Jesus Christ himself."

"Do you think he will testify?" I asked.

"Jesus?" the sweeper asked, and we both laughed. "Why not? He'll need a real miracle to cheat justice here in Herkimer." He pointed to the jail yard where Roxy Druse had been hanged, then grabbed his neck and made a comical face of being strangled.

I laughed but I knew that Justice was blind. It wouldn't take a miracle to fool her, only an illusion to create a false impression—a magic trick no one had ever seen, one that no one knew was a trick.

Dr. Henry Goddard took the witness stand. He was a psychologist at a training school for feebleminded children in Vineland, New Jersey. Psychologists were rarely used or accepted in court because they didn't have the medical training of psychiatrists, and this was Goddard's first time testifying. He had neither the arrogance of MacDonald nor his testiness as an advocate.

Goddard had written articles and books but was modest and didn't even mention the titles. He also didn't mention that his mother's name was Sarah, like mine and Jean's, which was probably why our three destinies became so intertwined. And he never told about his skill at using magic tricks to fool his students and keep them interested in his lectures. It was his research and experience with imbeciles that McIntyre wanted to hear about.

"I have been studying the problem of the mind for eighteen years," Goddard said. "For eight years I have been doing nothing but living with imbeciles and devoting my whole time to a study of their condition. I have visited and interviewed and inspected the inmates of a large part of the American institutions for the feebleminded, and in foreign institutions as well. I have observed at least 25,000 imbeciles in all."

"Doctor, to begin with, will you tell the jury what imbecility is?" McIntyre asked.

"Imbecility is the arrest of development existing from birth or in early age. It may be inherited; it may be acquired."

"And the condition of the mother during gestation will influence the offspring?"

"Without doubt."

"Is melancholia one of these conditions?"

"I regard it as one of the insanities that could affect the offspring's feeblemindedness."

"Have you recently developed a new classification to feeblemindedness, Doctor?"

"Yes, sir."

"Will you tell us what it is?"

"The older classification system called all defectives 'idiots.' Later on, when that term became too harsh, there was a tendency to call them by a milder and less offensive term and that was 'imbecile.' Later that became just as offensive as 'idiot' and we adopted the term 'feeblemindedness.' It was necessary to speak of different grades of feeblemindedness. The low-grade, those with a mental age of a one- or two-year-old child, we speak of as idiots. Those with a mental age of three to seven years are imbeciles. And from eight to twelve, they were once called high-grade imbeciles. However, to avoid confusion between this high-grade imbecile and others, I invented the term 'moron' in 1910, which means a high-grade imbecile with a mental age of from eight to twelve."

Goddard explained that he had visited Jean in jail for less than one hour in order to determine his proper classification. He asked questions of Jean from the Binet-Simon Measuring Scale of Intelligence, a 1908 test developed in France which he personally translated into English and revised for American children. According to the newspapers this was the first use of that test or any psychological test in a murder trial.

The Binet test consisted of a series of simple tasks and questions arranged according to their degree of difficulty for normal children of ages three to fifteen. It also included questions for adults. The test items asked children to identify objects, to make rhymes, to compose sentences, to copy figures, or to compare lines of different lengths, among other tasks. If the child could not answer the questions set for normal children of his age, then he was considered to be of a lesser mental age. The scoring was somewhat arbitrary but Goddard insisted it was highly scientific. Besides, after doing nothing for eight years but living with imbeciles and studying them, he knew how they should answer.

Most of Jean's answers seemed to be correct but Goddard said he was not fooled. From the group of questions designed for children of twelve, Goddard asked Jean for the definition of "charity." "Charity is giving," Jean said. Goddard scored this as incorrect because it failed to include the idea that charity is giving to the needy, a necessary answer for most of the normal twelve-year-old children he studied. Jean's answer, he said, was indicative of a mental age of only ten.

Goddard described his next set of questions to Jean. "I said I am going to tell you some little stories, some of them have some absurdity in them, something funny, something that you would not usually say. Now tell me what is wrong with these sentences: 'A painter has fallen off a ladder and has broken his neck. He is dead from the fall. They don't think he will get well.' Jean said, 'I would like to have seen him fall.' Then I told him another story: 'We found a boy locked in a room with his hands and feet tied behind him, and we think he locked himself in.' And Jean said, 'He must have been kidnapped.' I repeated: 'We think he locked himself in the room.' He said, 'Whose room?' I said 'Well, say it was my room.' He said, 'Well, you probably kidnapped him.'"

While Goddard failed him on both answers, I knew that Jean was just being a smart-aleck and you have to be smart and have a quick mind to answer like he did. Jean was not only smart but perceptive. When asked how old he would be on his next birthday, Jean answered "Supposed to be seventeen."

"Don't you know?" Goddard asked.

"I don't know," Jean said.

Again Goddard failed him on his answer. Goddard must have thought that the poor lad didn't even know how old he was. But it was the psychologist who had failed to appreciate that Jean understood the uncertainty of the trial outcome and the possibility of dying in the electric chair. That was why Jean had told me he was so afraid. On this simple question and answer, like so many of the others, it was Goddard who was dead wrong.

"Now, Doctor, as a result of the test which you have detailed here today, can you say what is the mental age of this defendant?" McIntyre asked.

"Yes. His mental age is ten."

"Will you tell us what other observations you made."

"He would interrupt me in the midst of a statement. He would laugh. He would turn to the stenographer and ask her about her work. While we were there in jail the dinner bell rang and it diverted his attention from the examination. His manner throughout the whole thing was not normal, I mean normal in view of the seriousness of the crime and normal in the sense of a reaction that is appropriate to his actual age. On the contrary, it fits his mental age of ten."

McIntyre read the same long hypothetical question given to MacDonald with the addition of new evidence presented by several witnesses who had testified before Goddard took the stand.

"Now, Doctor, assuming all these facts contained in the hypothetical to have been established by evidence in this case, can you express an opinion as to the condition of Jean Gianini at the time of the killing of Lida Beecher?"

"I can. He was and is a high-grade imbecile of the moron type."

"Doctor, have you observed criminal propensities in imbeciles?"

"I have."

"Do imbeciles sometimes act criminally because of delusions of fancied wrongs and fancied injuries?"

"They do."

"At about what age does the criminal propensity in an imbecile manifest itself?"

"The age from nine to ten is remarkable as being the time at which those propensities appear. We all have these tendencies at that age, but the normal person very quickly outgrows them and acquires normal control; the mental defective never does. He stops there and never gets the control over those things. He has no restraint."

"Do imbeciles masturbate without restraint, Doctor?"

"Almost universally."

"Did it increase the mental deficiency of the defendant?"

"I should say it did."

"And made him more disposed to criminal behavior?"

"Yes."

In the glaring light of the following day, Special Prosecutor Charlie Tom subjected Goddard to the longest cross-examination anyone could remember. He grilled Goddard for seven hours on the data and reasoning behind the test and his conclusions about Jean. He was able to show that Goddard had purposely changed the wording of some questions to lead Jean astray. Charlie Tom also pointed out that the stenographer's transcript contained differently worded questions and answers than those that Goddard remembered. Goddard was calm as he insisted the transcript was wrong, but defense attorney McIntyre raged. He huffed and puffed objections which were constantly overruled and he became so frustrated that when Charlie Tom finally asked his own long hypothetical question McIntyre screamed at Goddard, "Don't answer!" Goddard answered that he couldn't answer and everyone took a recess.

After the recess Charlie Tom was able to get Goddard to

admit that despite being an imbecile Jean knew the nature and quality of the act when he was killing Miss Beecher. McIntyre shook with anger and he asked for a mistrial. His motion was denied. On re-direct examination he tried to salvage what was left.

"Just tell us again what a moron is, Doctor?" McIntyre asked.

"A moron is defined as a high-grade imbecile, a person with the intelligence of someone from eight to twelve."

"Is it not a fact that an imbecile, even one of the moron type, never progresses in mental development?"

"Yes. They may acquire knowledge but not more intelligence."

"Is that true of a moron in the ten-year-old class?"

"He may know much more than any one ten-year-old child, but he will not have an understanding of anything that involves more than ten-year intelligence."

"So is it not a fact that morons are never more than morons?"

"Yes. I always speak of them that way. A moron is nothing but a moron."

10

Moron. I said the word several times. I liked it because it was easier for me to pronounce than "imbecile." It had a murmuring sound that rolled over my tongue as easily as "Mama." I wanted to know more about the term and gave myself an assignment to find out all I could. Dr. Henry Goddard had made it seem like there was a hidden tribe of morons lurking in shadows everywhere, a diaspora of defectives. I was hoping that I could find them in the library.

I needed a journal for my research and found a blank ledger that Uncle Sam said I could keep. It was a rather odd-shaped book, nearly a foot long and less than a half-foot wide, with hard blue-gray covers and red leather on the spine. Water had caused some of the red dye to stain the narrow ruled pages but they were still usable. I printed MORON on the top of the first page.

In the morning I put the driving goggles over my patch and walked to the library instead of the courthouse. The library looked more like the residence it had once been for a local judge than a public building, and although I had only been there once before, I felt like I was going home again. I went into the dining room which was now the library reading room and looked through *The Century Dictionary*. I was disappointed when I couldn't find the word "moron" but of course Goddard had only recently invented the word. I asked the librarian in the next room for books on medicine, afraid to embarrass myself by trying to pronounce "imbeciles." She directed me to a shelf with several medical texts.

I selected *The People's Common Sense Medical Adviser* and took it to a corner table in the reading room where I removed the goggles and raised my patch. The book, written by a Dr. Pierce together with a staff of medical experts, was an encyclopedia of medical diseases with over a thousand pages that included drawings and colored illustrations. It was printed in 1909, at a time when the term "idiot" was sometimes used by popular writers to refer to all feebleminded people including imbeciles and morons.

I learned there was a correspondence between the size and complexity of the brain and mental capacity. The brain of an idiot was very small and parts were much less complex than those of a normal individual and more like those found in baboons and other lower apes. This explained why idiots could never develop further and intelligence remained arrested. Idiots and "normals" were like different species.

Pierce's book explained how masturbation can lead to further degradation of mental capacity by softening the brain, thereby turning even a normal brain into an idiot brain. In addition to a wasted appearance and the other physical miseries of idiocy, or perhaps as a result of them, many self-abusers went insane and were either sent to asylums or committed suicide. While the Reverend Dr. Stall had warned of similar dangers, Dr. Pierce gave details of the actual physiological mechanisms. He even provided drawings of the microscopic appearance of semen. Healthy semen contained sperm with clearly defined heads and tails. The semen of self-abusers either had no sperm or, if present, they were defective, the heads severed from the tails. To lose one's head in exchange for a few moments of lustful enjoyment would certainly be something only an idiot's sperm would do. I was thankful that I had discontinued the vice and only prayed that I had stopped in time to avoid any damage.

I looked for related medical books and was thrilled to find a copy of Goddard's *The Kallikak Family*. This was the story of a family of morons that he named Kallikak from the Greek words *kallos,* for beauty, and *kakos,* for bad, to highlight the two distinct lines of descendants of a young man, Martin Kallikak, who fought with a militia during the American Revolutionary War. Martin met a feebleminded girl at a tavern frequented by his militia and sired her feebleminded son. Goddard traced the lives of the descendants of that illegitimate son and discovered that most of these were feebleminded. In addition, there were alcoholics, epileptics, criminals, and prostitutes. A few years after his unfortunate union with the tavern wench, Martin married a respectable girl from a good Quaker family, just like Goddard's own Quaker family. All of their descendants were normal and included doctors, lawyers, judges, educators, and other respectable citizens. Goddard concluded that feeblemindedness was hereditary and transmitted as surely as any other character. Furthermore, it was responsible for all the social sores of civilization.

But Goddard was not worried about the lower grades of the feebleminded—the idiots and the imbeciles—because they rarely reproduced. The danger came from the high-grade imbeciles, morons like the Kallikaks, who produced more than their share of offspring. They were social pests. They were dangerous and evil. Goddard included their photographs to help prove the point. I noticed that most of the Kallikaks had heavy black circles around their eyes making them appear larger than normal, almost like my own left eye. They were dark, ominous eyes that made me shudder. Having one deformed eye was bad enough, but two looked dreadful. There was one Kallikak who stood out among all the others with bright, lovely eyes. I tried to whisper her name, Deborah, but her picture took my breath away.

Deborah Kallikak had been born in an almshouse and had been living at Goddard's Vineland training school since she was eight. She was the one who had inspired his study of her family background. The frontispiece photograph showed that she was now a beautiful, well-groomed young woman of Miss Beecher's age. She sat in a chair reading a book with a cat on her lap. She wore her hair up like Miss Beecher, and even had a pinafore apron like Mama's. A series of other photographs showed her woodworking projects. Here were impressive chairs, stools, and even a shirtwaist box complete with mortise and tenon joints as well as exquisite paneling. I admired these photographs for many minutes, aching to do something, anything, with this beautiful and talented woodworker.

Goddard was afraid of Deborah Kallikak. He looked at her and saw only a moron, a direct descendant of a family of morons. He wrote that there were families like the Kallikaks all around us. They were multiplying at twice the rate of the general population. They formed a large percentage of society's criminals. Deborah was typical of the kind of girl who got into trouble, sexually and otherwise, and filled the reformatories. Morons like her had to be identified, segregated, sterilized. Such treatment did not seem fair. I slammed the book shut in protest and left the library.

When I returned to my room I opened the journal to a new section—RHYMES—and started copying the sweeper's poems from loose papers I had been keeping. Then I tried my hand at composing a poem of my own. The Binet test had shown that Deborah Kallikak was incapable of rhyming for herself. My poem was for Deborah.

I opened a book and was quickly smitten,
Hit over the heart by a lovely kitten.
Rescued from poverty Deborah's her name,
She grew to become a girl of great fame.
Descendant of a family called Kallikaks,
Goddard said they breed like alley cats.
According to him she's not the one,
Never be able to give me a son.
Everyone knows it would be of the kind
Born with nothing but a feeble mind.
So he locked her away in a training school,
There to become teacher's pet and fool.
Forgive me My Lord but it's been so hard
To look at my loss without hating Goddard.

That night the sweeper gave me a summary of the courtroom happenings I had missed that day. Several friends and relatives of Sarah Gianini testified about her melancholia and odd behavior. I now understood that the defense was following the same hereditary argument of feeblemindedness that Goddard had advanced with Deborah. In researching the Kallikaks, Goddard became so adept at identifying morons, even dead ones, he could do it solely on the basis of interviews with descendants and those who knew them. McIntyre was asking the jury to do the same with Jean's mother, thereby condemning Jean to the same defective heritage.

I didn't sleep very well that night, and I thought I might benefit from one of those bromides that Sarah Gianini was given to help her sleep. In the morning I wrote BROMIDES on a new journal page and returned to the library to research the word in a materia medica. I learned that bromides were powerful depressants of the nervous system. They not only calmed the nerves but hypnotized the brain so they were also useful in producing sleep. Bromides were given for the insomnia of overwork or pain, and were especially of value to women who had problems connected with their climacteric periods. Women who took too many bromides often appeared so stuporous, slurring their words and walking with tipsy gaits, that the bromide intoxication was mistaken for alcoholism.

Sarah Gianini had used bromides both before and during her pregnancy with Jean. Everyone thought she was drunk, but no one actually saw her drink alcohol that often. Everything said about her at the trial seemed to suggest that she had taken bromides for too long a period. She displayed the classic signs of a bromide habit: depression of spirit, self-neglect, dullness, mental weakness, melancholia, and loss of sexual interest. Even her rashes, loss of appetite, and fear of daylight suggested poisoning from the drug. Bromide sores would have made her skin unsightly and sensitive to the sun which may have been why she always covered herself in black clothing and only went out at night. She was in a constant stupor from the medication yet the doctors mistook it for alcoholism and prescribed more bromides. I did not know how this affected Jean when she was carrying him, but I suspected it was of little consequence since the bromide habit was acquired and not transmitted. People recovered once the medicine was discontinued, although Sarah Gianini took it until the end. Yet there was no permanent damage to the newborn children of such users. It was not hereditary feeblemindedness. It was not alcoholism. Her death certificate blaming alcohol was wrong. "It was bromism!" I shouted as I skipped out of the library.

It took me only a few hours of amateur detective work to figure this out. I assumed that the next defense witness on the stand, a man who was a professional medical detective, would not only have figured it out but would be able to explain it in terms that everyone could understand.

I watched as Dr. A. Walter Suiter, the local physician who was part of the defense team, took the witness chair and introduced yet another word: protoplasm. "It is the first principle of animal life," he said. "It is a shapeless mass inside the animal cells from which we are all created." He proceeded to lecture the jury on the process by which the protoplasm inside the developing fetus grows into a human being. Liquor was injurious to this process, he said, arresting development and disabling the individual. It was hard to imagine a fetus actually drinking liquor but Suiter used several charts to explain in garbled technical detail how it did so through the mother's body. His long-winded testimony caused much fidgeting and many yawns. Jean kept pushing his gum in and out of his mouth with his thumb. Everyone watched the clock.

Justice Devendorf stopped the proceedings for a supper break and told everyone to be back at 7:30 P.M. An evening session was unusual but he wanted to finish with Suiter, who had already been on the stand longer than the other defense experts. The courtroom emptied as spectators rushed down the street to find a quick meal. The hotels serving liquor seemed to be the most popular.

Charlie Tom had objected to Suiter's protoplasm explanation, arguing that it was absurd, impossible. He called it chimerical, a fabulous word that conjured images of a Chimera, the fire-breathing monster from Homer's Iliad with a lion's head, a goat's body, and a serpent's tail. The justice agreed with the prosecutor's objection but was willing to receive the testimony in order to be fair to the defense. Now that it had been unleashed, the Chimera was threatening to consume the People's case. Was I the only one who knew that sprinkling a little bromide on its tail would make it run away?

The court was packed for the night session. In addition to the locals who some newspapers called "Herkimerites," there were judges, lawyers, and district attorneys who had traveled from surrounding towns despite the forecast of showers. Word had spread that Suiter was planning a dramatic demonstration and everyone knew that Special Prosecutor Charlie Tom would be fighting hard to keep it out. Two regular court watchers sitting in front of me, who happened to be pudgy twins, obviously had had too much to drink at supper and now elbowed each other with excitement.

"Doctor, are you prepared now to make an experiment before the jury of the effect of liquor upon protoplasm?" McIntyre asked.

"Yes, sir. I could do so in a very few minutes."

"Now, will you show the jury the effect that liquor has upon protoplasm in an experimental way?"

"I will."

The press table came alive. Reporters got ready to prepare stories about the great medical detective who had created a winning case out of the ashes in the Roxy Druse murder. Now they expected he was going to do it again in what would surely be regarded as a great scientific and legal achievement.

Charlie Tom, who had been shifting around in his chair, stood. "I object to it and protest most respectively as it is incompetent, irrelevant, immaterial, unjustifiable and collateral."

"You mean a direct application of an alcoholic substance?" Justice Devendorf asked McIntyre.

"Yes," McIntyre answered. "Upon the protoplasm of an egg."

"Oh, no," the justice said, shaking his head. "I sustain the objection to that."

There were murmurs of disappointment in the courtroom. The twin court watchers kicked the back of the bench seats in front of them. I wondered what Dr. Suiter had been planning to demonstrate. Pour the alcohol on an egg, wait for it to hatch, then study the chicken? All chickens were imbeciles anyway, so what would that prove?

McIntyre was clearly annoyed and was left with little more to do than ask Suiter the hypothetical question. Suiter said that at the time of committing the murder Jean Gianini was a high-grade imbecile and did not know the nature and quality of the act or that it was wrong.

When Charlie Tom rose to cross-examine he was well aware that Suiter was not an alienist and knew little about imbeciles. Yet he was unable to change Suiter's final opinion. He paced back and forth across the room, asking the same questions over and over, parading the weapons and other ghastly exhibits in front of the jury, and howling like a wolf at McIntyre's constant objections. Finally Devendorf had to order him to stop displaying the exhibits so that the objections would cease and the trial could proceed.

"Now, Doctor, do you insist that your opinion is correct?" Charlie Tom asked.

"I desire to defend the position I have taken."

"Then you recognize that the position you have taken needs defense?"

"No."

"Do you recognize that the position which you have taken may not be right?"

"No, Mr. Thomas. You are the one who is wrong."

Charlie Tom finally stopped and slumped down in his chair.

After court I watched from the window of the darkened barbershop as Charlie Tom walked down the street to his office in a heavy downpour. He was not wearing a hat and seemed oblivious to the fact that he was getting drenched. His eyes were downcast and he walked in short spurts, stopping every few steps to stare at the rain pooling on the sidewalk. He did not look well. Bromides might have helped but it was now too late even if he knew enough to ask about them. He had been unable to get Dr. Suiter to give him anything. At the corner Charlie Tom stopped again and stared at the water pouring over the high curb into the street, watching the People's case being swept to the brink.

On May 22, Dr. Charles Bernstein, the fifty-seventh witness and last defense alienist, took the stand. Bernstein had been superintendent of the Rome State Custodial Asylum since 1904. He had personally evaluated over 4,000 applicants to the asylum but rejected 3,000 because they were not true imbeciles. Currently there were 1,370 in his asylum, most of them morons.

Defense attorney David Hirsch rose slowly. He had a cherub face, large owl glasses, and a nose that resembled a doorknob. The nose seemed to twist slightly as he asked the first question. "What was the result of your physical examination?"

"I observed the stigmata of degeneracy," Dr. Bernstein said.

"What were these?"

"Well, first I was impressed by the apparently small size of the head as compared with the body. Another stigmata was the defective eyesight. There was a defect of the physical constitution, the Darwinian tubercles, the so-called remains of the ape's ear. These are well-known characteristics of both brutes and criminals. There were irregular shaped ears, the inequality of the two sides of the face and cranium—you can't change those things by environment or exercise. Next his shambling gait was very evident when I asked him to walk across the room. These physical characters are the stigmata indicative of an abnormal organic condition."

"Now, Doctor, from the examination can you state with reasonable certainty as to whether or not there is any physical defect in the defendant's brain?"

"It was indicative to me of a defective brain. The size and shape of his head indicates there is a lack of a properly developed cerebellum."

Bernstein went on to describe the various types of imbeciles who exhibit the same physical stigmata. He had brought to the courtroom a large poster board that until now had been kept hidden. The board contained dozens of photographs of imbeciles, mostly morons, from the Rome asylum. I strained my neck to see the pictures but couldn't. However, before they could be displayed to the jury, Charlie Tom objected to them as inadmissable and the justice sustained the objection. After the trial, when I saw hundreds of similar photographs in Goddard's book *Feeble-Mindedness,* I became convinced that imbeciles did indeed look different.

Barred from using the photographs, defense attorney Hirsch tried to illustrate Jean's imbecility by directing the jury's attention to his courtroom behavior. "Now, Doctor, do imbeciles with defective brains exhibit nervous symptoms?" he asked.

"Yes, an automatic movement, a tendency to have some portion of the body constantly in motion."

"From your observations of the defendant in court, have you seen any such nervous symptoms?"

"The very evident automatic nervous movement of chewing gum by the defendant. This will take the place of other movements. If the jaws are not going, then the foot is going. If the foot is not going, then the jaws are going."

Jean burst into a forced laugh that could be heard in every part of the room. It was more a bark than a laugh and typical of disruptions he made in school. The entire courtroom stared. Jean immediately stopped chewing his gum, but now his foot was moving back and forth, much like it did when he was sitting at his desk in school.

"Now, Doctor, did you notice there were certain practices pursued by this boy?" Hirsch asked.

"Yes."

"I don't think it is necessary to characterize that any further; you know what I mean, do you?"

"Yes."

"Doctor, is that a common thing among imbeciles?"

"Very common. Masturbation is one of the main reasons for commitment to asylums."

"Now, Doctor, have you noticed a tendency on his part to grin or smile frequently?"

"I have."

"And is that grin characteristic of imbeciles and idiots?"

"It is very prevalent among them."

"It is a sort of password, isn't it, the idiotic grin?"

"Yes."

Jean suddenly became deadly serious and seemed deep in thought as he rubbed his chin the way Special Prosecutor Charlie Tom sometimes did. Charlie Tom saw what he was doing and grinned. McIntyre looked at Charlie Tom and grinned back. Justice Devendorf cracked a grin. They all knew the password. And it occurred to me that in a sense this trial was no different than the absurd trial that Alice faced in Wonderland—a trial run by imbecilic characters. The terror for Jean must have been that his was not a dream.

"Can you tell us in a general way, Doctor, the difference between an imbecile and the insane?"

"Yes."

"Do that."

Bernstein turned and faced the jury, still grinning. "A very simple description is that the feebleminded is the same as a poor man who never had money. He never had a whole mind. The insane is like a man that has had money and loses it. The insane man has had a full mind and lost it. This may not be technically correct, but I think it's a fair illustration of the difference."

"It is pretty fair. Thank you, Doctor."

Several jurors turned to each other and nodded. The pudgy twins nodded. Someone had finally explained Jean's condition in terms everyone could understand.

Hirsch ended by asking the defense's hypothetical question. Bernstein said Jean was an imbecile who did not know the nature and quality of his actions or that they were wrong.

On cross-examination, Charlie Tom questioned the witness

about the killing itself. It was clear that once Dr. Bernstein saw the stigmata, everything else followed. Jean was a moron and all his acts were interpreted as those of moron. When he attacked Miss Beecher, he did it from behind with the beastly instinct of a moron. When he hit her, she did not moan; it was Jean who moaned because morons moan and groan when they are exerting themselves. Jean confused his own sounds with hers, just like a moron. When he dragged the body from the scene of the killing, he left evidence behind and this was something only a moron would do.

"Doctor, then if he left her right where he killed her, you think it would have been better?" Charlie Tom asked.

"I would have done it that way," Bernstein said.

McIntyre fired a question out of order from his chair. "Anybody that is sane would?" he shouted.

"Yes," Bernstein answered.

Bernstein even saw Jean's behavior in the courtroom as characteristic of insane imbeciles. He noted that when the ghastly exhibits were displayed in court, Jean either smiled, grinned, winked, or smirked, all stamps of the imbecile. This conduct, so typical of the class clown I had known and liked, was pronounced by the doctor as proof that there was a crazed imbecile inside the clown suit.

"Doctor, will you watch the defendant just for a moment?" Charlie Tom asked.

"He stopped moving when you said that. Give me some motion and I will watch."

Charlie Tom walked back and forth in front of Jean, like he was trying to get the attention of a caged animal. "Doctor, do you see how he is observing me?"

"Yes."

"I don't suppose that he knows who I am?"

"I don't think he does."

"Do you suppose that he knows what I am here for?"

"No, not wholly. He's only partially conscious."

"Do you suppose he knows Sheriff Stitt?"

"Well, if you hadn't named him I don't believe he would."

Charlie Tom shook his head in disbelief. His lips were quivering and he could barely contain himself. He took a moment to drink some water and consult with District Attorney Farrell. A reporter at the press table overheard Jean speaking to defense lawyer McEvoy: "They must all think I'm a damned fool, don't they?"

Charlie Tom left the huddle with Farrell and approached the witness. "Now Doctor, when after having been punished severely several times and being assured that he would be punished again, he saw his father with a raised horsewhip and hollered 'Father, don't.' Was that in your opinion a normal reaction by a boy who apprehended physical injury?"

"It is a common reaction of an imbecile."

"It is a common reaction of most of us when we are about to be punished to holler, is it not?"

"The real tough hard boy, he will stand up and take his punishment."

"Yes, tough, I see. That is the distinction that you maintain between the normal and the imbecile, that one is tougher than the other?"

"I used to stand up and take my punishment and I thought I was normal."

"Well, I used to holler when the old man got at me," Charlie Tom confessed.

"Well, you are a nervous individual," Dr. Bernstein said.

"Well, do you think I was normal?"

McIntyre interrupted. "We don't want to characterize you, Mr. Thomas, because I don't want any expression of opinion concerning you just now." Several jurors suppressed laughs.

"Gentlemen, you may take a few minutes recess," the justice said.

When court resumed, Special Prosecutor Charlie Tom puzzled everyone with his line of questioning. "Is it a fact that when you answered questions about the defendant you considered matters not in the hypothetical and not observed by you in the physical examination?"

"Well, my observations of him in the courtroom."

"Anything else?"

"Not that I can think of."

"Any assumptions?"

"Well, of course, I am all the while comparing him to cases I studied."

"Isn't there something else going on here, Doctor? Now, with no disrespect , as a matter of fact you are a Hebrew, are you not?"

"I suppose my father was, but we never practiced the faith."

"I understand, no disrespect, but there is something about the Hebrew mind that bothers me," Charlie said.

"That is the trouble. It bothers many people. But my mind is not strictly Hebrew. Mine is a mixed one."

"Your father was a Hebrew and your mother was what nationality?"

"German."

"Now, Doctor, it is just that condition that concerns me. And with no disrespect to you or your parentage I assure you, is it not a fact that in giving your answer to the hypothetical question you did regard and consider matters not included in it?"

"No religious compunctions of any kind."

"I understand that, but I am talking about your Hebrew bent to—"

Hirsch and McIntyre jumped to their feet, screaming at the special prosecutor and objecting to this line of questioning. Justice Devendorf stopped it immediately with a series of sharp raps with his gavel. Cross-examination ended shortly afterwards. On redirect, Dr. Bernstein was asked if imbecility can be feigned and he said no, he could always tell an imbecile when he saw one. His simple nontechnical answer was viewed by the press as one of the most effective in the trial.

During a recess the defense team stood around the counsel table reading a copy of the same special edition newspaper I had just seen announcing that Lieutenant Becker, McIntyre's former client, had been convicted in his second trial. He was to be executed. McIntyre blanched and collapsed in his chair, sweating profusely. It had been rumored he suffered from a heart condition and now his colleagues must have feared the worst. When court resumed the defense unexpectedly rested and court was adjourned until Monday morning when the prosecution rebuttal witnesses would be available.

After lighting the Sabbath candles that night and saying a little prayer for McIntyre, Uncle Sam and I discussed Charlie Tom's questioning of Dr. Bernstein's Hebrew background. It had made me uneasy. Why would he raise such an issue as religion and the Hebrew mind? He was probably suffering from a delusion himself, the delusion of Jewish stereotypes. There were few Jews in the Mohawk Valley and most people didn't know any. They learned about them from the anti-Semitic stereotypes that were transmitted from one generation to another like a folk tale. I had encountered this once before with Zia Nardone, who believed Jews had big noses and were the embodiment of evil. Since I hid my background from the kids in Poland, I never heard the typical accusations of being a Christ-killer or a greedy Jew. No one taunted me with the anti-Semitic childish ditties which Father told me were used to taunt Jewish school children in New York City. But Charlie Tom was neither a stupid old woman nor a misguided school child; he was an educated gentleman, an officer of the court, a man with a great haircut.

"It bothers me, too, Noble," Uncle Sam said at supper. "I'd ask him myself, except I don't want to risk losing a good customer. I don't think he even knows that I'm Jewish. Most of my customers don't. I never did much more than light candles in my apartment and say a few words."

"He knows. You've got a big nose," I said, realizing I had made a rhyme. I made a mental note to record it later in my journal.

Uncle Sam laughed. "And I aim to keep it out of his business."

"To keep his business?" I asked.

"You're very quick tonight, Noble. Yes, and I suspect that Charlie Tom was going to suggest that Bernstein, being a Jew, was testifying for the boy only because he was paid a handsome fee. But I believe the doctor was just trying to be a good Jew, to earn his money and do a good job. Maybe he was trying too hard but I don't think he lied."

That made sense to me. After all, Bernstein rejected most patients from his asylum because they were not true imbeciles, let alone insane ones. He knew an imbecile when he saw one. It seemed highly unlikely that he would call Jean a moron if it wasn't true.

"Are you still going to cut Charlie Tom's hair after what he said in court?" I asked.

"What? And have you call me a greedy Jew?" He laughed. "I'll let Tony take care of him."

On Monday morning, defense attorney John McIntyre was back in fighting form as he tried to keep the first rebuttal witness, Dr. Charles G. Wagner, from testifying. Wagner was a large stalwart looking man. When he sat in the witness chair he was actually taller than McIntyre who was standing in front of him. It would have been no physical match if it came down to the brawl the newspapers were predicting but the defense attorney feared the doctor's strong opinions more than his size. Wagner had examined 200 imbeciles at the Binghamton State Hospital for the Insane and was one of the alienists who had examined Harry Thaw. The justice ruled he was qualified to testify.

Wagner, together with the other prosecution alienists, had met with Jean on four separate occasions. He testified that all the examinations, including another Binet test, were extremely thorough. The physical examination, including precise measurements of Jean's head, showed that everything was normal. Jean talked intelligently about his family, his school, and his friends. His answers to questions from the Binet test showed he had normal intelligence for his age. He was not an imbecile.

Charlie Tom grabbed a thick stack of papers from the counsel table and began reading the hypothetical question to Wagner. The question was the same one asked of the defense alienists with the addition of the transcripts of all examinations by the prosecution doctors. The hypothetical took over two hours to read and no one could recall a longer question in a murder trial. Wagner answered that in his opinion Jean Gianini was sane at the time he murdered Miss Beecher; he knew he had no right to do it; he knew the nature and quality of the act; he knew it was wrong.

"What in your opinion is his mental age?" Charlie Tom asked.

"He is at the mental age of sixteen, lacking in full education by reason of not having gone to school the full amount of time that he should have. He is therefore deficient but not defective. He is behind a year or two in educational advancement but not in mental development."

"Is that due to any mental or physical condition existing in the defendant?"

"Not a defect, but simply a lack of education."

"Is there anything wrong with him?" Charlie Tom asked.

"No. And I asked him that as well. He said all that was wrong was that he was all unstrung, nervous. He complained that people were saying he was buggy and dumb for his age. He was obviously upset about this."

Defense attorney McIntyre was all unstrung himself during cross-examination. He shook his jowls and snapped at the witness but Wagner refused to accept that the so-called stigmata was of any consequence to his diagnosis of Jean. Darwinian tubercles, shambling gait, all of that was worthless according to Wagner. Jean had poor judgement at the time of the murder, not defective judgement. He was not an imbecile. McIntyre threw up his hands in a display of utter disbelief. Then he ran over to Jean, grabbed him by the hair, and yanked his head back so hard that Jean swallowed his wad of gum.

"You examined his head," McIntyre screamed, "this head. Look at his forehead and state whether it is receding."

"I have already done that," Wagner said calmly. "It is not what is characterized as a receding forehead."

McIntyre jerked Jean's head back farther and pointed to the hairline. "Is it receding?"

"Certainly, but not beyond normal."

"Does any degree of recession indicate anything?"

"No, sir."

"Nothing at all?"

"No, sir."

McIntyre released Jean, who immediately began searching his pockets for another piece of gum. The court recessed until 7:30 P.M. and Justice Devendorf announced he was going to finish with Wagner that night no matter how long it took. The defense team went to the Allman House hotel on East Albany Street for drinks and a large supper.

McIntyre resumed the cross-examination looking flushed and distracted. I thought he might be drunk. His rambling questions made little sense. He appeared to avoid asking any question that would prompt Wagner to talk more about the Binet test which he had administered to Jean. Then McIntyre was silent for several minutes as he searched his notes. He put the notes down and strode directly to the witness chair, glaring at Wagner.

"Now, just one more question," McIntyre sneered. "Did you ever smuggle opium across the Canadian border?"

The question stunned everyone. Charlie Tom stood. The entire defense team rose. Everyone was speechless, staring at McIntyre. At the time, no one recognized that the question was one that McIntyre had once used to destroy a key witness in the Lieutenant Becker trial.

"I will withdraw the question," McIntyre said. "I will close the examination now."

It was 10:00 P.M. and everyone was exhausted. I watched as McIntyre strolled out of the courthouse with a tired shuffle, his derby riding so low on the back of his head that I suspected his bump of self-esteem had suddenly shrunk.

On Tuesday morning Dr. Charles W. Pilgrim took the stand. Pilgrim had worked as Dr. MacDonald's assistant at the Auburn Asylum for Insane Criminals. McIntyre blanched when he heard about the connection to MacDonald. Having the assistant to one of your own experts appear on the other side must have been a nightmare.

Pilgrim was asked the same long hypothetical question that had been presented to Dr. Wagner. During the two hour reading I watched Gertrude Trask, the girl from the Poland School who had been the last person to see Miss Beecher alive, whispering to Claude Barhydt, the newspaper boy. They were sitting a few rows in front of me and I strained to hear what they were saying. Suddenly someone next to me shushed them. Gertrude turned and smiled at the people all around her. I knew that the guilty smile carelessly about—until someone finally finds them out.

Pilgrim answered the hypothetical, saying that Jean was not an imbecile, not insane, and that he knew the nature and quality of his act and that it was wrong. He remained firm in his opinions during cross-examination. He was always polite and well-mannered even when McIntyre questioned his qualifications. Pilgrim did not think Jean was a moron but he agreed that morons are prone to laugh and do other things for either no reason or a trivial reason.

"Now, Doctor, wouldn't it be a trivial thing to a boy of sixteen with a normal mind to imagine being wronged by his teacher?" McIntyre asked.

"I think it is quite common for boys of sixteen, schoolboys, to imagine they are not properly treated by their teachers."

"Now, Doctor, in all your experience can you mention a single case where a boy killed his teacher because she wronged him, or as he stated, she snitched on him? Name a single case."

"I object," Charlie Tom said.

"Objection sustained."

McIntyre's final question disturbed many people. No one had ever heard of a pupil killing his teacher before. Years ago a teacher in Cooperstown, New York, flew into a rage and killed a six-year-old pupil when she couldn't spell a word. But no pupil had ever turned on a teacher. The act itself was so surprising and incomprehensible that it was assumed that something would have to be mentally wrong with such a person. I thought I knew Jean better than most and the killing was surprising to me as well but Miss Beecher really did snitch on him to Professor Robinson. Every pupil in school knew she did it and no one was happy about it. I suspected that the accomplice could have been another pupil who was also angry at the teacher, but I couldn't think of one who would want to smack her with anything more than a kiss, let alone a wrench. I glanced at Gertrude Trask who was whispering and smiling again.

Pilgrim was followed by Dr. Willis E. Ford from the State Lunatic Asylum in Utica. In answer to the long hypothetical asked by the special prosecutor, Dr. Ford said that Jean was sane, he knew he had no right to murder Miss Beecher, he knew the nature and quality of the act and that it was wrong.

On cross-examination, defense attorney Hirsch asked that if Jean knew all these things, and was so normal, how could he commit such a crime? Ford said he had asked Jean the same question and Jean's answer was that he lost his temper because he lost his seat in the classroom for throwing spitballs.

"Did you ever know, Doctor, in the course of your long experience, any boy of the age of sixteen who killed a school teacher because she complained about him throwing spitballs?" Hirsch asked.

"I object," Charlie Tom said.

"Objection sustained."

"Do you think it is normal for a boy to feel that a grudge can not be wiped out except by murder?" Hirsch asked.

"Oh, I don't think that. The normal boy doesn't commit murder. A good boy—a boy of good judgment, of good breeding, of good morality, of good surroundings, of good environment—doesn't commit murder as a rule."

"I believe that is correct, that the normal boy doesn't commit murder for such a slight offense, isn't that right?"

"Yes. Not if he's normal."

Hirsch has succeeded in making his point with the People's own alienist that the defendant was not normal. He stopped his cross-examination and sat down. The trial testimony ended and court was adjourned. Final arguments would begin in the morning.

A reporter stood on the curbstone and snapped a picture of Jean leaving the courthouse. Jean grinned, took the wad of gum from his mouth, and hurled it at the reporter's head for a direct hit. Then Jean held up his hands as if holding a camera and pretended to take a picture. His grin broadened as he snapped the imaginary shutter. This was the same old Jean I knew. None of the new words heard in the trial—feebleminded, imbecile, or moron—had changed that. He was still the class clown. He was still the confessed killer of our teacher. He was still my best friend.

11

The clock in the belfry of the Dutch Reformed Church tolled nine in the morning and already the steps of the courthouse were crowded with women. The sweeper and I watched from the shadows of a building across the street. At the top steps near the massive front doors were the young girls who had attended the three weeks of trial testimony and were eager to get a seat for the last day of final arguments. They were dressed in light gowns of pretty fabrics, chatting and laughing as they adjusted their hats or played with colorful parasols. The girls looked like so many summer flowers, bending and turning in the morning sun. There were also middle-aged women wearing the latest city fashions, trying to look young with blushed cheeks and forced smiles, and on the sidewalk were older matrons, gray and serious, standing like yesterday's wilted tulips.

"It looks like a garden party," I said, although I had never actually seen a garden party.

"A hanging party," the sweeper smiled. He grabbed his neck and pretended he was strangling on a rope. When he saw that I did not find his pantomime funny this time, he grabbed my neck and pretended to strangle me. I hung out my tongue and feigned dying only so he would let go. Little did he realize that I was guilty of knowing Jean's plan to kill Miss Beecher yet I had done nothing about it. Perhaps I, too, deserved to swing from the end of a rope.

In a few minutes the doors of the courthouse opened and the women jostled and elbowed their way up the steps. We watched hundreds of boys and men follow, then made a quick dash across the street and squeezed into the crowd. As we entered the courthouse and climbed the winding stairs to the second floor, I became separated from the sweeper. I turned around to look for him but the surging crowd continued to push me up the stairs and smack into a burly man with bushy sideburns and a big mustache standing on the top landing. He grabbed me by the shoulders and held me away from his body. I knew immediately that he was a detective by the way he looked down and studied me with a cold stare. For several minutes I stood frozen in his grasp as people rushed past us and into the courtroom. Then he released me. I ran into the courtroom just as the doors were being closed. Luckily, the sweeper had saved my usual seat in the back of the gallery.

Inside the courtroom the women craned their necks as Jean came in with the sheriff and slumped in his chair. The court crier's gavel fell and everyone stood as Justice Devendorf entered. Jean rose, still slumped over. The justice adjusted his black robe and sat down, signalling everyone else to do the same.

"Gentlemen, you may proceed with the case," he said.

McIntyre stood to address the jury. He spoke for more than two hours, glossing over many facts of the case and misstating others without a single objection from the prosecution. Then he appealed to the jury's native good judgment. "I am not going to ask you to consider the medical testimony but to apply the rule of common sense. Think of it, this boy standing without a living witness seeing the crime, without a scintilla of proof connecting him with the commission of the deed, and yet you find him confessing and furnishing the State of New York with proof to be used against him, proof that may send him to his doom in the electric chair. Gentlemen, well-balanced minds do not act that way."

He pointed to Jean. "He said he did it for revenge so why didn't he kill his father or his principal, Professor Robinson, the men who flogged him? Why did he tell his friends what he was planning to do?" McIntyre went through every aspect of the crime in this way, accusing Jean of irrational behavior. But the jury had heard it all many times before and they appeared bored. Several jurors glanced at the handsome women who were cooling themselves with fans and pretty handkerchiefs.

"Now, gentlemen," McIntyre said loudly, "pardon me, I may be tedious and maybe I am speaking on the subject too long but in the name of God and justice, bear with me. I have a duty to perform and if I appeared for one of you, you would expect me to do that same as I am doing for him. I crave your undivided attention until I have ceased." He glared at them until, one by one, they turned to look at him. Jean continued to gaze vacantly out the window.

"Now, I have not come to Herkimer to deceive twelve men. I have come here to be honest with twelve Herkimerites, to tell you he is not normal," McIntyre said as he pointed to Jean. He reminded the jurors of Dr. Ford's testimony that a normal boy does not commit murder without an offense. "That was the admission of the People's own alienist." He looked directly at the one juror—Jean's adopted "Pa"—whom he felt might agree. "How are you going to get away from that, Mr. Plattner? How are you going to get away from this admission, gentlemen? And Ford made another admission: he said that the mother of this boy was insane. Ford said the brother was an idiot. A mother insane, a brother an idiot. My God, was there ever a family more afflicted? Even the prosecution's Dr. Wagner said the same thing. I could only get the admission after laboring for an hour or more. It was like pulling hens' teeth out, but then I got the admission from him." McIntyre wiped his brow and continued running his hand back over his bump of self-esteem.

"And I say that Wagner knows little or nothing about imbeciles. His testing means nothing. Contrast Wagner's experience with the great Goddard of Vineland who lived with imbeciles for years and years. He developed the Binet test and is never fooled by imbeciles. Goddard says he is an imbecile, that he knows not the nature, the quality, the act that he did. Do you think that Goddard came here and lied? Do you believe that his experience is of no value? Who now will you believe, Goddard or Wagner? Wagner who may have seen only 200 imbeciles or Goddard who saw 25,000? I repeat, Goddard who lives from morning until late at night with these cursed of God, these imbeciles. If you are unable to decide, you have a reasonable doubt and under the oath you have taken it will become your duty to acquit him upon the grounds of imbecility." McIntyre was now perspiring heavily.

"Consider Bernstein's testimony. Bernstein says with positiveness he *is* an imbecile. Bernstein knows an imbecile when he sees one. He has slept in that institution night and day for ten years and inside there are now more than 1,300 of these afflicted creatures. Oh, I wish you could have seen the pictures of those creatures which Bernstein brought to court and then compare them with him." McIntyre pointed to Jean. "Gentlemen, you would not be out twenty minutes in this case."

McIntyre cleared his throat and delivered a theatrical closing. His words had a relentless momentum and he threw them at the jury with thrusts of his arms and hands and shoulders. "Gentlemen, I ask you in the name of God, in the name of this afflicted family, in the name of this unfortunate creature, not to send him to the electric chair. It is my holy duty and my duty as an officer of this court to save his life, to save him from the hands of that executioner who may one day take him into a dimly lighted death chamber, shave his head, slit his trousers on the side, fasten his arms into that chair, bring the electrode down on his head, the feet upon a wet mat, and another electrode on the right leg. Can you see the executioner dropping the handkerchief, a thrill going through the boy's body, a spasm afterwards, and death? I am endeavoring to save him from that. And why am I doing it? Because the evidence in this case discloses that he is not normal. May God Almighty aid you in your deliberations." McIntyre returned to his seat. The carpet where he had been standing was soaked with sweat like a wet mat. There was electricity in the air. The prosecutors were having a fit.

After a noon recess, the trial resumed at 2:00 P.M. By this time the courtroom was stifling. The young girls in the front rows were waving their fans so turbulently that people behind them had difficulty hearing District Attorney Farrell's address. For Farrell, the problem was simply trying to complete a sentence as McIntyre interrupted him with objections. Then Charlie Tom started objecting to McIntyre's objections and soon the jury was once again paying attention to a battle of the lawyers rather than the content of Farrell's argument.

Farrell pointed out this defense tactic that had been used throughout the trial. He noted other defense tricks including the misstatements of facts, the exaggerations, the illogical arguments. "Now, don't you men of Herkimer County be fooled by the counsel from New York," he said.

"One of the first questions asked by the defendant was 'Am I going to get the chair for what I did.' He knew that men were put to death for this crime, that they got the chair. He understood exactly what he did and the consequences. So then the refined counsel from New York says he didn't realize the nature and quality of the act that he had committed. Now gentlemen of the jury, don't be fooled by that awful statement of counsel that he is being honest with you.

"I know and counsel knows this was a crime done by a bad boy, not an imbecile boy. Consider the cleverness of it all. He had this grudge against Miss Beecher and he was going to get revenge which he wanted and which he thought she deserved. What an exercise of ingenuity, what a real cool deliberate cunning it must have taken for him to have convinced her that his father had moved up the hill, to lure her up that dark secluded road. When they got to that lonely spot, where there isn't a house, where she doesn't want to go any farther, he still urges her a little farther along. Then, after he got her to step in front of him, he—like a coward and a criminal, not like an imbecile—strikes from behind with deliberate and premeditated design to murder. He takes the wrench and strikes her on the back of the head and when she goes down, strikes her twice more." Farrell had picked up the wrench and now dropped it on the exhibit table with a loud thud, startling everyone.

"For fear that the blow from a blunt instrument might stun her, that she might recover, he took this knife and drove it into her because he says he wanted to finish the job, do a good job." Farrell stabbed hard at the exhibit table, leaving the knife quivering in the wood. McIntyre's jowls were also quivering now but he appeared too flabbergasted to object. "Did he know what he was doing? Did he know the nature and quality of the act when he says that he took the knife to finish her? He knew as you and I know exactly what he was doing. He was just as rational and cunning as any criminal who ever lived. And it is significant that other than his father there wasn't a single lay witness who came here to testify who ever saw Jean commit any act which to them seemed irrational.

"Now the experts for defense called him irrational and said he was an imbecile and didn't know the nature and quality of his act. MacDonald refused to explain it. Goddard confused all of us with his test. Bernstein came in here and spoke in a folksy way as if he was another 'Herkimerkike.'"

I heard the mispronunciation and wondered if it was deliberate.

"Use your common sense rather than analyze the jumble and division of opinion among experts. You have got to come to your own definite conclusion and your conclusion must be that this was not the act of an imbecile but it was the act of a bad villainous boy."

Farrell put down his notes and stood inches away from the jury box. "You have the opportunity here to set a precedent. Look well as to which way you set it," he pleaded. "There are thousands and thousands of young school teachers in our country. There are thousands of trusting young girls about to go into the world as teachers. Are you going to make them the victims of the vengeance of boys such as this or are you going to say to such boys that deeds such as this cannot be committed and must be punished? Remember you are sworn here to decide this case upon the evidence and your decision may have a wonderful influence. It may mean a great deal for the good of our country. I don't see how you can do anything else but bring this boy in guilty as charged in the indictment. Gentlemen, I thank you."

Justice Devendorf immediately instructed the jury and adjourned court. Jean left the courthouse so slumped over he appeared to be dying. The evening paper reflected everyone's feelings that the jury would finish the job and sentence him to the electric chair before another sunset.

I, too, felt like I was dying. The exceptional heat of the day must have gotten to me. By the time I returned to the shop my head was spinning. Bright lights flashed in the corners of my room and at first I thought that the detective had followed me and was taking pictures with flash powder, which was a silly thought because I was all alone. The lights squeezed into a circle around my head, then hammered mercilessly. I grabbed a small basin from a nearby shelf and vomited uncontrollably.

I searched through my shelves, looking for a handkerchief to soak and wrap around my head. I found one folded around a rabbit's foot Jean had given me for good luck. I took it back to bed with me along with the handkerchief.

The rabbit's foot was the size of a small cigar and covered with brown and white fur. I rubbed the soft fur against my temples, trying to get my mind away from the pain. Jean had cut it off the rabbit for me after we came across the animal lying in the road. The rabbit was not quite dead as Jean started cutting. He motioned to me with a finger and I approached hesitantly. He told me to hold it down and I cupped my hands around it without applying pressure. He managed to sever the last piece of skin when the rabbit wiggled out of our grasp and squirmed across the road into the brush, trailing blood.

As I recalled the story, I retched a second time and prayed for sleep to come and make my world normal again. When I didn't appear for supper, Uncle Sam came to my room with a bowl of soup. It tasted just like Mama's potato soup but I could only swallow a few spoonfuls. He changed my handkerchief, kissed me, then turned off the light as he left. In the darkness a giant clamp tightened around my head. I reached back to the headboard and listened to my nails scraping the wood.

In the delirium of the morning an apparition resembling Uncle Sam took away the uneaten soup and replaced it with a fresh cut flower. My first thought was that I had died and he had come to put a flower on my grave. The pulsing pain in my head told me I was still very much alive. I forced myself to sit up.

"You'll never guess who sent the flower," Uncle Sam said as he changed my handkerchief.

I was too weak to guess and simply shrugged.

"Your friend Jean Gianini," Uncle Sam said. A secret admirer, probably one of the young girls from the courtroom, Uncle Sam explained, had sent Jean a box of cut flowers. Jean gave the flowers to Mrs. Stitt but saved one for Sylvester to deliver to me at the shop. I smelled the flower, inhaling the first distraction from pain in days. Jean may not have defined charity properly, but he certainly knew how to hug a friend in need.

"Sylvester said the jurors have been deliberating all night without sleep," Uncle Sam said. "This morning they told the justice they couldn't agree but he demanded they reach a verdict and sent them back to the jury room." Uncle Sam laughed.

"What's so funny?" I asked.

"Jean was trying to bet Sylvester that he would be executed and forgotten but Sylvester wouldn't take the bet."

I would have bet the flower he was wrong.

In the middle of the afternoon Uncle Sam rushed into my room and announced that the jury had reached a verdict. He and Tony were closing the shop and going to the courthouse. I pleaded with him to take me. He sensed how important it was for me so he and Tony took my arms and practically carried me into the courtroom. I noticed that Tony's fingers were digging into my armpit and pinching the flesh. I thought it was deliberate but the sharp pain distracted me from the headache. Tony kept his hand there, squeezing, even after I took my seat in the last row of the gallery. I was too weak to protest.

Deputy Hinman brought Jean into the courtroom through a rear door. Jean forced a smile as he walked over to his chair and slumped down. The justice entered and nodded for the jury to be let in. The jurors looked red-eyed and totally disheveled as they filed in and took their seats. They huddled close together, glancing nervously at each other and refusing to look at Jean or his attorneys. Spectators whispered their guesses about the verdict. The pretty young girls in the front row appeared tense for the first time since the trial began.

The court clerk's voice was dry as he spoke. "Gentlemen of the jury, have you agreed upon a verdict in the case of the People against Jean Gianini, the defendant at the bar?" he asked.

"We have," the foreman said. He wasn't standing so I had a hard time seeing who was speaking but he certainly sounded like "Pa" Plattner.

"What say you? Guilty or not guilty?"

"Not guilty."

A distinct murmur swept through the courtroom. Several spectators half arose. The twin court watchers hissed and punched each other on the arm. Jean stood as a smile of triumph spread across his face. The justice glared at him and he sat down, still smiling broadly. The foreman handed a folded sheet of paper to the clerk who passed it to the justice. The paper shook ever so slightly in Devendorf's hands as he read it to himself, then aloud to the hushed courtroom: "We find the defendant in this case not guilty as charged in the indictment. Therefore we acquit him on the ground of criminal imbecility."

Everyone was astonished. McIntyre's jaw dropped. He later admitted that he fully expected a verdict of guilty.

Justice Devendorf didn't even look at the jury when he dismissed them without thanks. "Gentlemen, you are excused from further attendance." He turned to McIntyre. "Mr. McIntyre, the proper papers will be made out committing the defendant to the Matteawan Asylum for the Criminally Insane. Court is adjourned."

Jean grinned as he literally skipped out of the courtroom.

McIntyre caught up with him at the stairs where I was headed and grabbed him firmly by the wrist. "Don't grin," he growled. "You haven't won a victory. You're going to a madhouse and you're going to stay there."

They were the last words I heard before fainting in Uncle Sam and Tony's arms.

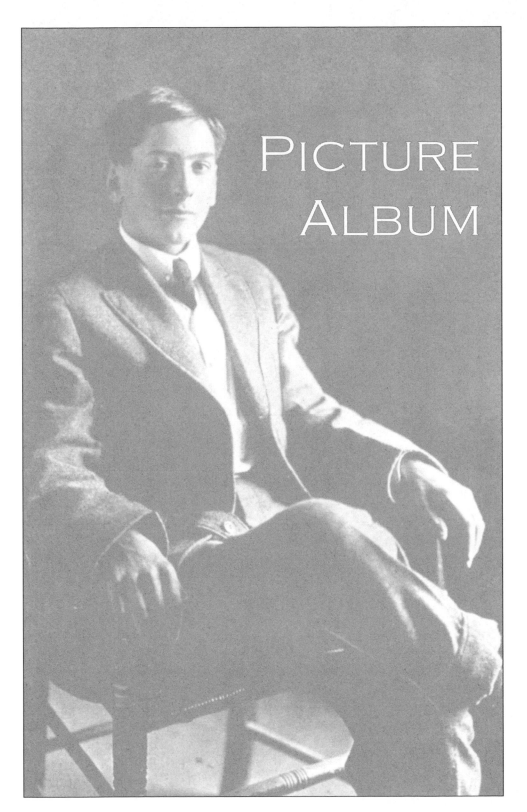

PICTURE
ALBUM

*Lida Lui Beecher, the first school teacher
in America murdered by a student*

*Jean Martinette Gianini in photograph
commissioned by his father for the trial*

Poland School

Jean Gianini, official photograph taken after his jail haircut

Jean Gianini being escorted from jail to the courthouse

Herkimer County Courthouse

Justice Irving R. Devendorf

Charles D. Thomas, special prosecutor

John F. McIntyre, defense attorney

Herkimer County Jail

Palmer House hotel where jurors and defense attorneys stayed during the trial of Jean Gianini

Henry Herbert Goddard, Ph.D., defense expert witness who coined the word "moron"

A. Walter Suiter, M.D., defense expert witness

THE EVENIN[G]

THE ONLY DAILY PUBLISHED

VOL. XVI, No. 171.   HERKIMER, N.

JURY DECLARES GIANI[NI]
TO BE AN [...]

RETURNS VERDICT OF NOT GUILTY AS CHARGED IN INDICTMENT. LIDA BEECHER'S SLAYER GOES TO MATTEAWAN

Murderer Laughs And Smiles As Verdict Is Read

Is Acquitted on Ground of Criminal Imbecility—Many Express Astonishment and Murmur Swept Courtroom On Announcement of Verdict—Had Deliberated Twenty Hours and Eleven Minutes—Herkimer County Jurors Equal in Intelligence To Those of Metropolis, Says McIntyre—Thomas Not Surprised—First Ballot 10 to 2 For First Degree Murder—Jean Wanted to Wager He Would be Convicted—Goes to Matteawan Next Week.

Jean Gianini will not expiate with his life, in the electric chair, the crime of murdering pretty Lida Beecher, the Poland school teacher, on the lonely Buck Hill road, on March 27th last. He is not even guilty of any degree of crime. A Thaw verdict has been returned in the case. A jury of twelve Herkimer Couty citizens has so decreed. They have further decreed that no criminal punishment is not guilty as charged in the indictment. Therefore we acquit him on the ground of criminal imbecility."

Gianini's Smile One of Triumph.

As the verdict of "not guilty" was announced, Gianini, the defendant, arose in his chair and a smile of triumph overspread his face, one of complete understanding. Noticing that he was attracting attention, he quickly sat down again.

No Commendation for Jury.

After a moment's pause, Justice Devendorf dismissed the jury with six words: "Gentlemen, you are excused from further attendance."

Committed to Matteawan.

Justice Devendorf addressing defendant's counsel said "Mr. McIntyre, proper committment papers will be made out committing the defendant to the Matteawan asylum for the criminal insane.

Mr. McIntyre's Suggestion.

Jean pulled 75c from his pe[...] while being taken to the jail and [...] to Deputy Hinman, "I'll bet you seventy-five cents that I am conv[...] of murder in the first degree."

At 7:20 the jury retired for fo[...] deliberation. The first notifica[...] officers got from the jury room—same room, by the way, in which [...] fate of Roxalana Druse, Chester[...] lette and other noted Herkimer C[...] ty criminals was decided—was [...] o'clock last night. Frank Jordan Herkimer, who had been elected [...] man, said that certain testimony desired. The court was quickly [...] ganized but by that time the jury sent out word that the testimony [...] not desired. The next alarm [...] 10:05 this morning. Foreman [...] dan told Officer Syllaboch when [...] latter opened the door, that info[...] tion was wanted. It took about [...] teen minutes to organize the cou[...]

"Gentlemen of the jury, have [...] agreed on a verdict?" asked J[...] Devendorf.

"We have so far been unable [...] agree" responded Mr. Jordan, [...] desire to have read to us that [...] tion of the charge defini[...] ferent degrees of murder and [...] slaughter."

The judge read the excerpt de[...] and the jury were about to re[...] to their room when they were [...] ped by the judge, who said: "I [...] gest that you retire to your [...] and conscientiously and care[...] confer and consider the eviden[...] this case, so that you may be abl[...] reconcile your differences. The [...] ple have a right to demand a ver[...] if it can be conscientiously render[...] Mr. McIntyre excepted to the [...] portion of the judge's charge.

Gianini Unconcerned About Fat[...]

The most unconcerned, care[...] and light hearted individual in [...] court house last night was Jean [...]

MBICILE

t the defedant was mentally de-
tive.

Attorney Thomas Not Surprised.

asked what he thought about the
dict Charles D. Thomas, who has
n associated with District Attorney
n. E. Farrell in the progress of the
e said:

I am neither surprised nor disap-
ted. Those who were in atten-
ce during the trial, observed its
s and courses, comprehended the
ngs of the court, some of which
r be said to establish new pre-
ents in respect to the introduction
evidence, appreciated the intricate
are of the scientific evidence pre-
ted and realized the force and ef-
of the eminent counsel who re-
sented the defendant, aided as they
e by sympathy engendered by his
had a right to expect such a ver.

While I regard the outcome as less
n exact justice to the defendant
ase act of murder was most atroc-
s, I share that degree of satisfac-
that is common to most people
e are familiar with the case and all
details.

kimer County Jurymen As

ntelligent as Those of Metropolis.
hen Mr. McIntyre was seen by a
egram reporter late this afternoon,
made the following statement:

t clearly indicates to my mind
t twelve men from Herkimer Coun-
re fully as intellectual and intel-
nt as any twelve men from the
ropolis on the scientific questions
olved in the case, as it was a case
d on scientific lines, and in my
gment, every juryman in the box
not fail to understand the obtuse
ations involved. I think it a
at triumph of Justice, when not-
nstanding the fact that a brutal
ng, horrifying in its details, that
jury could so clearly see that it
the product of a malform brain
he deed and the preparation.
lnt will be safe in the future, for

GIANINI JURY

* * * * * * * * * * * * * *

THE JURORS.

1. Warren W. Fenton, 26, typewriter assembler, Mohawk, married, two children.

2. Webseter Rasbach, 40, grocery clerk, Herkimer,
married, two children.

3. Luke Byrnes, 60, stone mason, Winfield, married,
three sons.

4. Bronson J. Plattner, 55, manager feed store, Frankfort, married, five children.

5. Horace J. Nichols, 38, cheese maker, Norway, married, two children.

6. Seward G. Bellinger, 49, farmer, Danube, bachelor.

7. Frank A. Jordan, 51, laundry proprietor, Herkimer,
married, four children.

8. Joseph Frinkle, 68, farmer, Ohio, married, three
children.

9. Edward J. Turner, 30, farmer, Columbia, married,
one son, one daughter.

10. George Homerighouse, 37, farmer, Salisbury, one
son.

11. Henry Sterling, 65, mill worker, Dolgeville,
daughter 22 years of age.

12. Terrence O'Day, 41, woodworker, daughter 11,

Newspaper announcing verdict

Herkimer Free Library

12

"JURY DECLARES GIANINI TO BE AN IMBICILE"

The misprinted headline seemed an appropriate end for the Alice-in-Wonderland trial I often thought it was. I laughed but it only made my headache worse. I was back in bed but at least now I was able to sit up and read the evening paper that Uncle Sam had brought me together with a little food that I ignored. The jurors tried to explain to the reporter how they had arrived at their decision over the course of thirty-nine ballots. They all agreed that Jean had murdered Miss Beecher and that the murder was premeditated. He was therefore guilty of first degree murder but they didn't want to execute him. Second degree murder carried a sentence up to life imprisonment but such a verdict implied that the act was not premeditated. This was so obviously false that the jurors feared such a verdict would have been set aside and Jean granted a new trial. And if they called him insane, he might be cured some day and released as had just happened to the murderer Harry Thaw. But imbeciles were arrested in development and never got better. The jury believed that finding him to be an imbecile would mean confinement to an asylum for life. This was just, they said. After all, he was not only an imbecile, but a moron. The criminal potential would always be there.

I accepted the verdict because it was one that would keep Jean alive while I figured out what to do. McIntyre told the court he would oppose any future release for Jean from Matteawan and this was added to the commitment papers. The only possibility of an appeal and rescuing Jean from dying of old age in a mad-house, I realized, was to find the accomplice and prove that he was the real killer.

The Burns detectives had been unable to identify the accomplice, let alone find a single suspect. Another article in the newspaper explained how inept they had been. William Burns was too busy to come himself so he sent a couple of junior detectives who did little more than interview the same kids who had talked to reporters about Jean's plan for revenge. They stayed only a few days in Poland, then watched some of the trial before returning to New York. "I regret the detectives were not successful," Mr. Gianini told the reporter, "and I have asked them to stop all work. It has been an unfortunate expense which could have been avoided if Jean told who put him up to the murder. However, I am content that Jean should go to Matteawan because I do not consider him safe to be at large and mingle with the public. It is my desire that he be locked up and that it all be forgotten as soon as possible."

Since the article mentioned that the prosecution's detective from Boston was also unsuccessful and now off the case, there was no one else looking for the accomplice. Despite the life sentence Jean still refused to turn on his partner in crime. I had to admire his self-sacrificing loyalty but it wasn't just. I knew it would be up to me to find the coward who let my friend take all the blame. The Goddess of Justice demanded another sacrifice. I raised an imaginary sword in the air and pledged: "Long life unto my valiant friend, and death to his accomplice." I had chosen words paraphrased from Shakespeare but I was alone on a stage with fright as to what my next act would be.

As I put down the newspaper I noticed an advertisement for the local Richmond movie theater on the back page. Tonight they were showing *Gianini*, a movie based on the murder and trial. The ad mentioned that the movie would include newsreel footage of Jean, the justice, the jury, and all the principals. Jean would have been amused because he always wanted to be in the moving pictures. Since the movie included scenes of the crowds at the crime scene, I wondered if the accomplice might have been caught on camera. If so, perhaps I would recognize him. I couldn't imagine a more important moving picture to see for my first one. It was to run for one night only and I had already missed the 7:30 P.M. show but there was still time to catch the one at 9:00 P.M. The theater was just down the street. I had the five cents for a seat. I trembled with excitement.

When I tried to get out of bed I wobbled on my feet and retched again. It was no use. I was too dizzy and weak. I turned off the light bulb hanging from the ceiling and fell back on the mattress. Afterimages of the light flashed like a flickering projection lamp. In the dark theater of my delirious mind I tried to visualize scenes from the movie of the murder.

My movie began with the scene where Jean found the rabbit by the road. I didn't even have to think about it as the flashing memories took on a feverish life of their own. Jean started to cut off the rabbit's foot. The legs kicked again and again as the knife cut away. Then I noticed that the feet had high button shoes. It was not a rabbit but...Miss Beecher! Jean and the accomplice were leaning over her body. Jean turned around, grinning. The accomplice started to turn. I screamed.

I woke drenched in sweat. Uncle Sam was shaking me, asking if I was all right. I mumbled something, then fell back to sleep.

When I woke again I recorded the dream images in my journal in a section where I had previously recorded other dreams about the murder, although this was the first time the accomplice had appeared. I was never sure if elements were from memories or fantasies, but I suspected all such phenomena were conjured from real pictures stored in my brain which was why I had entitled the section of the journal REMEMBRANCES. If I collected enough remembrances, I figured, I might be able to sort them out later and discover the reality they were based on. After all, if I could find myself in the mirror of books, what better book to use than the journal of my remembrances? And now I realized that clues to the identity of the accomplice might be buried in those jumbled images.

I looked at another newspaper Uncle Sam had left for me. Jean had given an interview to reporters who gathered outside his jail cell while yet another lynch mob massed outside the jail. The paper described Jean as jubilant, almost euphoric, as he chattered away.

"I was lucky, all right," Jean said as he leaned over to smell a bunch of pink roses and sweet peas on the table in his cell, another gift from an anonymous admirer.

"You bet you were," Sheriff Stitt said. "What do you think of the verdict?"

"I guess I was a pretty lucky kid," Jean repeated. "God. When that fellow said 'not guilty' it seemed just as if a knife was going right through my heart. I was so sure I was going to get the chair. I don't know how in hell they did it. I was ready to go to the chair. I said I would die like a gunfighter without being scared. Maybe you noticed I smiled when I came into the courtroom. I wasn't afraid."

A stone hit the outside wall of the jail. This was followed by a chorus of jeers and curses from the crowd.

"They didn't like the verdict, did they?" Jean grinned. "Herkimer County will remember this for a long time. I bet old Charlie Tom is madder than hell. He thought he was going to kill me. What does he say about it?"

"He called it atrocious," replied a reporter.

"I guess that's right," Jean said. He lit a cigarette and took a long puff. "I was lucky, all right. If a kid told me that he was going to kill a teacher the way I did, and wanted to know what I thought of it, I'd tell him not to do it because his old man might not have as much money to get him out of it as my old man did."

"What did you think of the experts, Jean?" asked the reporter.

"I got sore from sitting there and listening to them. I didn't like being called insane, although I may be feebleminded. I didn't want to sit up so the yaps behind me could gawk, so I slid down in the chair so much that I've got a blister."

"Jean, do you think you could pass the Binet test for us?" asked another reporter.

Jean laughed. "That's a great game, that is." He flicked the ashes from his cigarette, then swung open the iron door of his cell and pointed to Chester Gillette's name scrawled on the floor. "I was going to put my name there, too, but I've changed my mind now that I'm gonna live. Now I gotta go down to Matteawan where Thaw was. Who's gonna take me?"

"I will," Sheriff Stitt said. "Do you want to see your father before you go, Jean?"

"My father don't care a hell of a lot, I guess."

"Do you want to see Mr. McIntyre before he goes back to New York?"

"Every time I look at McIntyre he growls at me. I guess he don't want to see me very badly."

"Who do you want to see, Jean? Who's your best friend in the world?" a reporter asked.

Jean looked at the reporters through the bars of the door. After a moment he cupped his hand over his left eye and began swinging back and forth on the iron door, grinning and laughing. The article said that the response was positive proof of the lad's imbecility. I made a mental note to ask Uncle Sam to ask Sylvester to arrange another haircut with Jean so I could visit with him one last time. Then I fell asleep again.

Voices from the barbershop woke me. There was a wonderful aroma in the air and I turned to see that Uncle Sam had left breakfast for me on my table. I stumbled out of bed and began scooping handfuls of porridge into my mouth. It was the best tasting porridge I had ever eaten. I finished the bowl before I even noticed the spoon on the table.

There was a knock on the door and Uncle Sam entered with Dr. Bernstein, who was wearing a fresh haircut. Uncle Sam explained that Dr. Bernstein had been in Herkimer for several days to inspect a farm recently acquired by the state. He was considering using the farm as a work site for inmates from his asylum.

"Noble, Dr. Bernstein kindly offered to take a look at you."

"Good *Shabbes*," I said. The words came out as an unintelligible mumble because my mouth was full of the last of the porridge. A little dribbled from the corner and I wiped it off with my finger, then licked my hand clean. I was still starving.

"Do you still have a headache?" Bernstein asked as he moved closer to where I was sitting. The scent of witch hazel swirled around him.

I tore into a piece of bread and shook my head.

He asked if I had had bad headaches in the past. Had they lasted for more than a few hours? Did I have seizures? I mumbled my answers as I continued to eat. All the time I could feel Bernstein staring at my patchless eye. He was obviously intrigued by the massive growth yet he refused to get close enough to touch it.

"You had a megrim," he announced.

Me grim. I liked the expression. It sounded like an appropriate label. I was pretty grim.

"Did your mother have megrims?" Bernstein asked.

"Mama was always happy," I said.

Bernstein turned to Uncle Sam. "It's obvious the boy doesn't understand his condition. Did his mother or father have bad headaches or seizures?"

"I know his mother had frequent headaches," Uncle Sam said.

I nodded. I could see her fixing meals and cleaning the house, wearing a handkerchief headband and a beatific smile. The memory made me nostalgic and I closed my eyes, pretending the bread I was eating was Mama's black bread. Me grim turned into a big grin of remembrance. It was the first time I actually grinned and it felt awkward. I kept twisting my mouth into various grins, trying to find one that felt comfortable. I opened my eyes and noticed that Dr. Bernstein was watching as tiny pieces of masticated bread escaped from my lips.

When Bernstein asked me to walk back and forth across the room, I took the bread with me. I felt unsteady on my feet after so many days in bed but I managed to keep from falling by positioning my feet wide apart and taking short steps. He stared at me intensely as I returned to the table where I wiped the inside of the bowl with the remaining bread and ate it.

He asked me about school and I answered in Hebrew, hoping to impress him. He didn't appear to understand and asked Uncle Sam about my schooling. Uncle Sam explained that I had only attended school for one year but he bragged about my ability to read and write Hebrew and Russian.

"He's an excellent worker, too," Uncle Sam said with a pat on my head. I leaned against his hand, trying to make the pat last a little longer. Uncle Sam obliged and massaged my scalp for a moment. I grinned with pleasure and didn't object when he told me to get washed and dressed while he went back to the shop with the doctor.

As I was putting on my patch I could hear them talking in a whisper. I caught a few words: defective, arrested, moron. Bernstein was obviously talking about Jean and I rushed out to the shop to hear what he had to say. Uncle Sam asked me to go outside and take off my patch so the good doctor could take my picture. Fortunately, it was a cloudy day and I didn't object. Tony stared at me as I walked through the shop.

"Would you like to go to my place in Rome?" Bernstein asked as he fiddled with the camera. Uncle Sam was standing next to him.

I shrugged.

He approached and positioned me next to the barber pole near the front door. "It's the best place for you. You have nerve storms which cause the headaches and seizures. They will only get worse. There will be paranoiac imaginings...and strange urges. We can take care of you in the asylum and give you special schooling."

"They'll pay for everything, Noble," Uncle Sam said.

"You said I could go to school here in Herkimer as soon as the new term starts in the fall. I don't want to leave." How could I ever hope to find the accomplice if I left?

Uncle Sam looked uncomfortable and glanced nervously at Bernstein.

The doctor grabbed me by the shoulders and turned me toward the overcast sun. When he touched my shoulders I immediately flashed on Professor Robinson and reflexively stiffened. "It's really the best place for you," Bernstein said softly. His breath was hot and foul. "I don't take everyone into the school, but I'll make a special place for you. We have many other feebleminded boys at the school. You'll be our little Hebrew moron."

It took me a moment to realize that he was calling me a moron. Images of Dr. Goddard's Kallikak morons with their dark eyes and haunted expressions paraded across my mind. Now I realized that I was about to be photographed and enshrined forever in Bernstein's gallery. I could even imagine him showing my picture in a courtroom or medical meeting where it would be gawked at like a racy French postcard. Little Hebrew moron. It seemed like a knife was going through my heart. Bernstein wanted to stick me inside his institution like a specimen in a museum. I had listened to him describe his so-called "special school" in court. They didn't teach geography for fear the inmates would run away. They didn't teach history for fear they would fight. They didn't teach physiology for fear they would practice it. They only taught morons to be obedient specimens of an inferior species like bugs in a jar. Was this my destiny, to turn back into the insect that had once dreamed he was a boy?

I could feel the world spin as I reached for the barber pole in order to steady myself. The striped pole had once advertised the bloodletting services offered by barber-surgeons. The top ball represented the basin used to hold leeches while the red and white stripes represented the bandages stained with blood. My skin tingled with a thousand leeches. I gripped the pole tightly as the blood drained out of my face.

Bernstein backed up and readied the camera. "Look here," he said.

Click!

Just as he snapped the picture, I jumped behind the pole. The photograph captured only the right side of my body. My good right eye was peeking out from behind the pole, wide open in fear.

I bolted down Main Street, chased by an imaginary army of imbeciles with twisted faces, crossed and slanted eyes, and drooling mouths. If they caught me, I would become one of them. I ran as fast as I could. Run, run, I kept telling myself.

I ran through the village and up Steuben Road. The steep grade slowed me down as I entered the wooded area. My side hurt and I was breathing hard but couldn't seem to get enough air. "I've got to catch my breath," I panted as I slowed to a walk.

"Keep running," cried the trees.

"Drive on," said the Gryphon.

"No time to pine," rhymed the sweeper.

I picked up my pace and didn't stop again until I reached the edge of Mirror Lake which supplied water power for the village industries. After finally catching my breath, I kneeled next to the water for a drink, watching the ripples from my lips spread across the surface. Bernstein had said he could always tell an imbecile when he saw one. What did my mirror say? I studied my reflection in the water much as I had as a child. The young happy boy had drowned now. All I saw was the image of a terrible fish rising from the depths. A monster. A moron.

13

At sunset I left Mirror Lake and walked home to eat. An imbecile, even one of the moron type, always thinks first of his stomach, so say the experts. I was hungry and knew that Uncle Sam would be preparing supper. And he knew I would never miss a meal unless I was deathly ill. Did this mean he had always known that I was an imbecile? The possibility troubled me.

Yet there was something about Dr. Bernstein's diagnosis that cleared up all the questions I had about myself. He called me a moron and suddenly everything made sense. It was like an instant look in a full-length mirror. I now knew why I always felt like an outsider, watching and spying on people. I was not only different physically but mentally as well. My best friend turned out to be another moron like me. The only people who ever touched me in a loving way were my parents or Uncle Sam, family members who were stuck with me and had no choice in the matter. Everyone else either flogged me like Professor Robinson, kicked me like Tony, held me at a distance like the detective at the courthouse, or gawked and wanted to take a picture like Dr. Bernstein. In fact, except for Jean, no one even touched me in a friendly way aside from Miss Beecher.

I couldn't help but think about her as I made my way through the woods behind the lake. The area was not unlike the willow grove where she had lost her life. Would there ever be another soul so beautiful who would dare touch me knowing what I had become this day? Had I lost my chance of ever attending a normal school again, of ever having a normal life...of ever having a real wife? I began composing a poem in my head.

Miss Lida Beecher lost her life
To a criminal imbecile wielding a knife.
No one played a drum or fife
To mark the passing of a would-be wife.
Since that time my prayers were rife
To marry my teacher in the afterlife,
Putting an end to my daily strife
To find someone to call *ziskeit*.

I emerged from the woods at Steuben Road. If I turned left, the road would take me back to the village. If I turned right, I would eventually end up in Oneida County where Baron Steuben, the Revolutionary War General who built the road, had lived. There was a legend that the Baron had buried a treasure in gold there. I had always wanted to look for it but now I knew there would never be any gold for me at the end of the road.

As I turned left and walked down Steuben Hill I passed a small house with a vegetable garden surrounded by a white picket fence. There were young tomatoes and tall stalks of rhubarb ready for picking. I reached through the fence and pulled a stalk from the moist dirt. After carefully removing the poisonous blades, I bit into the stem. It was very acidic and needed to be cooked and sweetened but I chewed several bites and swallowed. In a few minutes I turned to the side of the road and vomited a crimson pulp. It was a bitter lesson. Here I was—a young moron, not even a day old—thinking only with my stomach. And by stealing the food I was already manifesting my natural criminal potential. Years before I had walked down Buck Hill to begin my new life as a schoolboy. Now I was walking down another hill to begin my new life as a moron. The rhubarb was only the appetizer. I wondered what courses my criminal instincts would serve up tomorrow.

During supper Uncle Sam behaved as if nothing had happened but I knew that he was acting. He kept his distance at the table, slyly watching me from the corner of his eye. Dr. Bernstein had explained that there was a nerve storm in my brain that was responsible for the headaches and seizures. The storm would continue to grow as surely as the flesh around my eye. My mental development was arrested and I would be unable to control the criminal urges sleeping within some dark repository of my mind. They could awaken and strike out like lightning bolts. Uncle Sam was watching for telltale signs of trouble. His jittery movements infected me with the same nervousness. I half-expected to see the reflection of a lightning bolt in his clear blue eyes.

He finally spoke as we were sipping coffee from china cups decorated with tiny roses. "Dr. Bernstein left on the noon train," Uncle Sam announced. He looked down and fingered the roses as he talked. "The doctor mentioned that all morons end their regular school life by age fifteen or sixteen. He said most are unable to advance further and it was useless to try. But he agreed with me that you are very special and he could help you at his special school. You're sixteen now, Noble. It's a good opportunity for you."

"No, Uncle Sam," I said. "I want to stay with you. Even if I can't go to normal school I can study and read in the library across the street." I paused for Uncle Sam to say something but he kept looking at his coffee cup. "You won't have to put aside money for my schooling," I continued. "Now you can save for that Maxwell automobile you always wanted. Please, Uncle Sam. I'm an excellent worker—you said so yourself—and I always keep the shop clean. Besides, I'm small so I don't need much food. I'm happy to stay in the storage room. I'll not be a bother and I'll keep out of the way," I promised. "Please let me stay. You're the only family I have left." He finally looked up at me and nodded, tears welling in his eyes.

I learned later that Dr. Bernstein had joined Goddard at a convention of alienists in Columbus, Ohio, where the case of Jean

Gianini was discussed. They compared Jean to Jesse Pomeroy, another moron who was only fourteen when he was tried for his crimes in Massachusetts. Pomeroy had also been whipped at school and at home, had practiced the solitary vice, and seemed to enjoy being a bad boy. His favorite game was to play "scouts and Indians" and pretend he was a scout torturing the Indians. He played the game with younger boys by tying them up, sticking them with needles, biting and doing worse things. After a few months in reform school, he was released for good behavior. Then he tortured and killed a four-year-old boy and slashed to death a ten-year-old girl. The total number of wounds on the girl was the same as Jean Gianini had inflicted on Miss Beecher. Like Jean, Pomeroy confessed and showed absolutely no regret for his acts. His lawyers and alienists argued insanity. The jury found him guilty of first degree murder and sentenced him to hanging. But Jesse Pomeroy, like Jean Gianini, was a lucky kid. The governor commuted the sentence to life imprisonment.

The alienists at the convention agreed that morons like Pomeroy and Gianini should never be free. All morons lack morals. All morons are capable of committing the most heinous and revolting crimes. All morons need to be locked up even if they have not yet committed any crimes. While I was now a member of the same fraternity, I could not conceive of living my life locked inside Dr. Bernstein's school. I could never imagine turning into a ghoul like Pomeroy. If I ever became such a monster I could not conceive of living at all.

Yet since I carried the moron's plague of criminal potential I knew I would have to remain vigilant for any signs of trouble. Jesse Pomeroy had described a sudden headache that preceded each attack of violence. The pain was accompanied by a feeling that he must lash out and attack his victims. An alienist testified that Pomeroy turned into a vicious tiger without the moral force to control himself. My headaches were different. They immobilized me; they didn't turn me into an immoral beast. I was as gentle as the cat purring on Deborah Kallikak's lap. You could touch me without fear of being scratched. Pet me and I would love you.

When I saw Jesse Pomeroy's picture in the library, my hair stood on end and I leaped from my chair like a frightened kitten. Pomeroy had a bad eye! The pupil of his right eye was covered by a pale film like a lace curtain. Some described it as a loathsome disfigurement. Jesse's own father couldn't look at it without shuddering. The headline in the *Boston Globe* called it "Pomeroy's Evil Eye."

I cowered with fright in the corner of the library. The picture of the deformed eye didn't bother me. It was the realization that I was not so different from Jesse Pomeroy after all. His eye looked like a small white marble. Mine was larger, a giant croaker. I could see the headline now: "Zoken's Evil Eye." I was terrified to read the story that might follow. If the stigmata of my disease was something as simple as the Darwinian tubercles which characterized Jean's ears, it would have been an easy matter to Van Gogh my own ears. But I was not so mad as to Oedipus my own eye. Now there was a lump in my throat. It felt like an invisible hand was choking me.

For the next several weeks I hid in my room, venturing into the shop only to perform the nightly cleaning and collect the daily newspapers. Almost every paper had editorials and letters to the editor condemning the verdict. Everyone blamed the jury's stupidity for allowing Jean Gianini to escape with his life. The businesses of some jurors were boycotted, other jurors were ostracized from their churches, and still others lost their jobs.

Reverend Beecher told a reporter that the verdict was not only a personal tragedy for him but a far greater tragedy for America. "And what will be the natural outcome?" he asked. "The prototype of Jean Gianini, who is to be found in every school district in the land, has been waiting daily for the morning and evening papers, scanning with eager interest the details of this trial. He is taught by this travesty of justice that he, too, may kill his teacher on some slight or fancied provocation and so get his name and picture in the papers and make himself notorious."

Then it happened. *The Evening Telegram* reported that in Fort Herkimer, just south of the village, school teacher Anna Kellner left her handbag on a desk in the classroom. A boy named Lewis stole four dollars from the purse but was caught and sent away to a reform school by a local justice. His brother was bitter and held Miss Kellner responsible. He made several threats against her and told other kids that he would get his revenge. "I'll give Miss Kellner what Gianini gave his teacher," he promised. He went to the school and drew a 22-caliber revolver on Miss Kellner. She wrested the gun from his hand and turned him over to the authorities.

"That boy must have been an imbecile to copy Gianini," said a customer in the barbershop the following day. "Or what's that new word they used in the trial?"

"Moron," Tony said.

"Yeah, that's it. Moron."

"Do you want to see one?" Tony asked. He didn't wait for an answer but rushed over to my door and threw it open.

I was standing at the sink with my back to the door. Tony walked in and kicked me. "Turn around," he yelled.

I gripped the sides of the sink and refused to budge, wishing that Uncle Sam had not gone to Utica for supplies. Tony kicked me again. My knuckles turned as white as the porcelain sink.

"Well, that's a moron," Tony said as he walked out and slammed my door.

I listened as he and the customer discussed my potential to imitate Gianini's example. They sounded fearful. But there was no need for them to be afraid of me. I was not a copycat, just a misshapen kitten.

"I heard what happened at the shop today," Uncle Sam said at supper. "I'm very sorry Tony hit you. I want you to know I fired him."

I felt guilty. "I didn't do what Tony ordered but he didn't hurt me."

"You did nothing wrong, Noble. It's not your fault."

"Will he be able to find another job?"

Uncle Sam shrugged.

"Are you going to hire another barber?"

"Not now. Business has been slow since the trial ended. I was thinking of letting Tony go anyway, so don't go worrying about him. Eat, eat." He scooped another helping of mashed potatoes on my plate. "Eat," Uncle Sam repeated. "It's not right to leave leftovers," he said, patting his paunch. I had no appetite but forced myself to eat everything.

That night I mentioned Tony in my prayers. I prayed he would never find another job. If he did, I prayed he would stick himself in the eye with his scissors. As the words rolled off my tongue, I was surprised by what I was praying for. Then I slept as well as I ever did.

I have mentioned that I stayed in my room for several weeks after the trial but that is not completely accurate. During the full moon on June 8, I went outside. As I walked through the alley and up Main Street I was full of an anger and rage I had never known. It had been sparked by the morning paper which I had only just read.

That morning, in one of the greatest newspaper scoops anyone could remember, the *Utica Daily Press* published Jean Gianini's farewell address to the citizens of Herkimer. The address was a poem that later ran in papers across the state:

"My name is Gianini I would have you know,
And I always have trouble wherever I go.
To be thought a tough, it is my delight,
And I am thinking and planning both day and night.

I killed Lida Beecher with an old monkey wrench,
And they took me before the judge on the bench.
The sentence they gave, it caused me to smile,
It was 'He is not guilty; he's an imbecile.'

Now here is thanks to the jurors who let me go free,
The foolishest men I ever did see.
When they came marching in it raised up my hair,
I thought sure they'd say, 'He must sit in the chair.'

Now soon I must leave you and bid you adieu,
And the dollars I've cost you they won't be a few.
I never will fear if I can find McIntyre,
For I really believe he could save me from hell fire."

I was fuming about the poem when I spotted the writer standing on the sidewalk near the jail. I ran as quickly as I could and leaped onto his back, circling his tall body with my legs as though he were an apple tree. The air rushed out of his lungs. I clawed at his shirt and slapped his sides. He reached around and threw me off onto the sidewalk. I rose and continued slapping his body in a wild frenzy, one blow accidentally glancing against his crotch. He reddened, then threw me to the ground even harder.

"What's wrong with you?" the sweeper asked.

"You did it, you did it," I yelled.

"What are you talking about?"

"You wrote that fake poem in the paper, the one supposedly by Jean Gianini."

"Did I?" He smiled his big jack-in-the-box smile. "Be sure of it; give me the ocular proof," he said, quoting Shakespeare.

"I have listened to your poems. They're your words and expressions."

"Morons rhyme all the time. They said so at the trial."

"You used that line 'he must sit in the chair' before," I said. "Remember? And you're the only one I ever heard say 'adieu.'"

He smiled. "So what's so bad if I did write it?"

"It's, it's dishonest," I stammered. It might have been criminal as well but I wasn't sure.

"O, the worst of words," he said, lowering his head and feigning shame.

I was shaking with anger.

"Why are you so upset?"

I didn't know. Maybe it was because I wanted to believe Jean was now truly sorry. In my heart I did not believe his was the unfeeling voice in the poem. Poetry was a mirror of the soul. As a person rhymes, so he is. I remembered how he waited for me after school when I was whipped. I thought about him turning Miss Beecher's body over, covering it with the raincoat and placing it under the apple tree. His was not a totally uncaring soul. I was certain Jean's farewell address would have been different than the sweeper's version. Even the farewell poems of condemned killers like Roxy Druse or Chester Gillette were filled with repentance. Gillette's poem spoke of being with God in the morning. Those condemned to life in prison or an asylum would be no different. They would want God to be with them. The sweeper's poem never mentioned God.

"It's dishonest," I repeated. "And ungodly."

"You're right, I wrote it," the sweeper finally confessed. "After all, morons can rhyme a word or two but they can not write long poems. Their words are few, their minds adieu." He laughed loudly.

He was still laughing as I turned and walked away. I was angry at him and even angrier at myself for acting in such an ignoble way by physically attacking him. Shakespeare's Cassio spoke for me: "O! I have lost my reputation. I have lost the immortal part of myself, and what remains is bestial."

There was a newspaper article a few days later about Jean Gianini's train ride to Matteawan. "Oh, what a damn fool I've been," Jean cried at the start of the trip. It sounded like he might be sorry after all. I continued reading the article hoping to find words of repentance.

In the early hours of the morning Sheriff Stitt had handcuffed Jean and whisked him away from Herkimer in his automobile. It would have been a simple matter to go down the street to catch a train but the sheriff feared another lynch mob and drove west to the Utica train station instead. They would take the long trip back to Herkimer and through the scenic Mohawk Valley, around the capital at Albany where they would change trains, then down the rocky banks of the Hudson River to Newburgh near the Matteawan asylum.

Once they were inside the smoker car on the train, the sheriff removed the cuffs. Jean looked out the window, smoking cigarettes and babbling in a nonstop stream of conversation recorded verbatim by the reporters who filled every seat. The newspapermen remained skeptical of Jean's words. They wrote that the bad boy of Poland was only feeling sorry for himself, not Miss Beecher or her family. But I knew that morons have exceptionally strong feelings for others.

Somehow the journey back toward Herkimer reminded Jean of *The Rime of the Ancient Mariner*. When prompted by a passing scene or thought, he recited lines from the poem. The reporters were astonished that an imbecile was quoting one of the glories of the English language but I could have done the same. The poem by Samuel Taylor Coleridge was the last thing we read in Miss Beecher's class before Jean left school. He and I would recite lines as we walked back and forth to the schoolhouse. As the train moved along the Mohawk River, Jean looked out at a small boat adrift on the water and recited:

> "Water, water every where,
> And all the boards did shrink;
> Water, water, every where,
> And not a drop to drink."

Although Jean mangled the last line, I was impressed by his memory. He turned away from the window and noticed that the reporters were staring at him in disbelief. "Say, what kind of a boob wrote that?" he asked with a hint of embarrassment. "He must have had the D.T.'s." Jean was acting like a smart aleck but the passing landscape and rhythmic rocking of the car soon lulled him back into the Mariner's boat. He mangled another line from the poem:

"The Sun came up...and out of the sea came he."

Jean turned to the reporters. "Thank God and John McIntyre I'm going east this morning instead of west to the chair."

As the train approached Herkimer, the whistle blew and Jean glanced up Main Street. "Well, so long, Herkimer," he smiled. "You brought me some pretty good luck."

In a few more miles, the train rolled through Little Falls with its blackened brick factories rising like giant tombstones in the sky. "Pretty near as high as the hall of columns at Karnak, isn't it," Jean remarked, impressing everyone with his knowledge of ancient Egyptian history. He said that the city looked as dead as Karnak. "She's dead," he said softly. "And I can't do it over again." He recited again from the *Ancient Mariner*:

"And I had done a hellish thing,
And it would work 'em woe;
For all averred, I had killed the bird
That made the breeze to blow."

The train moved through the outskirts of Schenectady. A little girl walked near the tracks, swinging a basket. She waved to the engineer on the train. Jean tried to recite another stanza but could only remember the first line:

"Her lips were red, her looks were free."

At 8:45 A.M. they arrived at the freight yard in Albany. "This is where I rolled off the train last July," Jean told the reporters as they left the train. He pointed around the yard where the railroad detective had fired a gun at him. "This is where the bull shot at me, and I ran over there and across the lot." Jean and the group walked into the station to change trains. A crowd quickly gathered to gawk, pointing fingers and whispering. Jean locked eyes with a pretty young girl wearing a clinging purple dress. He smiled at her. The paper said the girl turned pale, gave him an icy look, then hurried away. When the train's departure was announced, the crowd parted for Jean like he was a leper shuffling to the gate.

The sheriff, Jean, and the reporters climbed aboard the new train. It pulled out of the station and picked up speed as it headed down the Hudson Valley. Jean lit another cigarette, his thirtieth of the day, and looked back at the state capital receding in the distance. "I guess there are lots crazier folks in that town than I am," he said. "Once I thought I would be a criminologist. I got a bad steer and here I am a criminal instead—a criminal imbecile with depraved tastes, you know."

Near the edge of Dutchess County, a wreck held up the train for more than an hour. Jean appeared transfixed by the scene as he smoked another six cigarettes. When the temperature in the car started to rise, he licked his lips. "Water, water every where and not a drop to drink," he repeated. Finally, the train got under way again and soon arrived at Newburgh. Jean caught sight of the long brick buildings of Matteawan. "Damn," he said, turning away from the window. "I'll never come out until I wear a wooden overcoat." The reporters saw tears in his eyes.

I put down the papers and gazed up at the solitary window in my room. How like a tiny dungeon the room had become. I stretched out on the bed. Would this now be the place where I would spend the rest of my days? I reached back to the headboard. Would this become my wooden overcoat?

Jean and I had once sailed together on the riverboat of our youth. Now we were both like retired mariners, circumnavigating the memories of our shipwrecked lives. He was a castaway on the isle of Matteawan. I felt I was destined to endlessly circle the eye of a nerve storm. And each of us, like that ancient Mariner,

"Alone, alone, all, all alone.
Alone on a wide, wide sea."

14

I never owned a pocket watch or a clock; that small frosted window over my bed was a far more accurate timepiece harrowing the seasons of my existence. When I first arrived in Herkimer it was March and winter ice still coated the outside of the window. The light that shined through was as broken and fractured as the happy life I had left behind in Poland. I could lie on my bed and gaze up through the window at the brick building next door which was now reduced to a jumbled picture puzzle like the rest of my life. In spring the rains bathed the frosted glass, melting the ice but doing nothing to restore the clarity of my vision from the inside. In the summer I couldn't see the birds and bees flying freely outside, only angry flies buzzing against the inside glass, struggling to escape to the sunlight. I was condemned to listen to their incessant buzzing as it became more and more frantic just before they died. Their tiny corpses began to pile up on the windowsill. Every so often a spider would carry one away but I knew it was just a matter of time before the corpses buried the view of the buildings outside and obliterated all light in my life. For me there was no escape from this scene. It was the same torment that afflicted those condemned to live out their lives in the solitude of a prison. I was convinced that somewhere in the dark tombs of Matteawan, Jean Gianini was looking at a similar window, unable to alter his view of inevitable death. I thought about him a lot.

In the fall blustery winds rattled my window. I read that Jean Gianini began to die. He had become sullen, pale, and hollow-chested. His eyes were sunken. I suspected he was masturbating himself to death. Jean did not want to leave his room and even refused to go outside to exercise in the yard. He stopped jumping around and was rarely observed swinging his foot. Like a fly at the end of its life, he was buzzing less and less. The doctors at Matteawan said his condition was fatal. They gave him two years to live.

If Jean Gianini were to die it didn't seem fair that he should go down in history as the first killer of a school teacher in America when the identity of the accomplice remained unknown. Claiming sole responsibility for a murder you might not have committed by yourself was not the same thing as cheating on a test. I could understand how he might have been carried away by acting the role of the unrepentant murderer but now he might die playing out that part. Jean didn't want to snitch, but history as well as his best friend deserved to know the truth. And the Goddess of Justice still demanded another sacrifice. All guilty parties had to be held accountable. I renewed my pledge to find the accomplice. This time I picked up my pen instead of the imaginary sword.

I made a list in my journal of people I suspected of being the accomplice. First on this "A" for accomplice list was the person I was most curious about: Gertrude Trask, the last person to see Miss Beecher alive. Next was Claude Barhydt, the newspaper boy seen running down the hill after the murder. Both had testified they were friends of Jean but I knew that true friends do not testify against each other. While no one bothered to verify their whereabouts during the actual murder, it was hard to believe that the accomplice would have been so brazen as to agree to appear in open court. I would have expected the real accomplice to hide in the woods or disappear completely from public view just as Brainard Wilt had done. Brainard was a lumberman who lived in Gray, a small village along Black Creek. I had never met Brainard, who was only a little older, but Jean said he looked big and strong. The two rarely spoke but that didn't stop Jean from admiring him. "He wears a hat like a gunfighter in the moving pictures," Jean had said when he visited my house and told me that Brainard was one of the people he tried to recruit to help kill Miss Beecher.

When the first reporter had arrived at the murder scene, Brainard emerged from the woods and started babbling that Jean had done it. He admitted that Jean had asked him to help but said he had refused. "I was not a particular friend of his," Brainard explained, "but I guess he thought I was." Brainard told the reporter that Jean discussed his plan but he had disapproved of the way Jean wanted to work it. I suspected that Brainard, an experienced woodsman, suggested taking her into the woods away from the road. Brainard knew the woods hide secrets for a long time; he had once bragged that he had been in the woods for as long as two weeks and no one could find him.

After the encounter with the reporter, Brainard disappeared again. He never showed up at the Grand Jury hearing or at the trial. I was highly suspicious and moved his name to the top of the list. There were now three suspects on my list. Only Jean knew if the accomplice was one of them.

I decided to write Jean a letter and give him a last chance to snitch on the accomplice before he died. Although I had never written a letter, or received one, I found a book containing General Grant's correspondence during the Civil War. I studied those letters carefully, composed one to Jean in my journal, then copied it on fancy paper and mailed it to Matteawan.

Jean Gianini:

I received official word of your situation in the newspaper. Do not surrender. You must muster your forces and push forward to avoid defeat. Your rations should include plenty of hot tea and potato soup. This will help you recover lost ground. Make sure you peel and skin the potatoes first and add plenty of butter. If you need any stores I will attempt to have them delivered as speedily as possible. I know the flies can be particularly troublesome when you are wounded so try to keep them away from your quarters.

I fear for my own position. Dr. Bernstein attended me recently and informed me that I am afflicted with the moron disease. Now you and I must be united in our campaign. We have fought battles before but none so great as this one. I propose an exchange of letters with details of plans. I know you spoke in confidence to Reverend Beecher but he is no longer around. I can be of service in contacting the one who assisted you before and can be of most help now. I pray you inform me as to the name and allow me to do this. In the meanwhile, there should be no relaxation in your pursuit of health. Stay away from Harry who is a Confederate spy out to deplete your reserves. I need you to remain strong to fight for our Union. I miss you.

Very respectfully, your humble friend,
Croaker

While I was waiting for Jean's reply I tried to learn as much as possible about the suspects on my "A" list. Gertrude and Claude were still living at home but lumberman Brainard was apparently not to be found. The inept detectives never talked to him. Even the sheriff had been unable to locate him and bring him to court. Of course everyone had been looking in the area around Poland or Gray, Brainard's home. No one had bothered looking for the accomplice in Herkimer. What if lumberman Brainard had moved to Herkimer and found a safe place to hide like I had done?

The only lumberman I ever saw in the village was the one who handed Reverend Beecher the note calling for breaking into the jail and killing Jean before he blamed another. But who could have known that there was another to blame before Reverend Beecher revealed the existence of the accomplice to the press? The answer was obvious: only the accomplice could have known. I figured that the accomplice had written the note. The accomplice must have been the man in the checkered lumberman shirt. As I thought about it I became convinced that man had to be lumberman Brainard Wilt, my number one suspect. Brainard was the dastardly accomplice who had turned my best friend into a killer. And he had been right here in Herkimer!

I began to conduct nightly spy patrols in the woods surrounding the village, looking for lumbermen or their camps. I even purchased a wool lumberman overshirt so I could infiltrate their ranks when I found them. I purchased the smallest red checkered shirt I could find but it still fit like a coat and exaggerated the fact that I was too short to be a real lumberman. I failed to lure Brainard or anyone else into my path, only a bobcat who took one look at me, hissed, then ran away.

One night as I was returning from yet another empty patrol, I decided to remove my patch for a few minutes so I could feel the cool evening breeze over my entire face. As I turned a corner on East German Street I saw Charlie Tom's house, a gigantic structure of glass and yellow brick. The house looked like something one might expect to find at the end of the yellow brick road itself. Charlie Tom was always bragging about how architect Frank Lloyd Wright had designed his Prairie-style house but no one knew if the story was true. Now I spotted the sweeper clearing the leaves from the walkway, something he did for private homeowners to earn extra money. The sweeper had recently admitted to the local paper that he had written the Gianini poem and I was no longer angry. I still wanted to be friends.

"Hi," I said as I approached.

He didn't answer or look up.

"It's me, Noble."

He kept sweeping.

"I didn't know you worked for Mr. Thomas," I said as I stepped closer.

"Stay away from me," the sweeper said. He turned and gave me a strange look as if he found me disgusting. I realized I had forgotten to replace my patch. "You really do look like a moron, just like Tony has been telling everyone," he sneered. "You already attacked me once. Are you going to use a wrench and knife next time?"

I couldn't speak. The invisible hand was choking me again.

"It's best if you go on, you're just a little mor-on." He laughed.

The laughter followed me down the deserted street as I headed home. Part of me felt as dead as the leaves blowing across my path. Leaves crackled under my feet as the wind laughed. The sounds were sadder than any words. Since I still hadn't put on my patch, it must have been the wind that was irritating my eye and causing it to tear.

In September 1915, the local paper mentioned that Dr. Goddard had written a book about Jean Gianini. A copy had been ordered by the library and was expected to arrive shortly, but already there was a long list of people who had signed up to borrow it. I refused to add my name for fear that detectives who might investigate the case in the future could check such lists. Instead I returned to the library every day, waiting for the book to finally become available on the shelf.

There were other books to keep me occupied during the long winter of my wait. I found a new copy of Robert Frost's *A Boy's Will*, which had just been published in America. I had read Uncle Sam's copy but borrowed this one to show him. He was excited now that an American edition was available because it increased the likelihood that either President Wilson or some future president would read it and learn what was really important in life. Once I had hoped I might grow up to shake a president's hand like Father had done. Although I was arrested in my own development I now hoped that with the help of Frost's poetry a future president might grow up and one day be able to reach out and shake the hand of a moron like myself.

Among the library's recent acquisitions was a new novel, *Victory*, by Joseph Conrad. I had read a few of his short stories after Mama died and felt that his title "Heart of Darkness" captured my own pain. I was the first person to read the library copy of *Victory* and I was excited when I opened the blue cloth cover and caught the fresh scent of printer's ink. It was easy to identify with the main character who distrusted the world and exiled himself to the South Seas. There he helped a young woman who was later murdered. Only after her death did he recognize that he truly loved her. He must have been an idiot not to marry her when he had the chance. At the end he, too, was killed. The story was so close to my own heartache that I became convinced it had been written just for me. I had to remember not to act like an idiot when I finally met someone to marry.

Each day I watched the librarian open the mail and sort the new books as I waited for Goddard's book to arrive. One day she handed me a new arrival. I thought it had a strange title—*A Portrait of the Artist as a Young Man*, by James Joyce. The book had a blue cloth cover with gold lettering on the spine. The pages were crisp and smelled of ink. On the second page I read:

"Apologize
Pull out his eyes,
Pull out his eyes,
Apologize."

This was too grisly for me. Was I supposed to apologize for being a moron? Was that why the author wanted to pull out my eyes? What about the accomplice? He was the one who should apologize and lose his eyes. I closed the book and immediately handed it back to the librarian who closed her eyes and remarked "Well!" in a way that made it sound like I belonged in a well myself. I thought about telling her that after I found the accomplice, he would be the one at the bottom of the well without his eyes. The unexpected brutality of the thought frightened me and I said nothing.

The Goddard book, *The Criminal Imbecile*, eventually arrived and worked its way through the list of borrowers and into my hands. I stared at the thin volume for a long time before opening it. The cover was the same blue cloth with gilt lettering that adorned the Conrad and Joyce books. I was beginning to suspect that this was no coincidence but a clever conspiracy of publishers, a secret code that signaled the book was intended for morons like me. Blue was the color of melancholy and gloom, the color of morons. Blue was the color of the indecent and obscene, the color that set morons apart from the accepted. Blue was the color of the sea upon which we were hopelessly set adrift. Blue was the color of the sky which didn't notice us. I now knew why blue had always been my favorite color. When Mama took me to a store for the first time and let me pick out my own clothes, I selected a blue corduroy jacket and cap. I always wore that cap, always lived under a blue cloud.

Since the Gianini verdict Dr. Goddard had been living on his own cloud of widespread recognition as America's leading voice on morons and what to do with them. He wrote that "probably no verdict in modern times has marked so great a step forward in society's treatment of the wrongdoer. For the first time in history psychological tests of intelligence have been admitted into court and the mentality of the accused established on the basis of these facts."

Goddard knew that the verdict was unpopular and hard for people to accept but this was because most people did not understand the high-grade imbecile or moron. Unlike the village idiot who everyone recognized as "not all there" or "not quite right," the moron was not easily recognized. But the great Goddard argued that an experienced expert like himself could find a moron with his all-telling Binet test. The process, he said, was similar to diagnosing consumption. An expert physician could recognize the early warning signs of a cough and other symptoms that would eventually progress to tuberculosis, consume the patient, and infect others with the deadly disease. By asking people to cough up answers to his Binet test, Goddard could diagnose those who would eventually turn into criminal imbeciles and kill others.

In the case of Jean Gianini, Goddard wrote that it was the fires of sexual passion that consumed Jean and caused the death of

Miss Beecher. Jean lacked the power of control and the ingenuity to overcome the force of his sexual impulse. The signs of a sexual fire burning within were evident from an early age when he played Indian with little girls, then later teased his little sisters. The association with the young and beautiful teacher further fanned the flames until he made plans for playing Indian with her and conquering her. The violence against her was ultimately a sexual act.

But Goddard had never met Miss Beecher and could not have realized the seduction of her presence. He could not know what it was like to sit in her class and watch her handsome figure floating back and forth in front of the chalkboard; to be teased by the tips of her shoes as they peeked from beneath her flowing skirts; to be enveloped in the lavender cloud of her presence; to feel her gentle hand on your head, her delicate fingers parting your hair as she combed it with the same comb that only moments ago had caressed her own locks; to see her lips so close that you could feel the warmth of her breath; to see her day after day and to feel the sweetest sensations growing in your loins. Goddard could never understand the irresistible impulse to take her, to possess her. He could never understand that it might not have been a violent act of rage but an act of passion, a pupil's manifest destiny of love for a teacher.

Goddard saw Jean as an example of the criminal imbecile who was not fit to live among the rest of us for fear he might repeat his heinous act. The surest way to see that he didn't was to put him away. "It is certainly no great loss to society if Gianini is put out of the way," Goddard wrote. While Gianini was incarcerated for life, Goddard worried about all those other imbeciles with criminal potential who were infesting our society. Unless their mental condition was recognized and they were cared for in such a way as to make the expression of their sexual impulses and murderous rages impossible, he feared there would be many more Jean Gianinis and many more Lida Beechers. He ended the book with a proposal for a final solution to the imbecile question. Imbeciles will never get better. They will never have a full mind, never be free of following the suggestion of some wicked person or yielding to uncontrolled impulses. It will never be safe for imbeciles to remain at large. If we wish to save our teachers from being murdered or our daughters from being sexually assaulted, we have to be on guard for criminal imbeciles. We have to use the Binet test to find them. Then, like lepers, imbeciles must be colonized and segregated. They must not be allowed to propagate. Goddard promised that if we followed his plan, in a few generations they would be exterminated.

I closed the book and felt as though I was closing the book on my own life. I had lived for eighteen years but if my mind was no longer growing, what was? Inexplicably, I felt that I was standing still in space as time passed. Was I only an observer watching through the window? Was I destined to end up like a fly on the sill, an empty shell that died without ever feeling the sun on its grotesque eye again?

As I lay in my bed under the window, and another cycle of seasons passed outside, I felt that, like Jean, I was a prisoner in a looking-glass world. We were like Tweedledum and Tweedledee, two schoolboys forever arrested in development. The only hope of escape was time—to wait until the window broke of old age, or we did.

15

A ray of hope penetrated my gloom when I read Goddard's book on Jean Gianini for a second time. It was not unusual, he wrote, for an imbecile to commit murder while under the influence of an accomplice with "superior intelligence" who took advantage of his weak mind. There were many examples including Roxy Druse who had been bright enough to lure her pretty yet feebleminded daughter into assisting with murder. Although Jean had confessed to being the sole killer, Goddard claimed that his confession was unreliable because Jean was the type of imbecile who talked for effect, and loved show and notoriety. This was certainly the Jean I knew. And I had always wanted to believe he was taking credit for the actions of an accomplice who did some if not all the killing, an accomplice of superior intelligence who had gotten away with murder. Now Goddard's book confirmed that likelihood. I wasn't sure if a moron could catch someone of superior intelligence, but I was determined to outwit him.

So I spent my days reading about logging and lumber operations in order to better understand the habits of Brainard Wilt. I learned the difference between cedar, pine, and spruce trees. I studied how to strip bark for tanning, float logs and slash them into lumber. I filled my head with all this knowledge and kept my body fueled with an exclusive diet of lumberman food. I had wheat flour pancakes with black strap molasses for breakfast and boiled potatoes with beans for supper. I even ate my meals with the non-kosher pork grease and salted pork favored by loggers, telling myself God would understand. Then I set out on patrols during the new moons, venturing far north along West Canada Creek. My body grew strong and I started running to cover more ground. I followed footprints along the creek and chased shadows moving through the trees but the accomplice was always just out of sight.

On Friday night, February 9, 1917, I decided to change the scheduling of my patrols which had always been conducted during the darkest of nights. There was supposed to be a full moon that night and I thought it might help.

I had just finished lighting the Sabbath candles with Uncle Sam, who wished me "Good *Shabbes*" and shook my hand. My handshake was as now as firm and sure as his, but I would have preferred Mama's soft kiss and even softer "Good *Shabbes, ziskeit*." I longed for the gentle way she placed her hands on the sides of my face as she looked into my eyes when she said it. Suddenly, I was missing her terribly. I felt angry that she had left me.

"You're squeezing too hard, Noble," Uncle Sam said as he pulled his hand away. It shattered my reverie. "Let's eat," he smiled, rubbing his paunch.

After supper I went outside and looked for the moon but the sky was overcast. I could not see even a single star. It had been over a year since I last walked through the village during a full moon and I wondered if the sky might have changed during that period. Perhaps there was a permanent nightly overcast caused by the Great War. Germany was at war with most of Europe now. Bread was being rationed in Britain and Uncle Sam could no longer get his aftershave lotions and powders from France.

Conditions for us morons in the United States were not any sunnier. Goddard had given his Binet test to a group of immigrants at Ellis Island and found that eighty-three percent of the Jews and eighty-seven percent of the Russians were feebleminded. He encouraged the doctors there to screen better and to limit immigration. Congress expanded the definition of non-desirable immigrants to include idiots, imbeciles, and morons. A dozen states had passed laws permitting the sterilization of the feebleminded. Extermination seemed just a matter of time.

No wonder I could not see the moon or stars. I wasn't even supposed to be here. If the new immigration laws had been in effect when Mama and Papa arrived at Ellis Island, it was likely they would have been turned away. I might never have been born. Perhaps I never should have been born. A specter was covering my sky and I was certain that not even that new telescope they were building on Mt. Wilson in California would be able to peer through the gloom.

I forced myself to hike to the woods north of the village for my patrol. It was not only a dark night, but frigid as well. I was shivering despite my wool overshirt. I realized that even lumbermen would not be outside on a night like this. I headed back to the village, disappointed and freezing but not yet ready for bed. I reached into my jacket pocket and felt the box of friction matches I used for the Sabbath candles. In an alley on the Munger Block which housed a big department store I found a carton of old, smelly rags and ignited them. There was something on the rags that caused them to burn with enough heat to keep me warm as I sat against a wall and watched the flames flicker and dance in the night. It made a wonderful fire.

It was easy to understand how our early ancestors were fascinated by fire. Fire was the giver of heat and light. Naturally, it was the gift of a god, a fire god. As I basked in the warm glow I understood why morons are said to be attracted to incendiarism. It is not the destruction from the flames but the warmth of the light that draws us in. I raised my patch and exposed my eye to the roaring fire. The fire god lullabied me to sleep.

A loud explosion woke me in the alley just after sunrise. I ran to the street as a mammoth column of smoke rose from an adjoining building. In ten minutes the smoke turned into flames, store windows exploded, and flames leaped into the sky. In a few more minutes the building was roaring like a furnace.

The fire quickly spread to adjoining structures and three entire blocks in the heart of the Herkimer business district were burning before the first hook and ladder truck arrived on the scene. Firemen attached hoses to the hydrants but the tiny streams of water only had enough pressure to reach the first floor of the three-story buildings. The heat of the blaze forced the firemen back as their hoses dribbled impotently on the street.

The fire roared with a mesmerizing force. For the next two hours I watched as the Earl Block, the Masonic Building, and the Grange Building were reduced to smoldering timbers. Nothing higher than ten feet was left standing above the ground. Two hundred people lost their jobs at the Munger store that day. Attorney Charles Hane lost his office, as did many other lawyers, an assistant district attorney, and several stenographers. *The Evening Telegram* office was destroyed and the First National Bank was partially burnt but the new fireproof safe protected the money. A cashier from the bank went among the crowd assuring people that there was no need to worry. The bank would open for business the following day in the nearby Star Restaurant. There would be coffee and doughnuts for all.

The Utica paper published a photograph of the devastation. The photo was spread over four columns with a large-type caption: "When the Fire God Had Finished at Herkimer." It was taken at the corner of Main and Green Streets when the fire was practically out. I thought it looked like one of those war photographs from Europe showing a city in ruins. In the foreground was a crowd gawking at the smoke and destruction. I recognized myself standing near the remains of the alley where they said the fire started. I was worried because I now suspected that the rags I had ignited may have accidentally spread sparks to the adjoining buildings. Fortunately my back was to the camera but I still feared someone would be able to recognize me. A good detective like William Burns might even be able to discover it was me, then deduce it was my campfire that started the inferno. The lump in my throat was back.

The smell of a drowned fire lingered in the air for months.

Soot covered the outside of my window, turning the ice black until the spring rains melted it. The scuttlebutt in the barber-shop was that local businessmen had hired private detectives to find the arsonist. Charlie Tom, who had lost his office in the fire, announced that he was volunteering his services to prosecute the suspect as soon as he was apprehended. He said that this time he was certain to get the conviction that had eluded him on the Gianini trial. When I heard this I nearly shouted a question from behind the crack in my door but Uncle Sam beat me to it.

"What's the sentence for arson?" Uncle Sam asked.

Charlie Tom sneered as he drew a finger quickly across his neck. The invisible hand was choking me once more.

The only bright spot was in October when I read that Jean Gianini did not die as predicted and was recovering. Obviously the hot tea and my potato soup recipe worked. I expected that he would now answer my letter but when no mail arrived by December I sent him a postcard wishing him a speedy recovery and a healthy birthday. I humbly beseeched him to write.

A year passed with no reply from Jean and no sightings of Brainard Wilt. After my birthday in 1918, Uncle Sam took me to the bank which had been remodeled following the fire. I was now twenty-one and he gave me a savings account that contained all the money from the sale of Father's apple farm. I was surprised that he had kept it for me for all these years. In addition to the interest paid by the bank, Uncle Sam had deposited money every week I worked in the shop. And, unknown to me, there was additional money from an account my father had main-tained at the National Bank of Poland. I counted the number of noughts in the passbook balance several times but each time I came up with the same answer: I had over eight thousand dollars.

On the way back to the shop I stopped to buy several boxes of *Zu Zu* snaps. I couldn't think of anything else I wanted except a letter from Jean. I mailed him a box of snaps and signed my name, hopeful he would at least write to say thanks. A few days later, after the New Year, I noticed an advertisement for another perfect present in *The Evening Telegram* and wrote the company for a demonstration. The next week a man from nearby Frankfort drove up to the barbershop in a new five-passenger Maxwell touring car. I purchased the automobile on the spot for Uncle Sam. It was his turn to be surprised. He walked in a circle around the car, all twenty-five feet and four inches of it, touching the oversized curved fenders, smelling the seats, and patting the white-walled tires. Then he hugged me, picking me up in his huge arms and laughing. He circled the car again, rubbing the black finish, stroking the steering wheel, and shaking his head in joyous disbelief.

Uncle Sam didn't know how to drive so he left the car exactly where the salesman had parked it. Each day he shined and polished the body to a mirror-like finish. "Maxine," as he affectionately called the car, was his pride and joy. Sometimes he would sit in the back seat and read the paper, nodding and waving to passersby as if he were an important politician. Occasionally he would invite them to sit in the car or try the horn but most of the time he would stare at Maxine through the shop window, stroking his mustache and smiling.

Maxine was good for Uncle Sam and good for business, too. There were more customers in the shop than ever. And after he had the brilliant idea to give a frightened little boy his first haircut in the car, so many mothers brought their sons to the shop that he had to hire another barber. He certainly got a lot of mileage from a car that never moved.

All through 1919, I kept looking at advertisements in the papers, hoping to find something to buy for myself. One of the shelves in my room was now full of *Zu Zu* snaps, the library was still free, and there was nothing I really needed. Then I came across an advertisement that almost knocked me out. It had a picture of the most hauntingly beautiful girl I had ever seen. And she was just down the street. I decided to treat myself to my first moving picture show.

I sat in the first row of the darkened theater as the screen flickered to life. The words of the title, *Broken Blossoms or The Yellow Man and the Girl*, were shaking on the screen as if the entire theater was trembling with the pounding of my heart. Next, the list of characters appeared including the girl, Lucy Burrows, played by Lillian Gish, whose picture had been in the newspaper advertisement. There was also the Yellow Man and "Battling Burrows," Lucy's father who was a professional boxer. When I read the names of two minor characters I thought I would have a heart attack: The Spying One and Evil Eye. It was obvious that this was my movie. I moved forward on the blue velvet seat.

I watched as Lucy's story unfolded on the silent screen. She grew up on London's foggy waterfront without a Mama and with only a brute for a father who used her as a punching bag for his drunken rages. All of this was magically reflected in her facial expressions and poetic movements as she sat on a large coiled rope on a wharf looking cold, hungry, alone. She was as helplessly lost in the fog of her hellish existence as I was in mine. I extended my hand to the screen in a vain attempt to assist her.

Lucy entered her home where her drunk father was threatening to give her another beating with a whip unless she smiled. She lifted her hand, spread her index and second fingers, and pushed up the corners of her lips into a ghastly, fixed-mouth smile. The pitiful gesture satisfied the old man and reminded me of my own awkward attempt to smile for Jean when I saw him on his way to the Herkimer County Jail.

Later, Lucy prepared to go shopping and adjusted her hat in a wall mirror, bending over toward the mirror as one might bend over a flower for refreshment. She seemed disappointed with her image. "But you are a flower," I said aloud. As Lucy moved among the shops, the man called Evil Eye, with a swollen right eye and droopy lid, approached and wanted to outrage her. The Yellow Man, who was a shopkeeper on the street, appeared and stepped between them, saving me the trouble.

Lucy went home where her father beat her savagely with a whip. She staggered into the street, then collapsed inside the open door of the Yellow Man's shop. He tended to her wounds and carried her upstairs into his bedroom. There he nursed her back to health. He gave her a magical silk robe to wear. She looked into a hand-held mirror and smiled for the first time as he gazed lustfully at her. His heart was on fire and so was mine. She moved to touch his face. The camera did not show the sex that followed, but I am certain that it happened.

Days later the Spying One, who was nothing but a snitch, told Lucy's father where she was staying. He arrived at the shop after the Yellow Man had gone out to buy some blossoms, and dragged Lucy home as she pulled against him like a terrified puppy. He reached for the whip again. Lucy squirmed away and locked herself inside a closet. The father attacked the closet door with an axe. Lucy panicked, whirling around with no place to escape to. She cowered in a corner and gnawed on the back of her hand.

Then the Yellow Man discovered her missing and headed for Lucy's home with a gun. "Hurry Yellow Man," I yelled.

The axe fell again and again against the closet door. With each blow, my heart was banging against my rib cage. The closet door splintered as the father tore the broken wood away and pulled little Lucy through the opening. His face was that of a gorilla snarling in rage. Her silent screams were almost too much to bear. I moved back in my seat and watched in disbelief as he beat her to death with the whip.

The Yellow Man arrived, shot the father, then carried Lucy's body back to his bedroom. He draped the silk robe over her. I stared with amazement as he knelt by her side and plunged a knife into his chest. But he was smiling. I believe he was happy to have escaped from such an unjust and cruel world.

The lights in the theater came on. I was breathless, stunned, heartbroken. I understood why they called this a moving picture. I was moved beyond my ability to endure. I went back to my room to tend to my wounds. Sometime during the closet scene I had gnawed the back of my hand. I knew my hand would heal but the tears in my heart would never mend.

16

The seasons passed by my window like the same movie playing over and over again. When the barbershop was empty I would always look out the window and think of Jean. I wrote him several more times and included the little news I heard about Poland from talk in the shop and the papers. I hoped by now he might feel the need to tell me about the accomplice. While I was certain it was Brainard Wilt, I did not want Jean to feel like he was snitching so I simply dropped the names of all those I had once suspected, hoping he would say something that would implicate the actual culprit. I mentioned that Claude Barhydt's father who ran the barbershop in Poland had visited Uncle Sam one day. I told him that Brainard Wilt might have been in Herkimer. In case I bumped into Brainard, I asked Jean if he had any message for him. I also asked if he had heard from Gertrude Trask who always used to write him notes in school. Each day was filled with the anticipation of receiving a reply, which never came. Each night was filled with dream-like remembrances of Jean and the murder, always with the same missing scenes and faceless accomplice. Day and night, my life was as empty as the mailbox.

During one unbearably hot summer I stayed sequestered in my room with the light off, replaced by the lights from my headaches which seemed to be occurring more often. I lay naked on my bed with only a wet handkerchief around my head and my trusty wooden vice grip on my penis. The flies were particularly bothersome, but I was in too much pain to shoo them away from my sweating body.

I was not the only one who was miserable. I read that Lillian Gish, who had played Lucy Burrows in *Broken Blossoms*, had contracted the Spanish flu and had survived a close brush with death. At least twenty million others perished. The pandemic ended but people were now dying for a drink as they desperately sought ways to circumvent the new Prohibition. All I ever drank was wine on Friday nights or at the Passover *Seder*. Uncle Sam went to Utica and got two cases of wine bottles from the orthodox Jewish congregation which had a special permit. It was more than we could ever drink. He wanted to taste the wine as soon he got back although it was still afternoon and not even a Friday or Passover. After three glasses he pronounced it good and promptly fell asleep on the sofa. I had only one glass but curled up next to him and allowed his rhythmic snoring to lull me to sleep.

We drank more wine during the years of Prohibition than ever before. When Sheriff Stitt died suddenly, we said a prayer and sipped wine at supper. "Stitty was a decent Scot with a great mustache," Uncle Sam said as he raised his glass. I raised mine, not to the jailer of Gianini but to the jailed. May he outlive them all, I said to myself.

Wine toasts became a regular feature of our Friday suppers. In the years that followed we toasted the election of Warren Harding, the end of the Russian civil war, Robert Frost's Pulitzer Prize, and the newest women's fashion of skirts above the knee. When we couldn't think of anything special to toast, we toasted Prohibition. I had mixed feelings about toasting the principals from Jean's trial as they passed away: District Attorney William Farrell, defense lawyers John McEvoy and John McIntyre, who had become a judge, and defense alienist Dr. Carlos MacDonald. The death that upset me the most was Charlie Tom's. On the day before Christmas one year, I went shopping for a birthday present for myself. It was a dark afternoon and my driving goggles made my vision worse. As I turned a corner I bumped into a man carrying a tall stack of presents. We both took a bad tumble. I tried to help the man pick up his presents before searching for my goggles and patch which had come off. He looked up to thank me, then gasped at my exposed eye. I found myself staring at Charlie Tom. He gathered his packages and ran off as if he had just seen a Christmas ghost. The following day he had a heart attack and died. At the next Sabbath meal, I not only toasted him but got drunk for the first time. I didn't like the feeling because it made both my eyes tear so I never got drunk again.

My headaches grew worse. There was now a searing pressure behind my left eye, and the pain was so bad that my brain bled with dreadful visions. The flashing lights became comets streaking across the ceiling, heralding a great disaster. Objects were suddenly looking unfamiliar. The shelves in the room appeared to be tilted at impossible angles, the very walls seemed ready to crumble, and fracture lines filled the air itself. Something terrible was going to happen. I rarely wrote in my journal but when I did I found my writing to be digressive. Afterwards, I could hardly read the tiny compressed script. It looked like someone else's handwriting. I was becoming a stranger to myself.

The pain became relentless and Mama's handkerchief trick was no longer working. I found myself standing outside the massive wooden door of Dr. A. Walter Suiter's office on the corner of Main and Court. "Hit me," said the Wonderland Gryphon carved on the door. "Go on. Don't be all day about it." I knocked and in a few moments Dr. Suiter opened the door. He appeared different than he had been at the trial. Now he was almost as pale and skinny as I felt. He looked down at me and smiled. I was not fooled. This was the same man who had helped send my friend Jean to Matteawan.

I told him my head hurt and he escorted me through the long foyer to his office. He asked me a lot of questions, scribbling on a small pad as I recited the history of my seizures and headaches. When I described my visions, he nodded as if he had heard such things before. The nods were very comforting. He directed me to a small examining room where he unbuttoned my shirt and held a cold metal stethoscope against my chest. While he was examining me, I had a sudden urge to ask about Jean Gianini. "Hold your tongue," said the Gryphon. I remained silent as Dr. Suiter removed my patch so gently I didn't even feel it, then just as gently felt the folds of tissue with his fingers. When he strapped a head mirror to his forehead and peered into the eye, I looked away to avoid seeing my reflection. He poked and probed the fleshy growth as if he were looking for a foreign object, a splinter that didn't belong. I hoped he could find such a thing and pull it out. When he finally worked his way down to my eyeball, he asked me to look directly at him. I did this in order to help him find the splinter and forced myself to ignore the light reflected from the head mirror.

Time seemed to stand still. I knew the light was streaming into my eye, but I withdrew. Somehow I stepped back and found a place deep inside my brain where it couldn't reach me. From a distance I watched Dr. Suiter peering into my eye as it dripped tears. Suddenly the light must have found something because Dr. Suiter's face froze only inches from my own. My body stiffened as I felt an unexplainable urge to hit him. He jerked away just in time.

"Von Recklinghausen!"

It sounded like he sneezed. "*Gesundheit*," I said.

He smiled. "It's the name for the condition of your eye. I've read about it but can't say I've seen it before. A man in England had the condition all over his body. They said he looked like an elephant." He examined my eye again with a magnifying lens. "Yours is just a growth confined to your lid and nothing to worry about," he announced as he put away his instruments. "The seizures are epilepsy but I believe you may also have a blot on your brain that is causing all the megrim headaches and at least some of the visions."

Blot? I didn't understand. "If you don't know what a blot is, you're an idiot," said the Gryphon. I decided not to ask for an explanation and simply assumed it was something like a blood clot. After all, I felt as if my brain had been bleeding with apoc-alyptic visions. If a clot formed, perhaps the visions would stop.

Dr. Suiter gave me a box of aspirin pills and told me to take one with strong coffee whenever I felt a headache starting. He said if it didn't work I should come back to see him again. I should also come back if I experienced any strange sensations or other disturbances—signs that the blot was growing. "Things may not always appear the way they really are," he said. Again, I didn't understand what he was saying. As he opened the side door on Court Street for me to exit, I reached into my pocket and produced a few coins and bills. "How much?" I asked.

He smiled. "Use the money to buy yourself some candy or to see a picture show," he said, ignoring the wad of money in my hand and ushering me out. He turned and walked briskly to a little marble alcove where he proceeded to wash his hands. As I left I heard him wheezing and coughing.

Dr. A. Walter Suiter died at noon on the following day. The newspaper said his first name was Augustus. I had been his last patient and he was the last doctor I would ever allow to look at my eye.

When Halloween approached I took Dr. Suiter's parting advice and purchased candy, enough to fill up a giant bowl for the customers in the barbershop. There were penny candies, caramels, Hershey Kisses, Walnettos, and a few wrapped bars. Uncle Sam came to my room and asked me to remove all the bars of Goldenberg's Peanut Chews. He said it was a mistake to buy them. "People don't want Jew candy," he whispered. Judging from the growing anti-Semitic talk in the shop, I knew he was probably right. But before I could go out and remove them, the mayor came into the shop for a shave. I listened as he raved about Henry Ford's essays which had been running in all the papers. The mayor had the annoying habit of nodding as he talked.

"Ford says Jews are hucksters," he said. "They don't want to produce. They want to make something out of what somebody else produces." A nod. The mayor suggested that Uncle Sam show his support for Ford by trading in the Maxwell for a Model T like his own. Another nod. He reminded Uncle Sam that one of the "kike" peddlers who came through the village drove a Maxwell. A big nod. As the mayor grabbed a handful of candy on his way out, I silently wished he would choke on a Goldenberg Peanut Chew. My chin did a double nod.

By Halloween eve all the candy in the shop was gone and I was left with Peanut Chews. I ate too many and couldn't sleep. I tossed and turned as my mind filled with a waking dream of trick-or-treating. In my dream there was a knock on the door to the alley, and I opened it. Someone stood there wearing a Halloween mask with Miss Beecher's picture pasted on the face. The mask came off. It was Miss Beecher, cackling like a witch. Her face was slashed and dripping with blood. I bolted from the bed and ran to the sink where I vomited a mass of undigested candy. The ancient Druids believed that on Halloween eve the veil between the world of the living and the world of the dead was at its thinnest, allowing for the souls of the dead to cross and roam the land. I was ready to believe that it was I who they were trying to scare to death.

I followed Dr. Suiter's recommendation about drinking strong coffee at the onset of a headache. Whenever I noticed the flashing lights in the corner of my visual field, I poured coffee grinds into a glass of water and swallowed it with an aspirin. This turned out to be surprisingly effective in either blocking the headache entirely or greatly reducing its intensity. However, the coffee made me restless and prevented me from sleeping. At such times I resumed my nightly patrols in the woods for the accomplice, taking care to avoid the sweeper when I returned through the village.

One night during a new moon I stood on the corner of Church and North Prospect Streets and admired the home of Justice Devendorf. It was built in the Federal style of architecture and seemed a fitting home for a jurist. A light was flickering inside one of the downstairs rooms. I looked through a window and saw a small fire in a large green marble fireplace. The fire was dying but there was enough light to illuminate bookshelves lined with the most beautiful leather volumes I had ever seen. I longed to run my hands along the spines and smell the leather. Almost automatically my feet took me to the rear of the house. The back door was not only unlocked but ajar, a clear sign that I should not bypass this opportunity.

I entered and tiptoed down a hall, past a wide twisting staircase and into the room with the fireplace. As I stood on the hearth, a warmth radiated on my face while my hand rubbed the cool marble. A thick wooden mantle covered the top of the marble, and above that was a giant mirror that took up most of the wall and reflected back the entire room. I saw that the room was unoccupied. Unoccupied? I looked again and realized that my image did not appear in the mirror! Puzzled, I quickly averted my eyes, more out of habit than fear, and tried to understand the significance of what had just happened. Was I losing my eyesight? My mind?

I surmised that this had to be just another Halloween hallucination, a waking dream conjured up by the blot on my brain to scare me. It was now influencing my grip on reality just like Dr. Suiter had warned. I grabbed a candlestick from the mantle and heaved it at the mirror, fully expecting the noise to cause me to wake up in my bed. The candlestick hit the mirror with a snap and fell to the floor. Now a giant crack ran drunkenly from the top right corner of the mirror down to the bottom left corner. I felt it with my fingers. The crack was there all right but I was not. The noise of the breaking glass was immediately followed by footsteps coming down the stairs. I slipped out of the house and into the night.

There was only one explanation for the absence of my reflection in the mirror—I was a ghost. After years of spying on people, of trying to be unseen, of wishing with all my heart to understand the magic of the looking glass, I had transformed myself into a mirror. Mirrors do not see themselves. And a person does not see the mirror itself, only a reflected image. People didn't see me, only reflections of what they wanted to believe were there. I had moved out of my body. I had become a ghost, a creature from people's nightmares, the vampire who came out at night to feast on their fears and suck them dry of reason. I was the Jewish huckster pretending that the mental reasoning I possessed was the product of my own brain, not siphoned from someone else. Here, outside a justice's house I had just burglarized and vandalized, the verdict was unanimous: I was a criminal imbecile, a moron, a ghost of a man.

The last piece of Dr. Suiter's parting advice had been to see a moving picture. It was, of course, advice I dared not follow for fear of becoming overwrought. After *Broken Blossoms*, the only movie I ever wanted to see was *Orphans of the Storm*, also starring Lillian Gish. I found a novel of the same title that was based on the screenplay. The book even contained photographs of scenes from the actual film.

Lillian Gish played Henriette, a poor peasant girl caught up in the Reign of Terror following the French Revolution. She was jailed and sentenced to the guillotine. I was fascinated by the description and pictures of this machine, which was uglier than the gallows and had a knife blade the size of a plough share. Henriette was strapped on a board and her swan-like neck placed in the round-holed crossboard which prevented her from moving back. A picture showed Henriette looking up in horror at the awful edge of the knife. At the last moment, a deformed hunchback, who happened to be her devoted admirer, rushed from the crowd and stabbed the executioner. Henriette was saved and I breathed for the first time in several pages. My breath was taken away again by the final words of the novel: "For Love is stronger than Death, and must prevail."

Even a ghost of a man can keep the man's dreams.

17

When I became a ghost I made it my job to haunt the Herkimer Free Library, living among the ghosts of writers and their characters. I read my way through the stacks of books with the same steadfastness I had applied as a child to the encyclopedia.

I mentioned that Mama had taught me how to read. Long before she taught me the meaning of words she showed me the essence of reading itself. My earliest memory was watching her sitting next to the window cradling a book in her lap, her head slightly bowed as if in prayer. There was a glow on her face like an illumination radiating from the very pages of the book. I often wondered if the light came from her or the book or the sun from the window, then decided they fed each other in a magical way. Mama was absorbed in that glow. She was a picture of reverence. She showed me there was something magical, something almost sacred about reading.

When I did start reading for myself, I discovered the same special communion with books. Later, sitting in the dark corner of the library amidst the storm of the trial, I found that reading provided an island of calm. But there was another storm—a nerve storm—brewing in my brain. Headaches knifed like lightning across my eyes. Dr. Bernstein had called me a moron and the word clapped like thunder against my ears. He had invited me to seek shelter at his school but I thought that I was in no danger and could ride out the tempest on my island.

Then the storm clouds grew darker. The stock market crashed. The Great Depression swept over the land like a terrible deluge. I spent more and more time on my island, a castaway from a world that was more than willing to be rid of me and my kind. I was afraid. The invisible hand squeezing my throat was becoming more powerful and more visible with each passing year. By 1931, twenty-seven states had enacted sterilization laws for the feebleminded. Prohibition ended in 1933, but I saw nothing happening that was worth toasting except Justice Devendorf's passing. The Nazis had just published a new German edition of Goddard's *The Kallikak Family* at a time when they were burning other books by non-Nazis and Jewish authors. Then the Third Reich began the forced sterilization of Germans with feeblemindedness or epilepsy, thereby giving Goddard's warnings against mixing "good blood" with "bad" a chilling reality. It seemed as though the great Goddard had unleashed a ravenous octopus which had grown to a colossal size with tentacles stretching across the ocean, threatening to devour all misshapen fish like me.

The Nazis began a policy of killing the incurably ill, including idiotic children, feebleminded adults, and mental patients. One technique was to inject phenol into their hearts. Death was almost immediate. Phenol was also known as carbolic acid, the same antiseptic substance Dr. Cole had used in his office in Poland to get rid of my stench. I wondered if Dr. Cole was a Nazi sympathizer who gave them the idea. Thinking about that possibility made me angry.

Some of the incurably ill were killed by the Nazi guillotine. The execution itself was so fast that it seemed to be all over in the twinkling of an eye. There was no time for prayer or fear. The victims never even had time to kick or fight. The only ones who screamed were the crippled, whose bodies had to be forcibly straightened as they were being tied to the board.

I tried to imagine what was going on in the mind of the victim during those last moments. Judging by the stories from the Reign of Terror that told of decapitated heads blinking and looking about, even trying to speak, I figured that consciousness could survive for awhile. The hero of Dostoevski's *The Idiot* fancied that consciousness could last for five seconds. If the severed head of an idiot continued thinking for seconds, I fancied that a moron's could last for minutes, maybe longer.

The horrors of the Nazi totalitarian state made me feel helpless. I was grateful for my island in the library where I could grow old and die a natural death. I was now past the age when Mama died and I began to contemplate what it was like in the afterlife. At least Mama would be together with Father.

Then I read in the barbershop's newspaper that Charles A. Gianini, formerly of New York, had died on Halloween in 1935. Who would be with him? His first wife Sarah? What if she still wouldn't talk to him? The obituary mentioned that his second wife and children were still alive. I remembered how my own father's death affected me, so my thoughts naturally turned to Jean. Since the article didn't even acknowledge that Jean was a son, perhaps the family hadn't bothered to tell Jean of the death. I knew that when a parent dies, a son senses it deep inside and I had no doubt that Jean sensed a great tear in the fabric of his being. He deserved to know for certain what had happened. I clipped the article, changed my clothes, hastily collected my wallet, and set out on the next train to Matteawan to see Jean. Although there was a risk I might be identified by the Matteawan alienists as a criminal imbecile and locked away myself, I reminded myself that Mama always taught me to do good deeds for others.

At Matteawan the guards waved me through the gates, probably because I was wearing my best clothes, a tie, and a derby with a wide rim hiding my face. The walk through the mazy corridors of the main building to the visiting area seemed almost as long as the train ride and just as noisy. I had said at the gate that I wanted to visit Jean, and after a few minutes a guard told me the prisoner was ready to see me. Jean and I sat across from each other, separated by a solid wall with a small glass window. The window was no larger than a picture frame and revealed only his head and shoulders. Scratches and smudges on the glass made him appear as worn and marked as his old school desk. His hair was gray and was covered with a greasy pomade that glistened under the bright overhead lights. A dirty piece of adhesive tape held part of his glasses together. He looked like one of those railroad hoboes in need of a bath and shave. I was not sure how I looked to him but we both stared for quite a while.

"Did you get my letters?" I finally asked.

"You really are a moron," he said with a familiar smirk. The words came through a tiny steel screen below the window. "There was no return address, just a loony line: "From Head-Quarters, Army of Tennessee."

I was dumbfounded. I had copied General Grant's address. What a moron I was, I thought. But Jean was laughing now and I laughed, too, shaking my head in embarrassment.

"It is good to see you," he smiled. His voice was sincere.

"Did you hear about your father?"

He stopped smiling and shook his head. "He never writes me," Jean said.

I took the obituary and held it up to the window for him to read. It covered most of the glass and his face.

"Daddy!" The word came out of the screen like a faint cry from a faraway crib. "Dadddeeeeee!" he wailed. This time the word screeched like chalk on a blackboard.

I pulled the paper away.

"No, leave it," he whimpered.

I held it up again and listened to him sob his way through the article. I had read it myself several times on the train ride from Herkimer. It said that Charles Gianini had been sixty-seven when he died in St. Luke's Hospital in Utica following five days of illness from pneumonia. Most of the article was devoted to listing his accomplishments: nationally known sportsman and magazine writer, author of several best-selling books, acclaimed photographer, and honored member of many archeological and historical societies including the National Geographic Society. I thought it was odd that Mr. Gianini had written so many articles and books, yet not one letter to his son Jean.

"Okay," Jean said. I took the article away from the window as Jean removed his glasses and wiped his eyes with a sleeve. "I wanted him to love me but he never did. As far as he was concerned I was dead. The paper didn't even mention me. I might as well be dead."

"The article mentioned a son, Gerald," I said. "The papers are always making mistakes with your name. Once they spelled it with a 'G,' so why not Gerald?" I wanted Jean to feel better but I knew he was right. The old man had never cared about him. I probably should have cut off the last paragraph of the obituary which listed the survivors, but I wasn't thinking rationally—just like a moron.

"Gerald is my half-brother," Jean explained. "He was born after the trial. I heard that in school the other kids called him a murderer and a moron and threw stones at him. All because of me. He must hate me now. Nobody loves me."

I didn't know what to say as Jean cried softly.

"My old man was always hitting me," Jean continued, "sometimes for no reason. Why did he do that? Or he was laughing at me. Once when I was little I was playing with a toy train and couldn't put the tracks together. Instead of helping me he sat there and laughed. Later I asked him to help me with the tracks and he punched me because I interrupted him. Why did he do things like that?"

I shrugged. I had heard this story in court but pretended that I was hearing it for the first time.

"He still cared about you," I said. "Why else would he have gone to such a huge expense to save you from the chair?"

Jean shook his head. "He had the money and felt he had to spend it to show he was a proper parent. But he didn't really care a whole lot."

He started sobbing again, saying "Daddy" under his breath.

It was difficult to endure. I felt my own eye tear under the patch and tried to change the subject by telling him happy news about his friends from Poland whose lives I had followed in the newspapers. Morris Howe had become a hero in the Great War, had married and now had three little girls. Leon Coonradt owned a lumber business in the village of Cold Brook near Poland and was married with two sons. Estus Compo was also married.

"Say, are you married?"

The question bothered me. "No," I said. My answer bothered me even more. "Not yet," I added, to make myself feel better.

"I'll never get married," Jean said. "I'll never get out of here."

"What's it like here?"

"I'm getting good care. The food is okay. Sometimes the staff pushes us around. You have to do everything they say. I think about ways to get my revenge but all I can do is yell at them." He looked at me with sad eyes. "You probably think I'm some kind of boob."

I shook my head.

"Didn't you ever think about revenge on someone?" he asked.

I admitted I used to think about burning down Zia Nardone's house when I was a kid but that was a long time ago.

"It might make you feel good," he said.

I could see the Herkimer fire and feel the satisfying warmth of the roaring flames but the invisible hand of a detective tightened around my throat. I shook my head to loosen the grip.

"No? Well, if I were free, I'd burn it down for you," he smiled. "So what do you do now?"

I told him about my job cleaning the barbershop and explained my technique of holding the broom and pushing it with one hand while pulling it with the other. He said it was a crazy way to sweep but I argued that it wasn't crazy if it got the job done effectively. I said it was very satisfying to sweep the shop every night and know when I finished that I had done a good job.

"Then you're lucky because you must sleep well," he said. "I don't."

"Do you have bad dreams?" I asked. I knew I was touching

on areas even best friends didn't discuss but I had to know if Miss Beecher bothered his sleep as much as she did mine.

"I cover myself with the blanket to keep away the dreams," Jean said.

"Does that work?"

"Yeah, or sometimes I stay up talking to one of the boobs we call Albert Einstein because he's good with numbers. Einstein knows all about cockroaches and is up all night watching them. He says they're really smart and know how to survive. He catches the stupid ones and eats them. He's a funny boob," Jean smiled.

"Do you have a library? Books to read?"

"Nothing. They said I was arrested in development. I guess they mean to keep me that way."

"But what do you do with all your time during the day?"

"They arrested time in here."

The profundity of his remark stunned me.

"Maybe it would have been better to get the chair," he continued.

"Don't talk like that, Jean," I said. "That's horrible."

He grinned. "Did you know that some people spontaneously pollute themselves in the electric chair right at the end? How horrible can it be?"

I jolted in my own chair. I considered asking him if he was sorry about what he had done. But the murder now seemed like a bad dream in a distant life. I couldn't very well ask Jean to apologize for something he did inside my dream.

Suddenly two attendants holding large rings with jangling keys came to Jean's side of the window and announced that the visit was over. I noticed they pronounced his name, Gianini, as "Ninny" instead of "Ja-nin-ny." I was upset but Jean seemed used to it. The attendants had eaten the *Zu Zu* snaps that I had brought for Jean and sneered as they handed him the nearly empty box. They grabbed him by the arms and lifted him off the seat. "God bless you, Croaker," Jean said in a breaking voice. "I love you."

The attendants took him away so quickly I could almost see an afterimage of his face in the window. "I love you," I whispered to Jean's ghost. The light was turned off on his side and the image disappeared. "What about the accomplice?" I asked the darkness. The only answer was the distant slamming of an iron bolt.

I mentioned that I spent much time haunting the stacks of books in the library. But I also spent time reading my collection of newspaper clippings about the murder. I had arranged them in chronological order inside the wooden box in my room. Each day I removed one and put it on the wall next to my bed. There it would become my meditation for the day as I read it over and over, scrutinizing the lines for hidden messages about the accomplice. On the following day I would replace the clipping with the next article. The only one I kept up all the time was the picture of Miss Beecher wearing a smile and my favorite dress. If I ever met another teacher like her I would not miss my chance to keep more than her likeness in my bedroom forever.

I paid particular attention to those early accounts of Brainard Wilt's statements to reporters. He seemed nervous. When people are nervous they slip up and either say things they shouldn't or don't say things they should. I looked for both. By the time I finished studying the clippings, I knew everything about Brainard. I read between the lines and knew what he wasn't saying. I knew what he was thinking. I knew what he had done. I knew what he was capable of doing again. It was not some paranoiac imagining; he was dangerous. So each night I set out on my patrol for lumberman Brainard armed with a razor from the barbershop. I told Miss Beecher's picture I had use for it. It was only a weapon for defense, but I knew I would use it without hesitation if need be. I recognized the violent urge I was feeling but excused it under the flag of love for a teacher. After all, this was 1939, war time in Europe again. Nazi spies were already at large in America. So was the killer accomplice. All was fair in love and war. And each morning I returned to my room and apologized to Miss Beecher for failing to find him. She was always there, next to my bed, smiling, reminding me of revenge, haunting me.

After three years, Miss Beecher's picture was yellowing and I could tell she was unhappy with my failure to find the accomplice.

She expected me to do better. I wrote Jean again with news of recent events. Estus Compo had died as had Leon Coonradt. James Dayton Countryman, who owned the boarding house across the street from Jean where Miss Beecher and Ethel Clark had stayed, also passed away. I told Jean the sad news and asked about him. Was he sleeping better? I confessed I wasn't. Could he please tell me about "A"—the code I used for the accomplice? I needed to know. This time I included stamps and a General Delivery return address rather than the barbershop for fear the detectives would try to track me down. Despite the fact that no one had mentioned the detectives for years, I believed they were still looking for me for starting the Herkimer fire.

Jean wrote back and sent two dollars which he wanted me to use to buy flowers for Mrs. Countryman. He said she had always been nice to him and had never laughed, even when Miss Beecher and Ethel Clark made fun of him. I didn't have the heart to write him that Mrs. Countryman had died many years ago. He also wrote that it was finally time to tell me about the "A," which he misunderstood as meaning the "apples." Jean described how he had stopped by my farm to visit but no one was home. He loaded up several bushels of apples in Peck Newman's cutter and drove off. Jean said it was Peck's idea to steal the apples but he was sorry and hoped I would forgive him. This was not the "A" I had in mind, and learning that my best friend would steal from me hurt. I realized it was sometimes difficult if not impossible to communicate with a moron, especially when you happened to be one yourself.

The worst part of World War II for me was the rationing of coffee which began in 1942. Until that time I had been able to keep my headaches under control with coffee as soon as the sparks started to fly across my visual field. The coffee quickly dampened the fire in my brain and helped me read with incredible speed. I drank over thirty cups a day and was like a one man army on a blitzkrieg through the library bookshelves. I also expanded my patrols for the lumberman accomplice by conducting forced marches through the woods around neighboring villages. I had been encouraged by fleeting glimpses in the corner of my eye of a checkered pattern darting around the trees.

The decree to ration coffee was tantamount to a death threat for me. Americans were being asked to use only one cup a day but when I tried this my headaches became unbearable. Uncle Sam received a ration book with stamps for coffee and other items but I refused to register as a member of the household and get my own stamps for fear the detectives would be able to find where I lived. I intended to remain a ghost in official records as well as in the mirror. Uncle Sam managed to trade his gasoline coupons for extra coffee stamps for me but I still cut back on my use, more out of a sense of patriotism than anything else. I hated the Nazis more than any headache. With less coffee I no longer had the energy to conduct my patrols for the accomplice. My reading slowed and I worried how I would ever keep up with the flow of new books arriving at the library daily, let alone get through entire sections of the library I had not yet attacked. Hemingway, Faulkner, and others were all expecting me to read their latest works.

I drank just enough coffee to keep the megrims from completely paralyzing me but the nearly constant pain in my left eye kept me agitated. I had a difficult time sitting still at the library table and became as restless as Jean Gianini at his school desk. It seemed as though I was spending as much time pacing back and forth among the stacks as I did reading. I started doing a strange thing with my right hand. I held my fingers out with the thumb stretched underneath, then began opening and closing the hand like it was a bird trying to talk or chew gum. It became a reflexive response to my pain that was so fast that even if my hand could talk I doubted anyone could have understood such rapid-fire babble. When I did sit at the table I ground my teeth and made little sounds in my throat. This was no good. There was nothing more potentially dangerous than a criminal imbecile who couldn't keep quiet, especially in a library.

One of the newest treatments for such behavior, I had read,

was the lobotomy, a surgical procedure performed by trephining small holes in the skull so that a special wire knife could be inserted into the brain. The surgeon twisted the knife this way and that, like a paint brush, thereby severing the fibers connecting the frontal lobes and cutting off emotions. In 1941, a young moron girl was asked to sing while the surgeon twirled the wire knife in her brain. When the girl stopped singing, he knew the operation had been successful. The problem was that she became so quiet she never sang again and could barely talk. She went from moron to idiot in the stroke of a wire brush.

I was not quite desperate enough to try such a risky procedure, and I investigated other treatments. I was surprised to learn that Dr. Bernstein, who was just a short train ride away in Rome, New York, was reporting much success with morons. He had now opened sixty-two "colonies" for housing morons throughout the state and some of the morons were improving enough to be discharged. Although he had once told me that I would not get better, perhaps he had discovered some way for an incurable like me to at least feel better.

I decided to see Bernstein. First, I wanted to get a new suit so he would realize that I was grown-up even if I had not changed in size. I went to see Nate Meyers who ran a clothing store on South Main Street. Nate was a regular in the barbershop and may have been the only one who knew Uncle Sam was Jewish. The two became friends and, when alone in the shop, they would speak in Yiddish. Sometimes I came out of my room and joined the conversation. Nate was about my height yet I always looked up to him. When Nate had been a vagabond peddler, before he opened the store, he carried his wares in a cart pulled by a blind pony that he had rescued. He loved that animal when no one else did. This made him very tall and special in my eyes.

Now I stood in a back room of Nate's store as he fitted me with a new suit. I wanted a blue one, but all he had in my size was a shiny black three-piece suit that seemed more appropriate for a funeral than a visit to a doctor's office. However, he convinced me that it was the right color and a good fit.

"But do I look like a *mensch*?" I asked him. I had to know if I looked like a decent person.

"It looks good on you," he said.

"Am I a *mensch*?" My voice was loud.

"Don't get your bowels in an uproar. It fits."

"Am I a *mensch*?" I yelled.

He stared. I visualized Dr. Bernstein staring at me. I took off my patch and stared back. Nate turned away. "I'll ring up the total," he said as he hurried to the cash register.

The next day Dr. Bernstein died. My first thought was that somehow I had been responsible for his death by glaring so angrily at the mental image of him in the store. His obituary only mentioned that he had died following a long illness, but why now? Why was this day different from all other days if not for my vicious glare?

I returned to the library and continued reading to the throbbing beat of my headache. One day I noticed a pencil-thin shaft of light fall on the book that was open on my table. I thought someone had moved the curtain on a window and allowed for a ray of light to peek through. When I moved the book slightly, the light followed. I glanced at the window and saw that it was an overcast day, then I looked back at the book. The light was still there, only now it had expanded. It seemed to glow like my memory of the light on Mama's face when she was reading, illuminating the space between my eyes and the pages of the book. The light became so dazzling I could no longer read the words on the center of the page. They simply disappeared. Some partial words on the edges were visible but I couldn't make sense of them because when I moved my eyes to read them, the light followed. The spot of light occurred with both eyes, just like the flashing lights that preceded the megrims, but the spot was so large it wiped out half of my visual field. Wherever I turned and looked it became a searchlight, vaporizing all I gazed upon. It was as if I had looked at the sun too long and was blinded by its brilliance.

Then came a most peculiar terror. As the days passed the spot did not go away, as had always happened with the megrim lights. It became a permanent aspect of the way I saw the world. The light fell on objects and erased parts of them—the leg of a chair, the corner of a shelf, half the front door. I knew they came back when I turned away just as I was certain the words reappeared when I closed a book. After all, they were solid, inanimate objects. But what happened to the people I looked at?

I had always sensed that people were affected by the sight of my eye because they turned away or averted their own eyes. When someone talked to me they did so with sidelong glances, too frightened to look straight at me but nonetheless helpless to keep from staring at my deformity. They knew. Zia Nardone knew. The rabbi who circumcised me knew. I suspected that deep down Mama knew, yet she was always denying it with her endless *"kine-ahoras."* Now there was no denying it. A great change had taken place and the fire that had been kindled in my brain for so many years was now roaring. A malevolent stream of light energy was pouring out through my eye whenever I looked at something. The dazzling truth was right there in front of me, on every page, on every wall, on every face. Now I knew I had the evil eye.

I was actually relieved by this insight. All those strange coincidences were no longer strange or coincidences. The jumbled pieces of my past fell into place and the picture they created explained everything. It explained why bad things happened to those I stared at. The rabbi fell off his horse. Zia Nardone fell down. Jean Gianini lost his freedom. Tony lost his job at the barbershop. Charlie Tom died. Dr. Suiter died. Dr. Bernstein died. My eye, that single part of me that had never stopped growing, had always been malicious and harmful, and now it was deadly.

Zia Nardone had a word for me. She called me a *jettatore*, the wielder of *mal occhio*, the evil eye. As a child, I thought it had been a lie. In her home town of Messina a story was told of a *jettatore* whose glance was so fatal that he was struck dead when he accidentally caught a glimpse of himself in a large mirror. Zia knew a *jettatore* when she saw one. They could be identified by stigmata which distinguished them from other human beings: a thin, sallow face; deep-set eyes; a big hooked nose. I had all those features. This explained why I could never look at myself in the mirror. A terrible seizure always knocked me down. As an orthodox Jew I believed that the soul was reflected in the mirror. I no longer saw my reflection because I no longer had a soul. I had looked in the mirror and killed myself. Who would be next?

18

I did not accept my fate as a *jettatore* without a fight. I fought against the evil that had invaded my eye with the same panicked desperation that my distant relatives in Russia were mustering against the Nazi evil that was invading their land. I nailed a horseshoe over my door. Each morning I spit three times on my chest. I even placed a lock of my hair in the barbershop spittoon so others might help drown my evil. I made it a point to wear my underwear inside out. I carried a packet of salt in my pants. It was unclear if such folktale measures would keep me from hurting someone else but they certainly did nothing to stop my own pain.

When coffee rationing ended in July 1943, I immediately resumed drinking as much as possible. The coffee kept most of the megrims at bay but there was now a constant throbbing over my left temple that seemed to keep pace with my pounding heart. The bird in my hand was constantly jabbering. The dazzling spot of light never went away. The new moon looked anything but new. When I tried to resume my patrols for the accomplice, the light prevented me from finding my way, let alone the elusive lumberman. After I got lost in the woods for two days, I shut down the patrols. I explained to Miss Beecher's picture that it was only a temporary setback. I vowed I would still catch the accomplice. And each night her picture watched as I sharpened the razor.

I mentioned that I could no longer read but that was not exactly accurate. I could still read a few things such as large newspaper headlines, but anything printed in smaller type would take many minutes for me to read. Even a single line was difficult as I would have to constantly move my head back and forth across the page in order to glimpse a letter at a time. It was an awkward, frustrating way to read and neither I nor the bird had any patience for it. We were much more at ease looking at picture books in the children's reading room or flipping through magazines.

Sometimes I would read the headlines from out-of-town newspapers or browse through magazines at the In & Out Shop on Main Street. The shop was the size of a large closet and almost as dark. There was barely enough room to walk in, grab something from the overfilled display racks, and walk out. George, who sat on a stool behind a small counter with a Camel cigarette in his mouth and his dog, Caesar, at his feet, let me browse for as long as I wanted.

One day he pointed to a display rack hidden behind the door. "I got some new funny books over there," he said. "Go take a look."

That was how I discovered comic books. They were easy for me to read because they told stories with pictures and the few words were printed in large letters. But most comic books showed silly animals doing stupid things. They seemed to be written for idiots. There was one worthwhile series, Classic Comics, that appeared to be picture stories based on real books, some of which I had read. They were only ten cents so I gathered up a handful. I also bought a small book of cartoons that cost thirty-five cents but it had my name on it and I had to have it: *Little Moron*.

Back in my room I stared at the cover of *Little Moron*. It showed a caricature of a boy with an uncanny resemblance to Jean Gianini, complete with protruding ears, dark hair and eyes, and a mindless grin. The cartoons that followed were either stupid or sick or both. One featured the little moron shooting his parents with a shotgun. The text read: "Do you know why the little moron killed his mom and pop? So he could go to the orphans' picnic!" Sick. The last pages contained caricatures of the little moron's father, mother, brother, and sister. They all had protruding ears, dark eyes, and big grins. It was a family tree that Dr. Goddard and his Nazi eugenicists would love to cut down. I hated the book. There was nothing funny about depicting morons as idiots.

I turned to the Classic Comic books and selected *A Tale of Two Cities*. The blue cover depicted a handsome man standing before a huge guillotine, a priest to his side and the executioner holding a rope behind him. There was a look of brave resignation on the face of the condemned man. It was a mesmerizing scene, more vivid and heroic than I had pictured when I first read the novel by Charles Dickens.

The story took place in the period before and during the French Revolution and the Reign of Terror. There were many interesting characters but the only one I cared about was Lucie Manette, a beautiful girl with long dark hair like Mama's. Lucie appeared on the second page of the comic wearing a blue dress which she had obviously put on for me. The last panel of the comic showed her in a crimson dress, as if stained by the bloody events that had transpired during the intervening years.

Between the blue and red dresses had been many executions by guillotine. The executions were always accompanied by the carmagnole, a wild demonic dance performed by the crowd. A large panel showed the dance. Men and women were moving furiously, spinning around, waving their arms, clutching at one another, screaming and singing. It was a dance of raving lunatics that only stopped when participants dropped in sheer exhaustion. I studied the indistinct faces of the commoners in the mad crowd. I thought I recognized a withered hag standing in the middle of the street, shaking her fist and screaming. Yes, it was Zia Nardone. My throat tightened.

I closed the book and stared at the cover again. Why did they call it a funny book? I wondered. I saw fresh blood dripping on the cover and realized that my hand was bleeding from where I had gnawed open an old wound.

In 1943, Robert Frost was awarded his fourth Pulitzer Prize for a collection of new poems entitled *A Witness Tree*. Uncle Sam was so excited he gave me a copy at supper one evening. I didn't have the heart to tell him I could no longer read the narrow columns of words in poems, but I thanked him as I tried to divine the contents by studying the drawing of a tree on the dust jacket. I peeked under the dust jacket and noticed that the cloth boards were blue. I looked at the tree again. The tree had gnarled bare branches like a willow in winter and it seemed to be bending ever so slightly toward the reader as if to whisper a secret. Here and there were blood-red brush strokes pooling around the trunk. I felt a cold wind start to blow through the branches of my mind. It filled my ears with a doleful moan.

"Noble, you're crying!" Uncle Sam said.

"My eye is bothering me again," I said as I excused myself and returned to my room.

The war ended and the Nazi octopus was finally defeated. I was hopeful that it might be safe to celebrate so I went to see a traveling carnival that came to a field on the outskirts of Herkimer. There was a small midway with a Ferris wheel, games of chance, cotton candy and other treats. Everyone seemed to be enjoying the sights and no one seemed to notice me as I walked around wearing my driving goggles and licking an ice cream cone.

I came upon a group of men crowded around a woman who was standing on a small platform. Her face was painted with heavy makeup, her hair was an ill-fitting wig the color and consistency of straw, and she wore a thin, silky outfit that exposed her navel and hips which she moved rhythmically back and forth. Folds of fat moved with them.

A barker invited the men to come inside a small tent to see her show. The first to line up was a young man wearing a lumberman overshirt. He appeared to be in his teens, too young to be the accomplice but I wanted to ask if he knew lumberman Brainard Wilt. I lined up with the others, paid fifty cents, and entered the tent where I stood next to him, waiting for a chance to talk. The woman dancer stepped onto a stage to the cheers and applause of the crowd. She began moving her hips again, turning in circles. "Take it off," someone shouted. The men clapped. The dancer smiled, took off her scarf and moved it over her hips. She looked directly at me and blew me a kiss. I dropped my ice cream cone and watched as she removed her top, exposing her bare breasts. A memory from infancy flashed in my mind.

"Mama!" I cried.

The woman smirked, tried to restrain herself, then burst out laughing. The crowd turned to me, gawking and laughing.

"The shrimp's an imbecile," said a tall man.

"I am not an i-em-bee-sill. I'm a moron."

The crowd pushed and shoved me. Invisible tentacles wrapped around my neck, choking me. The crowd threw me to the ground and began pulling off my clothes. The packet of salt fell from my pants and spilled open.

"Look!" the tall man shouted. "He's wearing his underwear inside out!"

Everyone howled with laughter as I gathered my clothes and ran all the way home.

On the first Fourth of July after the war I lay in bed and listened to people setting off fireworks in nearby Myers Park. I had my own, a star-spangled headache that left my white sheets striped with blood from my bitten lips. I didn't think I would ever have peace.

After World War II there was a big increase in commitments of people to asylums and mental hospitals. By 1948, the number of morons was growing at an alarming rate. Everyone, including me, was desperate to find new treatments.

I developed my own method to temporarily relieve both the

ever growing pain and the agitation. I filled up the sink in my room with ice-cold water and submerged my head. The cold numbed my head as I took the opportunity to clean the folds of tissue around my eye. I repeatedly dunked my head, each time holding my breath as long as I could. If I did this long enough, the numbness would last so I could get to sleep.

By this time the lobotomy had been perfected and thousands of morons were being operated on throughout America and in other countries. The reason for the new popularity was the use of an old tool: the ice-pick. The surgeon would insert the ice-pick into the roof of the eye socket and tap it with a hammer. This would cause the pick to puncture the skin and thin bone, then plunge directly into the brain. A swing of the pick would sever the prefrontal lobe. The entire procedure was over in the time it took you to say "Zip-a-dee-doo-dah," one of the popular songs that year. But singing it yourself afterwards was another matter.

I tried to imagine what the operation would be like and found my father's ice-pick in the tool box. His initials, "A.Z.," were carved on the wooden handle. I ran my fingers over the letters and then smelled the wood, remembering a time when all I wanted to do with the tool was to help Papa chop ice for making my favorite vanilla ice cream. Now I took the pick and held it along the side of my head. It was longer than my skull. If someone were to insert it into my eye, the point could penetrate my entire brain and come out the back. If my problems all stemmed from a scar on my brain as Dr. Cole had told me as a child, I didn't understand how making another scar could help. I was suffering from a nerve storm, a fire in my brain. Even a moron knew that sticking a poker into a fire only stirred things up. It made sense to keep soaking my head.

Perhaps things might have been different if I had gone to one of the asylums that Dr. Cole had recommended. Things certainly would have been different if he had used the phenol on me instead of on the mess I made in his office. I shuddered with embarrassment at the memory of vomiting in front of him. I certainly would never have developed an evil eye if Zia Nardone had had her way. The witch was always threatening to break my eye or "wall me," which I had since learned meant burying me alive inside the wall of a building. I shuddered again, this time burning with enough anger to almost ignite the friction matches in my pocket. It was impossible to rest with questions about a Nazi sympathizer and an evil midwife tormenting me.

I found myself on the next train to Poland. I now wanted to find Dr. Cole and ask him if he had ever told the Nazis about the phenol. I also wanted to see Professor Robinson. He had testified at the trial that he had done nothing wrong by whipping Jean with a rubber hose. I had read that he was now the superintendent of schools, ordering similar punishment for hundreds of pupils throughout the entire school district. I wanted to save these kids from such cruelty and tell the Professor that it was time to retire. As I remembered the pain from his rubber hose, I feared he might try to whip me again, so I put the razor in my pocket for protection.

When I arrived at the Poland station I walked directly to Dr. Cole's old office. But there I learned he had moved to Inlet, near Old Forge, sixteen years earlier. He had died recently but nobody could tell me how. I wondered if inhaling fumes from phenol for all the years he had used it as an antiseptic could have had anything to do with his death. If Dr. Cole had actually told the Nazis about phenol, then such a death was just.

I knew that when adults return to childhood places everything appears smaller than remembered because, of course, they have grown. But Poland seemed the same to me. The Hotel Carlton was still standing and seemed just as big as ever, although the name was now the Kuyahoora Inn. I was sad to see that the Poland Union Store was closed but the building looked the same. As I pressed my face against the boarded window I could almost see Mr. Lamb handing out samples of candy to Jean and myself as we stood gawking at the glass cases. Of course there were many modern changes in town but none made me feel like I had grown. Instead, they confirmed the fact that I was truly arrested in my development. The old covered

Cameroon Bridge over West Canada Creek where Jean and I had played had been destroyed. But I stood there and watched a memory of Jean and me holding hands and jumping into the water. We were both arrested now, caught in the currents of the past with no bridge to the future.

Another thing that hadn't changed was my old schoolmate Nicholas' house. The front steps still needed repair, I realized as I climbed up to the porch and rang the doorbell. When Nicholas came to the door to greet me, I saw he was emaciated with lusterless eyes and a hollow-chested posture. He had a shock of white hair and an equally shocking drool in the corner of his mouth. I handed him the copy of Rev. Stall's book on the dangers of masturbation and apologized for not returning it sooner. He said he didn't mind and from the looks of him the damage had already been done.

"I have something for you," Nicholas said. He went to a drawer and returned with a large monkey wrench. I began to tremble uncontrollably.

"I found it on Buck Hill Road when I went to look at Miss Beecher's body," Nicholas said. "I wanted it for a souvenir. I cleaned it real good," he explained, turning the wrench over. "That's when I saw the letters." He pointed to the initials "A.Z." scratched on the handle, then handed the wrench to me.

I was unprepared for the weight which caused my open hand to sink like an anchor. Memories began to bubble up from an ancient well. "It belonged to my father," I said. "When I was moving everything to Herkimer, the wagon hit a bump and a box fell on the road. The wrench must have fallen out of the box." It must have, I repeated to myself. I remembered there had been another wrench at the trial.

"I thought it was the murder weapon. It was covered with crud, like bl—"

"Rust," I corrected. I had to force the word past the lump in my throat. "It was always getting wet and rusty from fixing our well pump."

"Then it's yours. Keep it."

"Thanks."

I left in a daze and allowed my feet to carry me around the village until the sun was setting. I had forgotten about wanting to see Professor Robinson. I still had a little time before the night train left for Herkimer so I took a walk up Buck Hill Road. As I climbed the steep grade the wrench swung in my hand like a pump. Memories began to trickle out from some underground vault. The wrench fell from my hand. I picked it up and brushed off clumps of dirt, unearthing yet more buried memories. Now I remembered holding another wrench, one that was much larger and heavier, on Buck Hill the night of the murder. I knew that larger wrench had been the murder weapon. The willow trees had witnessed it all. I stopped at the bend in the road and gazed at the willows, watching images rushing across my mind with all the force of reality.

I was walking down Buck Hill to find Jean in order to say goodbye. I looked at the setting sun and had a seizure. When I recovered it was dark. I was still woozy and continued down the hill. There were voices in the fog. "I won't go any further," Miss Beecher said. I moved closer to the two figures in the mist. Jean was there and saw me. "Croaker," he smiled. I waved, more out of habit than anything else. Then he took a wrench from his pocket and struck her. She fell to the ground with her hands raised. Her mouth was open as if to say something. He leaned over and stabbed. I could not believe what I was seeing. I stared at her shoes as her feet kicked again and again, like a little bird with broken wings flapping helplessly on the ground. Jean grabbed her legs and pulled her into the woods. He motioned to me with a finger and I followed hesitantly. Her face appeared covered with deep cuts. Her hand was pointing at something like a red ribbon around her neck. She made an awful sound. Jean ran away. I knelt beside her, took her hand and held it, noting the fineness of the skin. Her eyes were looking up, questioning me. Air rushed from the ribbon. "Don't die," I heard myself whisper. I put her bloody hand on my head. "*Ziskeit,*" I said, patting my hair with her hand. My hand was trembling; hers was lifeless. Blood seeped invisibly through her red dress, then steamed when it reached the frozen ground. I moved her under the apple tree and adjusted her raincoat. I picked up the huge wrench from the road where Jean had dropped it. When I saw hair and pieces of flesh on it, I threw it to the side. Then I retched so hard I gave myself another seizure. I walked back to the farm in a daze.

Now my eyes were wide open in terror as I rode the night train back to Herkimer. I had discovered the unprettified truth that, unlike all my previous dreams and imaginings about the night Miss Beecher died, this had been my real memory. The bird was flapping its mouth, trying to say something. I hit the bird with Father's wrench over and over again. I wanted to break its neck so it could never tell anyone about the accomplice it rode with on the train, the one who once had his teacher's blood on his hair, the one who now had her blood on his hands. Oh, my agitated heart.

I said my prayers that night inside my room. All night. In the morning I put on the *tefillin*, wrapping the leather thongs around my arm and forehead as tight as humanly possible. They were still not tight enough. I retied them around my neck. Yes, here they could be pulled even tighter. I kept pulling, furiously spinning around, waving my arms and clutching at the air, jumping up and down, dancing a mad demonic dance as Miss Beecher's picture watched. Voices screamed the charges: "Accomplice!" "Pervert!" "Monster!" The crowd roared in my ears as blackness descended.

19

My hand was broken and so was I. I noticed that my middle finger was permanently curled and useless. Although it hurt to hold the broom, I refused to see a doctor. But I felt an urgency to write Jean. He had never snitched on me. It was the ultimate act of charity and friendship. Yet it still troubled me that he had never apologized for the murder. I couldn't figure out what to say to him. Then I realized that it didn't matter because I discovered that my hand could no longer hold a pen and write. My wrist and fingers didn't seem to work that way. Perhaps it was just as well; Jean knew what we had done. And if I confessed my role, then I, too, would be locked up in Matteawan. More words were not about to free either of us from the moron curse. Perhaps when I died someone would cut off my middle finger and preserve it in a museum as had happened to Galileo's finger. Mine should be labeled "Noble's Revenge," and it would be my last wish that all alienists be forced to look at it.

The roar in my brain never went away. It had always reminded me of the roar of the ocean inside a seashell. Now I feared the shell itself would not hold up to the constant stress. Every so often I heard a crack like the sound of a walnut shell splitting open. It was sharp, painful, and it was followed by the sound of air rushing in my ears. I feared that my head would soon shatter. Whenever I heard a crack I made it a point to remember exactly where I was and what I was doing. Those cracks punctuated the only important events in the empty shell of my life.

The cracks began when Dr. Henry Goddard's newest book, *Our Children in the Atomic Age*, arrived in the library in late 1948. The blinding spot of light was expanding so fast that it took me until 1949 just to make out the first few pages. Goddard's book had blue cloth boards, although the blue was so dark it could have been mistaken for Nazi black. His purpose in writing the book was to tell parents how they could insure the success of their children and help build a better race, born and bred for the new world of the atomic age. "We must have men, big men and many of them," he wrote. Big men, of course, excluded little Hebrew morons like me. "One world or none," the great Goddard wrote. He might just as well have written "*Alles für Deutschland!*"

After deciphering these introductory words I finally lost the ability to continue reading small print. It was impossible to read the twenty pages of tiny text in the book's appendix where Goddard reproduced the complete Binet-Simon Measuring Scale for Intelligence, the exact same test he had given to Jean Gianini. There were additional pages describing the testing procedure and scoring. I might have taken the test and finally determined my true intelligence but God didn't want me to know and blinded me with his light.

I still enjoyed looking at the Classic Comic book versions of great literature but I missed being able to read the text in the talk balloons. Colors were also a problem. The spot of light was washing out the hues, turning everything into shades of gray. I was reduced to viewing the stories as still scenes from a silent movie in black and white. Life seemed just as bleak. The world was moving forward into an atomic age of motion pictures in full color and I was falling backwards to a more primitive level of existence.

In the summer of 1949, I picked up a copy of *The Hunchback of Notre Dame* Classic Comic at the In & Out Shop. George thumbed through the book as I paid for it.

"This guy looks like a moron," he chuckled. "What's the story about?"

I had never read the novel by Victor Hugo so I just shrugged and waited for him to hand the comic back.

Inside the library, I put the comic on the table and tried to make sense of the story. The hunchback looked a little like me: short in stature with chestnut hair and a deformed left eye. He wore a blue tunic throughout the story. People made fun of him, threw things at him, even whipped and tortured him. A lovely girl gave him some water to drink while he was being tortured. I could tell from the way he looked at her that he wanted to marry her. Later, she was sentenced to the gallows but he rescued her and carried her to the cathedral where he fed and clothed her, and even gave her his bed. She kissed him for his kindness. At the end, soldiers stormed the cathedral. The hunchback fought bravely but fell from the bell tower to his death. He had died protecting the girl, who managed to escape and marry a handsome, normal man. George had been correct. The hunchback did look like a moron yet he acted like a saint.

Crack!

In August 1949, the earth shook. I felt it inside my head. The headline in the paper confirmed it: "**ECUADOR QUAKE KILLS 4,000.**" There had been a gigantic fault. My fault.

A few weeks later I saw a meteor shower in the night sky while saying my prayers. I must have angered God by causing the quake. Why else would he be throwing stones at me? If one hit me, it would surely crack my shell wide open. I knew I could no longer trust a God who allowed a moron to go crackers. I stopped praying and set out on a walk around the village.

I ended up in front of the Quackenbush Factory. The yard was littered with scrap metal used for making nutcrackers. I recalled that the court clerk in the Gianini trial which condemned Jean to the nuthouse was a Quackenbush. And it occurred to me that the family had been conspiring to crack open nuts ever since. I walked around the factory, listening to the machinery inside. The stamping sounds were making my head pound. It was the worst hell. They had obviously perfected a machine to crack nuts like me with sound alone.

Crack!

On a hot September day while I was trying to hold my head together with several handkerchiefs, a Herkimer woman called Mrs. Weinberg, who came regularly to see Uncle Sam, brought her son into the barbershop. Her son's hair didn't grow as fast as her visits but that didn't stop her from coming in and asking Uncle Sam to fix a few hairs she insisted he missed the last time. "Fix it and don't charge me," she always said with a coquettish wink and smile. Her real purpose was to flirt with Uncle Sam. He enjoyed the attention and went along with the game.

The little boy climbed into the chair and Uncle Sam gave him a Mickey Mouse comic book from the stack he kept for kids. The black Maxwell automobile had been sold years before to make room for customers to park their own cars and the comic books worked just as well to keep the little boys entertained.

"I'm getting a *shtunk* from the colony," Mrs. Weinberg bragged. "That will give me more time to visit with you, Sam," she winked.

The Rome State School, the new name for the asylum started by the late Dr. Bernstein, had recently purchased the old Lanthrop Mansion on North Main Street in Herkimer and had opened a colony there as a residence for female patients. The women slept in the mansion but were available to work during the day in private homes as domestics. Most worked for wealthy families in the village and it was a sign of high status to have a "colony girl" in your home. All the women were mentally deficient to varying degrees and most were morons, but none were *shtunks*. This was a vulgar Yiddish word that implied the person was a fool, a dope, a jerk. I hated the word. You had to practically fill your mouth with spit to pronounce it properly. I also hated the fact that Uncle Sam ignored it and pretended he didn't understand Yiddish. The little boy knew. He held his nose when his mother said the word. Her ignorant prejudice was being transmitted to her child like a virus.

The few hairs on the boy's head were "fixed" and he jumped off the chair with the comic book. His mother put her high-heel shoe on the footrest of the chair, hiked up her tight skirt and adjusted her stockings, smiling and flirting with Uncle Sam. Meanwhile, the boy wandered around the shop and suddenly was looking through the crack in the door at me! His face was only inches from my own.

"Hi," he smiled.

I was caught totally by surprise. "Hi," I said.

He ran to his mother and tugged on her coat. "Mommy, Mommy. I saw a little pirate."

She turned and smacked him across the face. "Don't interrupt," she said, and raised her hand to hit him again.

I rushed from my room and stood between the two of them, glaring at her.

She turned to Uncle Sam. "What's with this *dreck*?" she asked.

I was enraged. She was calling me a piece of shit and not even looking at me.

"Hey, lady," I yelled.

She turned around, her face full of disgust. I raised my patch and bit her with my eye. She gasped.

"Go back to your room, Noble," Uncle Sam said sternly.

As I shuffled to my door I heard him whisper. "I'm sorry about that, Mrs. Weinberg. He's a moron."

"He's *dreck*. He should drop dead," she said as she grabbed the boy's hand and pulled him out of the shop.

As they left, the little boy turned and waved to me. "Bye," he said.

I waved back. I liked the boy because he didn't cry but I still worried about what would become of him. It broke my heart that Uncle Sam no longer worried about what would become of me. He knew that I had become a moron.

Crack!

An atomic bomb was getting ready to explode in my brain and I could feel the pressure. My eye had already turned into a mushroom cloud and I knew my head would be next. The headaches were getting so bad I could no longer hold down the coffee. The headlines didn't help: **"RUSSIAN ATOMIC EXPLOSION SPARKS RACE FOR WEAPONS. FUTURE OF**

CIVILIZATION MAY HANG ON OUTCOME." I tried to make light of the situation by creating a little moron-type joke: Why didn't the little moron worry when the headline said everyone's head was going to be on the line? Because he didn't have one!

It hurt to laugh. It hurt even more not to. God in heaven, did it hurt.

Crack!

A terrific thunderstorm woke me up. For a moment I feared that atomic war had started. I sat up in bed feeling terribly alone and guilty that my eye might have been responsible. I felt like a Gorgon, one of those hideous monsters of Greek mythology who lived alone on an island because their gaze was so power-ful it would turn people to stone. Then it started to rain. I saw lightning through the window—Zeus was hurling thunderbolts from the heavens. Perseus, his son, had once managed to approach one of the Gorgons, Medusa, and cut off her head by the trick of looking at her reflection in the mirror of his shield. Later, when the storm cleared, I went outside into the alley to look for the constellation Perseus to pray for him to come down and Medusa me before I turned all the people I ever knew into tombstones.

Crack!

In the fall the Nobel Prizes were announced. My headache should have won one. William Faulkner won for literature. I never did get around to reading him. Dr. Egas Moniz, who developed the lobotomy, won the Nobel Prize for Medicine. There were five thousand lobotomies performed that year in America. That made five thousand and one people who would never read Faulkner.

By that time I was questioning my ability to read even Classic Comics. I had one open on the table in the library and kept flip-ping the pages back and forth as I tried to piece together the story. There was very little action in the panels, just a lot of char-acters talking. Since I couldn't read the text, I had no idea what they were saying. I was so confused and frustrated that I was tearing the pages as I turned them.

"It would make more sense to read the book," a voice said.

"I like to look at the pictures," I said. Then I realized that someone had just sat down across from me. Nobody ever sat at my table in the library and nobody ever talked to me. I quickly covered my exposed eye with my hand, lifted my head from the book, and looked across at her.

She looked like a young girl with her perfectly smooth skin and short black hair. Her most interesting feature was her narrow eyes. They appeared slightly Oriental. She looked like one of the Mongoloid idiots I had seen walking around the enclosed grounds of the colony on North Main Street. Goddard said a Mongoloid idiot was like a pet and should be kept inside like a cat or bird. They didn't let them out, so what was she doing in the library?

"You don't mind if I sit here do you? You seem a bit old to be looking at comic books. Wouldn't you like to read the actual book?"

Why was she talking to me? Why was she asking so many questions? Was she a detective? The bird resting in my hand started to tremble.

"You do know how to read, don't you?"

She was still grilling me. I uncovered my eye and faced her. "Girlie, do I look like an idiot?"

The girl looked but said nothing. The shape of her eyes made it appear she was squinting, which I knew was an expression of distaste. I was bothered by her haughty attitude.

"Say something. Don't you see anything wrong with my face?"

"Well, you do have a big nose," she finally said with a smile.

I put the patch back on my eye. She was trying to be friendly now. Was she a Mata Hari spy after my secret? Had she been sent on a mission to unmask the accomplice? Was she searching for the arsonist who had set the Herkimer fire? Would she try to seduce me? My hand was shaking.

"I've upset you," she said as she reached across the table and placed her hand on mine. "I'm sorry. I ask too many questions. Sometimes I act like I'm still in school."

Her hand was soft and warm. The tremor stopped and immediately moved into my heart.

"Look," she said, holding up a shiny Mercury dime in the fingers of her other hand. "I'll pay for my mistake." She put the dime under the table and rapped it three times against the underside. Then she withdrew her hand, turned it over and showed me that the dime was gone. "You have it now," she said.

I didn't understand.

She removed her other hand from mine. "Look under your hand."

I picked up my hand. The dime was there on the table! It was a wonderful effect but I considered the possibility that she was playing a trick on a moron just for the laughs.

She smiled. "I use magic tricks in my class at school to keep the pupils interested."

It was difficult to believe she was a school teacher. She looked so young. "How old are you?" I asked.

"I was born in the year of the rabbit," she said. "The Chinese calendar uses twelve different animals, one for each year. What year were you born?"

"1897."

She scratched her head and counted to herself. "The year of the rooster," she announced. "That's good. Roosters are not afraid to speak their mind."

But roosters are imbeciles, just like chickens, I thought. "I prefer to think of myself as being born in the Hebrew year of 5658," I said. This always made me feel that I had been born old.

"See, you are a rooster," she smiled. Her eyes narrowed even further. "You say what you think."

"Are you a rabbit?" I asked. I was fascinated by her eyes.

"Yes. Rabbits are lucky and happy."

Except when they lost their feet, I thought.

She continued, "And they have many children, which I want some day." She went on to explain the cycle of animals used in the Chinese calendar. I calculated that she had been born in 1927, which made her twenty-two, the same age Miss Beecher had been when she died. But this girl didn't look at all like her. She was shorter than my teacher and closer to my size. Her face had both Chinese and American features. If Lucy Burrows and the Yellow Man had had a daughter, she would have looked exactly like this girl sitting across from me in the library. Was it possible that Lillian Gish and the actor who played the Yellow Man had actually had a child? Suddenly I wanted to know everything about her. Was her father Chinese? Was her Mama an American actress? But I asked nothing. Her mere presence satisfied all my desires for the moment.

When she finished her long explanation about the calendar, I suggested I call her Miss Rabbit.

"Okay. But shouldn't I have a first name?"

"Lucy. Miss Lucy Rabbit."

She smiled and bowed her head slightly. "Pleased to meet you. And you are?"

"Noble," I nodded. "But my best friend calls me Croaker."

Lucy Rabbit appeared puzzled.

"Because of the eye," I said. "Looks like a croaker."

"Why not Cyrano de Bergerac because of the way your nose looks?" she smiled.

She seemed impressed when I recognized the reference and laughed. Then we laughed together.

After she left the library I studied the dime. Mercury was wearing a little cap with wings, which was supposed to symbolize freedom of thought. My thoughts were freely flying all over the place. I rubbed the coin and it was her hand I was touching. The magic was continuing. I put the dime in my pocket and it was she I wanted to put in a place that was all mine, to touch and feel whenever I wanted. I would never spend such a coin. It would be my lucky keepsake. I would keep it, shine it, and protect it always. And I would never let anyone else have it.

20

Lucy Rabbit came to the library almost every afternoon after school. I watched her enter the foyer, take off her winter coat, then hang it on a hook on the wall. She would turn to the opposite wall and face a small mirror which she used to brush the snow from her hair and adjust her clothing.

When she gazed into the mirror there was a special look on her face, a look of inner reflection. She brushed her bangs with her fingers or fiddled with a gold necklace holding a single pearl, all the while seemingly tinkering with some inner dream. What did she dream about? There were a few clues. She had mentioned she wanted to have children and she was at the age when it was almost past the time to start, especially considering the fact that she had said "many"children. Every now and then she would stop moving and freeze in the mirror. Hers was the look of innocence wishing to lose itself. For a brief moment she was probably dreaming about the man she would marry.

Did she see me in that dream? I was certain she did, because every so often she would notice me watching her and a smile would creep onto her face. Then she would gather her books and papers and come into the reading room. She had a choice of seats but always chose to sit at my table, directly across from me. It was not an accident. She pretended to be just a friendly patron in the library but I knew. The mirror had betrayed her intentions. Her pretense was for others.

She worked silently, grading papers, preparing lessons, often with the tip of a pencil resting alluringly on her lip. I brought books from my room—not comic books but novels, some in Russian. I had read all of them before so if she asked me about them I could tell her without appearing to be an idiot. She never did ask but I was always prepared. When she worked I pretended to read, all the while studying her, inhaling her smells, listening to the pattern of her breathing, deciphering her mystery. I kept my patch on in order to avoid accidentally biting her with my eye. Besides, I didn't need the eye to read books I had already read. A sudden glance from my other eye was all I needed to see what she was doing. If she caught me looking, so much the better. Such darting eye movements were more likely to inspire a love interest than the steady glare of my croaker.

Of course we talked a little, but long conversations were unnecessary. We only had to say hello and sit at the table. Our relationship was more like a silent movie, the thoughts and feelings fully visible without the need for words. When she asked where I lived I considered saying "I dwell in a lonely house," a line from the poem "Ghost House" by Robert Frost. But I simply said "Here" because it was only here with her that I felt alive.

One day she asked if I liked movies. I did not want to lie so I explained that I could no longer attend movies because of my eye but that Lillian Gish was still my favorite movie actress. Lucy Rabbit said that her all-time favorite was *Snow White and the Seven Dwarfs*, the Disney animated feature she had seen as a child. As she told me about the movie I had the strangest feeling that my fingers were slipping through the pages of the book on my table. I saw the pencil in her hand bending like rubber. Everything was fading. A peculiar odor filled my nostrils. I struggled to ignore all this and concentrate on her voice but I kept feeling like I was drifting away, almost as if Mama was reading a bedtime story and I was going off to slumberland. I didn't catch everything Lucy Rabbit said but even an idiot could figure out why the movie was her favorite. She longed to be kissed by a handsome prince who would give her many children. When she finished talking she smiled at me. The smile was a kiss that brought me back from my momentary spell, waking me from my own long sleep. I was as happy as a dwarf who had just been patted on the head by Snow White.

When Lucy Rabbit left the library that day, I searched her place at the table for the source of the strange happenings. She had left behind a pencil but there was nothing rubbery about it. Was she just playing another trick on me or was the blot on my brain acting up? I looked everywhere and when I came to her seat I detected something very telling. The seat had been impregnated with her smell. That night I knew it was time to remove the vice grip.

Unfortunately that did nothing to relieve the pressure and pain inside my head in the days that followed. Eventually my headache became so bad that my walk turned into a permanent shuffle, as I had to stop every few paces to hold my head. One day I was looking down in agony when I noticed a quarter on the sidewalk. It seemed to be moving all by itself, yet there was no wind, only waves of pain inside my cracking head. I picked up the coin and it changed into a bottle cap. It wasn't the first time that something like this had happened. I remembered Lucy Rabbit's pencil bending. And I often saw bottles on the counter in the barbershop lean over as if to fall, then quickly right themselves. Maybe Lucy Rabbit's magic was continuing after all. My head was spinning and extraordinary things were happening to ordinary objects all around me. This must have been what people meant by the expression "crazy in love." I put the bottle cap in my pocket in case it changed back into a quarter.

I stopped at the In & Out Shop to browse the girlie magazines, a new interest sparked by the removal of my vice grip. The pictures were exciting and much better than the ones in the medical textbooks in the library. I opened a magazine on the floor and lowered my head, scanning the photos by moving my eye back and forth only inches from the page. My back was to George so he couldn't see my eye.

"Are you going to lick it or buy it?" George asked.

I lowered my patch and took the magazine to the counter.

He thumbed through the pages. "Glad to see you're finally graduating from the funny books. You know what I'd like to do with this one?" He pointed to a woman with her legs spread open.

I shrugged. Then George told me in lurid detail all the things he would do. There was not one part of her anatomy that he would leave untouched. I pointed to pictures of several other women and asked what he would do to each of them. He told me. I learned all about sex that day in the In & Out Shop. Later that night I began practicing with the magazine.

Lucy Rabbit was arousing more than my desire to sit at a table with her. I wanted to know if my feelings were reciprocated. Her eyes could tell me but I couldn't see them. When she first looked at my bad eye without a twinge of fear, I knew it was possible she could trust me. Now I sensed she might love me and might soon desire to consummate our relationship. But I had to see her pupils to know for certain. Did they open up into dark receptive pools that could hold my gaze and welcome me, or did they narrow into pinpricks of unease that would cause her to turn away? True lovers would be able to hold each other in their stare.

Her Oriental eyes were the problem. There was an extra flap of skin over the upper eyelid that gave her a Mongoloid slant. This I knew had been the evolutionary adaptation of her ancestors to icy conditions, a shield of flesh against the cold. Her eyes were so well shielded I could not make out the color, let alone the pupil.

The need for the Oriental eye to be protected from the cold suggested a possible solution to penetrating her shield: a reversal of temperature conditions. If Lucy Rabbit's eyelids had grown to insulate her from the cold, perhaps applying a little heat might cause the flaps to recede, thereby uncovering the pupils. Voices inside my head made crazy suggestions. Burn her a little and those little slanted eyes will open up real big. Nothing like a little incendiarism to incite passion. "Stop," I shouted, shaking my head as if to rid my ears of evil. A moron's fascination with fire was one thing, but burning a girl alive for some erotic interest was medieval. I could picture her eyes wide-open in fear, like Lucy Burrows' horrified look inside the closet in *Broken Blossoms,* or Henriette on the guillotine in *Orphans of the Storm.* These pictures suggested another solution. If I could get her inside a dark closet or other scary place, her eyes might just open enough so that I could see if she truly loved me and would marry me. I decided to wait for such an opportunity.

Lucy Rabbit was busy with her own plan. Christmas was approaching and she was going to put on a magic show for her pupils and their parents on the day before Christmas. One of the parents had donated the use of a meeting hall. I could tell Lucy was a little nervous. She told me that she had just purchased a large boxed set of magic tricks at Play World, a big toy store in Utica, but she still didn't have enough tricks to fill out a long program. Fortunately, she owned several volumes of the *Tarbell Course in Magic,* which contained instructions on how to make and perform hundreds of tricks. She brought these to the library and began making a list of the ones she would put in the show, occasionally describing the effect and seeking my reaction.

I had never seen a magic show so everything she described was fascinating to me. She wanted to start with a big production trick known as "The Temple Screen." This was a three-panel screen, each panel about a foot square and decorated with handsome Chinese calligraphy. The screen was shown on both sides, then folded into a triangle. A tap of the wand and she would pull out dozens of colorful silks and let them float over the stage like a rainbow. The silks would be used in the next series of tricks. Some would be tied in knots and mysteriously untie themselves. Others would change colors in her hand or disappear, only to be replaced by eggs or colored balls. Finally, everything would disappear back inside the screen. This sounded unbelievable and I begged her to show me. She accepted my enthusiasm as approval of the opening routine but insisted I wait for the show itself.

Next, she would illustrate a series of truly mystifying effects. One was "The Enchanted Paper," a piece of colored tissue paper that would keep appearing and disappearing in her hand or in a handkerchief. There was also a little ping pong ball that danced and floated in the air. She listed dozens of other tricks including "Chinese Linking Rings" and "Oriental Rice Bowls," but she didn't know how to integrate everything into a solid program. I suggested she needed a theme to help organize the show.

"So what's my theme?" she asked.

"It's obvious. Most of your tricks are Chinese. Have a costume to show the theme. Do you have a silk robe you could wear as a magic gown?"

"Yes. I have one that belonged to my grandmother."

"Is it blue?"

"No, white. Is that all right?"

"Yes, it's perfect." I knew that brides in America wear white on their wedding day. "Do you have a title for the show?"

"Not yet. Maybe 'An Evening with Lucy Rabbit,'" she smiled. "Although I don't have a rabbit trick."

"How about 'Some Enchanted Evening?'"

"That's my favorite song," she said with surprise. "I listen to Ezio Pinza singing it all the time. How did you know?"

"I follow you home every night and listen by your window."

Lucy Rabbit's face twitched and her neck snapped like a frightened bunny's. "No, you're teasing," she said nervously. "It was a lucky guess, right?"

I didn't want to lie so I just nodded. Then I added for good measure, "All your tricks are enchanting, not just the tissue paper."

"I still need a final trick," she said as she flipped through one of the Tarbell books. "I'd love to have a big stage illusion but they're impossible to build."

"What kind of illusion?"

She showed me pictures of an illusion called "The Egyptian Mummy." It was basically an upright coffin that was empty, with only a mummy figure hanging inside.

"The cabinet is closed and opened again to reveal that the mummy has been transformed into a beautiful princess," she explained. She smiled and struck a pose with her sweater pulled tightly across her chest. I was smitten.

"I could build something like that," I said.

"You could?"

I explained that I had very strong hands and a good set of tools. I had made coffins before and this mummy cabinet was no different but it was not really appropriate for the theme. I thought I could build an illusion where she, the enchantress of the evening, executed an impossible death-defying escape. Something Herkimer County would remember for a long time.

Lucy Rabbit was excited to know what I had in mind but now it was my turn to refuse to tell. "I'll show you when it's ready. It'll be a surprise."

Over the next few days I gathered parts and in my room began construction of the illusion. I tore apart the storage shelves for the wood and kept Uncle Sam from entering by telling him I was making a special Chanukah present for him. Since I had made tables and benches for him in the past, he accepted this explanation. A few parts had to be ordered from the local hardware store and this delayed the construction.

I decided to buy a couple of girlie magazines at the In & Out Shop to pass the time. But when I reached into my pocket I discovered I had no bills, just a pocketful of change. I grabbed a handful and dumped it on the counter.

"Do you think I'm a moron?" George asked.

I stared at the pile of bottle caps on the counter.

"They're magic quarters," I said, waiting for them to change back into coins.

"You're the goddamn moron," George yelled. "Get out of here. Go on or I'll sic Caesar on you." The dog growled.

The last parts for the illusion didn't arrive until a few days before the Christmas show. I realized I would need to work day and night to get it ready in time and told Lucy Rabbit I could no longer come to the library. Instead, I suggested that she come to my room behind the barbershop with her silk robe for a dress rehearsal of the trick on the evening before the show, and then I would help her move it to the meeting hall. If she wanted, I would be her assistant for the trick in the show.

"We could bill it as 'Noble's Amazing Rabbit Trick,'" I said.

She laughed several times, hard.

I didn't like that. It was not nice to laugh at someone you were going to marry. It angered me that she did not yet recognize we were destined to be a team. And that's when I knew it would be necessary to proceed with my plan. The trick would force her to open her eyes so I could tell if she loved me or not. If she didn't, and the trick still worked as designed, she would fall in love with me just like the Yellow Man who rescued Lucy Burrows or the deformed hunchback who saved Henriette.

I worked without sleep for three nights. My only food was a can of coffee grounds that I kept mixing in water and drinking. I ignored the megrims, the lights, the searing pressure in my left eye, everything but preparing the illusion. My entire life had come down to this one construction project. I took a break from the work one night to say my prayers in the alley for the first time in months. I couldn't see the stars. I didn't know what had happened to God.

On the night of the dress rehearsal, I worked feverishly to put the final touches on the illusion. Lucy Rabbit was to arrive soon and my room was in shambles. The shelves were all torn up. My bed was a mess. My patch was in shreds on the floor and I didn't have time to make a new one. But it didn't matter that she would see me this way. She knew what I looked like. The important thing was that my vice grip was off and tonight I would have the chance to know her. Something told me to put Miss Beecher's picture back in the box.

Suddenly there was a cold draft in my room and I discovered that the window had been cracked by the ice storm raging outside. I entertained a passing pleasantry: perhaps God wanted to give the idiot flies a chance to escape from the mad moron. An ice-cold breeze now blew through the room but at least the flies would no longer be trapped inside a cold unjust world. I put on the black sweater that Mama had knitted for me and felt much warmer as I continued with the final adjustments.

I walked around the illusion admiring my work, then opened the door to the barbershop and turned on all the lights. The lights bounced off the mirror and filled my room with a bright glow like a spot light. It fell directly on the apparatus. Perfect.

The voices were mumbling in my head. I turned to the spotlight and imagined the shop full of people who had come to see the show. I announced the trick, a death-defying illusion. "Done without mirrors," I laughed. I walked around the apparatus, explaining the mechanical workings to the audience. There was a murmur of approval.

"I will tie her up and place her here," I said. "There is no escape. She will be helpless and entirely at my mercy."

Somewhere in the back of the barbershop, Ezio Pinza started to sing: "Once you have found her, never let her go."

The voices started again. I heard a familiar whistle and hoot. Jean Gianini shouted, "Indian her, then Miss Beecher her."

"No, no," I protested. There was something repugnant about destroying a woman's body that could give birth to life. I was aware that some judges during the Reign of Terror copulated with the bodies of condemned girls but I could never do such a thing. "I will not hurt her," I promised. I had designed the apparatus to trick her into falling in love with me when I saved her from certain death.

"It won't work," Dr. Henry Goddard said. "She can never love a moron. You can't mix good blood with bad."

Suddenly I was worried. While I was building the apparatus I never considered the possibility that the trick might not work. What if all my efforts were useless? The question shattered my dream and turned it into a nightmare. Hideous fantasies that I had once cast from my mind as ones which only a criminal imbecile could conceive now crept back like a serpent tempting me with forbidden fruit. Should I consummate the relationship anyway? Transform the virgin princess into a mommy? Change her into many children and give her what she always wanted?

"It might make you feel good," Jean shouted.

"Don't do it," Henry Goddard yelled. "They'll all be morons."

"Go ahead, moron her," George from the In & Out Shop chuckled.

"Don't be a dimwit, spare the rabbit," rhymed the sweeper.

"You're a moron and nothing but a moron," Goddard said. "Your kids will be morons. They should never be born. You should never have been born. The criminal potential must be extinguished."

A knock on the door hushed the voices.

Then from above, on a whisper of wind from the broken window, I heard Mama calling that single word she spoke at my circumcision: "Noble." I thought it was quite remarkable that my eyes would choose this moment to weep.

I climbed on to the table, then checked the secret latch controlling the blade's descent that would stop it before it fell all the way. I wiped the upright rails with a handkerchief and a little mustache wax to insure smooth sliding. Then I stretched out on my stomach and put my head in the collar of the machine. I glanced at the Sabbath candle burning on the table. The flame was blue, getting ready to die.

"The door is open," I said.

I pulled the cord and listened to the noise of the blade coming down. I was aware that the guillotine had been designed by a famous German harpsichord maker. Would it play a tune for me? A lullaby? Suddenly the entire table rocked and I regretted not using something heavier than the pine headboard from my bed. There was a squeezing sensation on my neck. I couldn't breathe. It was like a monstrous hand pressing down harder and harder. I felt the sides of my neck joining together. Then the pressure stopped. It was all over.

I am terrified with uncertainty. Did I set the blade to stop short of my neck or to cut through it? I look around and find that all is well. I watch the handkerchief float from my hand down to the floor where it comes to rest next to my face. It is a strange feeling to be here on the floor when I know the rest of me is twitching on the table above. You must not let that scare you away. We are so much alike. You have those curious eyes that love to read. I know mine don't look quite right and the rest of me is quite a sight. There is probably blood all over. But I am in no pain. There is a sardonic grin on my face but it is the best I can do for a smile. I feel surprisingly light and I know why: for the first time in my life I am free of my label, free of the lump in my throat, free to tell you everything. I can't seem to talk but you can read it in my eyes.

Look into my eyes.

Read my story.

Hurry.

My lips are trembling with a word...

Mama.

Mama was my first teacher. She died when I was fourteen, and Father sent me to the Poland School near our farm in upstate New York. Since I was small for my age and had no formal education, the principal put me in Miss Lida Beecher's sixth grade class. Miss Beecher was only twenty and this was her first teaching position. I was nervous about being in a classroom for the first time and I could tell that she was too. It didn't make it any easier for her when the boys kept staring because she was so beautiful. All of us wanted to marry her when we grew up....

Author's Epilogue

•During the three-day Christmas holiday in 1949, there were 611 accidental deaths in America. These included deaths from fire, traffic, and two from miscellaneous causes. Actually, there were three miscellaneous deaths but a moron who killed himself didn't count. Even Jewish custom denied mourning rites to a suicide victim, so Noble Zoken's uncle simply read a few lines from Shakespeare:

"Now cracks a noble heart.
Good night, sweet prince,
And flights of angels sing thee to thy rest!"

•Zia Nardone's house had been destroyed by fire in 1948. No one knows what happened to her.

•Henry Herbert Goddard died on June 18, 1957, at his home in Santa Barbara, at the age of ninety. He considered his invention of the word "moron" to be his greatest contribution to the world. His papers, including a collection of moron jokes and rhymes, are housed in the Archives of the History of American Psychology at the University of Akron. One of those rhymes, known as "The Happy Moron," has become world famous:

"See the happy moron,
He doesn't give a damn.
I wish I were a moron—
My God, perhaps I am."

The author of the rhyme has remained anonymous. However, an undated copy was discovered in Noble Zoken's journal with Goddard's address penned next to it.

•Professor Burt M. Robinson died in 1960, in Largo, Florida, where he had been living since his sudden retirement in 1948.

•Robert Frost read his poetry at the inauguration of President John Fitzgerald Kennedy in 1961. By that time the diagnostic term "moron" (IQ of 50 to 75) had been replaced by "mild mental retardation," but it was revealed that President Kennedy's sister, Rosemary, had been classified as a moron and given a lobotomy in 1941. Kennedy's administration passed landmark mental health legislation and improved care for the mentally retarded.

•Brainard Wilt died at the Herkimer Memorial Hospital in 1978. He had been living in the town of Ohio, New York, for fifty years.

•Jean Martinette Gianini became psychotic as a result of his confinement at Matteawan and was transferred to Kings Park Hospital in 1966. One year after arriving at the hospital he was given a job as a sweeper. He had an unusual technique of holding the broom, pushing it with one hand while pulling it with the other. He died in 1984, at the age of eighty-six and, denied interment in the family plot in Poland, was buried on Long Island. The director of the hospital said that Jean was an intelligent person who might have done well in life. He had outlived all the principals in his trial.

•Lucy Rabbit now lives in California where she performs magic tricks for her many grandchildren.

Acknowledgements

This story is based on historical archives, court records, trial transcripts, school and hospital records, newspaper accounts, journals, diaries, letters, and oral histories gathered from many sources over the years.

I am indebted to Steven A. Gelb, Ph.D. (University of California, San Diego) for the generous sharing of files and materials on the trial of Jean Gianini. Susan R. Perkins of the Herkimer County Historical Society provided outstanding research assistance and graciously provided space for my work. Other historians and archivists who gave valuable assistance were Wilda Austin (dec.) and Jane Spellman (Herkimer County); Paula Johnson (Town of Russia); Muriel Elizabeth Fenner (Town of Newport); Jim Folts (New York State Archives); and Eileen M. Gallagher (Central New York Psychiatric Center). I thank the staff of *The Evening Telegram* (Herkimer) for access to their archives. For interviews, oral histories, letters, and helpful conversations I thank: Amy Gianini, Gerald A. Gianini (dec.), Donald Giffune, Michael Golden, Susan Heller, C. Richard Hulquist, M.D., M. Paul Keesler (dec.), Beatrice (Gianini) Kurfess, James Myers, Larry Oakley, Patty Putnam, and Rudy Tambone. For advice and encouragement during various stages of the writing I thank Sally Arteseros, Reid Boates, Lynne Gilberg, and Stephen Peters. I thank Philip March for assistance in preparing the photographs. I am especially grateful to Sheila Orlin and Rob Igoe, Jr. of North Country Books for bringing this book home to upstate New York where it all began. And kaddish for all the noble men and women who suffered and perished during the times depicted in this book. May they rest in peace.

About the Author

Ronald Keith Siegel is a modern alienist, both a psychologist and an expert witness in high profile criminal trials throughout the United States. He is also on the research faculty in the Department of Psychiatry and Biobehavioral Sciences at the UCLA School of Medicine and the author of several books including the critically acclaimed *Intoxication, Fire in the Brain*, and *Whispers*. He was born and raised in Herkimer County, scene of the trial of Jean Gianini.

Praise for Ronald Keith Siegel's Books

Intoxication: Life in Pursuit of Artificial Paradise

"A fascinating, eye-opening book
that challenges conventional wisdom..."

—*LOS ANGELES TIMES BOOK REVIEW*

"Compelling...fact-packed...thought-provoking...
reads like a well-crafted novel."

—*AMERICAN LIBRARY ASSOCIATION BOOKLIST*

Fire in the Brain: Clinical Tales of Hallucination

"Mesmerizing, fascinating, chilling...Siegel is a skillful writer
and seems a learned and compassionate scientist."

—*WASHINGTON POST BOOK WORLD*

"With a novelist's skill, Siegel evokes bizarre and
transcendental visions of imaginary companions, voices, and
events. His investigations are worthy of Sherlock Holmes."

—*PUBLISHER'S WEEKLY*

Whispers: The Voices of Paranoia

"A well-crafted tapestry...horrifying and utterly fascinating.
Whispers is a hard book to put down."

—*LOS ANGELES TIMES*

"Siegel is a skilled writer who effectively takes us into the
paranoid world of each individual...Reading *Whispers* is like
reading about an exotic and dangerous travel adventure."

—*THE WASHINGTON POST*